Living in a Material World

Social and Economic Papers No. 19
Institute of Social and Economic Research
Memorial University of Newfoundland

Living in a Material World

Canadian and American Approaches to Material Culture

Edited by Gerald L. Pocius

ISER

Institute of Social and Economic Research

© Institute of Social and Economic Research 1991
Memorial University of Newfoundland
St. John's, Newfoundland
Canada
ISBN 0-919666-67-1

Printed on paper
containing over 50%
recycled paper including
5% post-consumer fibre.

Printed on acid-free paper

Canadian Cataloguing in Publication Data

Main entry under title:

Living in a material world

(Social and economic papers ; no. 19)

Based on papers presented at a conference held in
St. John's, Nfld., 19–22 June 1986.
Includes bibliographical references and index.
ISBN 0-919666-67-1

1. Material culture -- Research -- Canada.
2. Material culture -- Research -- United States.
3. Material culture. I. Pocius, Gerald L.
II. Memorial University of Newfoundland. Institute
of Social and Economic Research. III. Series.

GN406.L58 1991   306'.072071   C91-097674-0

For Don Yoder

Contents

Acknowledgements

The papers in this volume grew out of a conference, "North American Material Culture Research: New Objectives, New Theories," held in St. John's, Newfoundland, June 19–21, 1986. I organized this conference as part of my tenure as a National Endowment for the Humanities Research Fellow at Winterthur Museum, Winterthur, Delaware, in 1985. The final format of this conference was shaped by discussions with colleagues at Winterthur: Kenneth L. Ames, Eugene Metcalf, Barbara MacLean Ward and other members of the Office of Advanced Studies; Patricia Mercer provided the mascot pig. Financial support for the conference came from a number of sources: Social Sciences and Humanities Research Council of Canada; Institute of Social and Economic Research, Memorial University; Department of Folklore, Memorial University; Government of Newfoundland and Labrador, Department of Culture, Recreation and Youth, Historic Resources Division; Winterthur Program in Early American Culture, University of Delaware; Winterthur Museum. It was the financial commitment of Michael Staveley, Dean of Arts, Memorial University, however, that finally made the conference a reality. Those who ensured the smooth running of the meeting included: Shane and Moire O'Dea, Margaret Allan, Sharon Cochrane, Lori Cook, Lin Kirby, Laurel Doucette, Marie-Annick Desplanques, Elke Dettmer, David Foy, Susan Hart, Kathy Kimiecik, Lynne Macdonald, Mary-Kaye Macfarlane, Richard MacKinnon, John and Maura Mannion, Isabelle Peere, Walter Peddle, and Heather Pocius. The Editorial staff at ISER worked admirably to transform conference papers into a publishable volume: Robert Paine, Susan Nichol, and Jeanette Gleeson; Bill Barker, Sarah Carter, and Iona Bulgin also helped with the editing. Finally, I would like to thank all the authors who have waited so patiently for this volume to appear.

Gerald L. Pocius   St. John's, August 1991

Notes on Contributors

Jeanne Cannizzo is a cultural anthropologist, curator and sometimes broadcaster for the Canadian Broadcasting Corporation.

Ann Gorman Condon is Professor of History at the University of New Brunswick at Saint John. She is author of *Envy of the American States: The Loyalist Dream for New Brunswick*, and has published numerous articles on the Loyalist experience in Canada, as well as on material culture. She is a Director of the New Brunswick Museum, and a founder of the Graduate Programme in Material History at the University of New Brunswick.

Jean-Claude Dupont is Professor of Historical Ethnology at Université Laval in Quebec City. His many books on the material culture and folklore of French Canada include *L'Art populaire du Canada française* (1971), *Le pain d'habitant* (1974), *Le sucre du pays* (1975), *Le fromage de l'Ile d'Orléans* (1977), *Héritage d'Acadie* (1977), *Habitation rurale au Québec* (1978), *L'artisan forgeron* (1979), and *Histoire populaire d'Acadie* (1979).

Michael J. Ettema is a curator at the Henry Ford Museum and Greenfield Village. His essays dealing with furniture, museums and other aspects of material culture have appeared in various collections and journals, including *Winterthur Portfolio* and *Art and Antiques*.

Henry Glassie is College Professor of Folklore at Indiana University. He has been a Guggenheim Fellow, and a Fellow of the National Institute for the Humanities. His major books include *Pattern in the Material Folk Culture of the Eastern United States* (1968), *Folk Housing in Middle Virginia* (1975), *All Silver and No Brass* (1975), *Passing the Time in Ballymenone* (1982), *Irish Folktales* (1985), and *The Spirit of Folk Art* (1989).

Alan Gowans taught in the Winterthur Program in Early American Culture for ten years, founded the Department of History in Art at the University of Victoria, where he acted as its Chair for sixteen years. His many books include *The Comfortable House* (1987); *Styles and Types of North American Architecture* (1991) and *Reading the Visible Past* (1991). He is now actively at work on another volume, *World Civilizations in Architecture*.

Bernard L. Herman is Associate Director of the Center for Historic Architecture and Engineering at the University of Delaware, where he is also Associate Professor in the College of Urban Affairs and Public Policy and the Department of History. His books include *Architecture and Rural Life in Central Delaware* (1987), *A Land and Life Remembered*, with Svend Holsoe and Max Belcher (1988), and *The Stolen House* (1991).

Adrienne D. Hood is Assistant Curator in charge of the Textile Department at the Royal Ontario Museum in Toronto. Her PhD dissertation from the University of California, San Diego, "Organization and Extent of Textile Manufacture in Eighteenth Century, Rural Pennsylvania: A Case Study of Chester County," was awarded the 1989 Allan Nevins Prize for an outstanding dissertation in American Economic History.

Stanley Johannesen is Associate Professor of History at the University of Waterloo, where he teaches courses in American Cultural History. He is editor of *Historical Reflections/Reflexions historiques*, and has published essays on material culture in *Canadian Collector* and *Canadian Antiques and Art Review*. He is currently conducting research on a Canadian Pentecostal congregation.

Eugene W. Metcalf is Associate Professor of Interdisciplinary Studies at Miami University in Ohio. He was a NEH Research Fellow at Winterthur Museum in 1984–85, and has acted as a consultant for a number of folk art exhibits. He has published widely on the topic of folk art, and is currently completing a major study, *The Common Man in American Art: A Social History of American Folk Art Collecting*.

Gerald L. Pocius is Director of the Centre for Material Culture Studies at Memorial University, Associate Professor of Folklore, and member of the Archaeology Unit. He was a NEH Research Fellow at Winterthur Museum in 1985. He is currently an Associate Editor of *Journal of American Folklore*. His publications include *Textile Traditions of Eastern Newfoundland* (1979), *Dimensions of Canadian Architecture*, with Shane O'Dea, and *A Place to Belong* (1991).

Jules David Prown is Paul Mellon Professor of the History of Art at Yale University. He has been Curator of the Garvan Collection of

American Art, and Director of the Yale Center for British Art. He is author of *John Singleton Copley* (1966), *American Painting from Its Beginnings to the Armory Show* (1969), and *The Architecture of the Yale Center for British Art* (1977). He has also published numerous articles on material culture studies.

David-Thiery Ruddel is Senior Curator of Industrial History and Technology at the National Museum of Science and Technology in Ottawa. He has published extensively in the fields of early industrial history, social and cultural history, and urban history. His publications include *Les apprentis artisans à Québec, 1660–1815*, with Jean-Pierre Hardy (1977), *Canadians and Their Environment* (1983), and *Québec City, 1765–1832* (1987).

Thomas J. Schlereth is Professor of American Studies at the University of Notre Dame. He is a Contributing Editor for the *Journal of American History*, and has published twelve books in American cultural, urban and landscape history, as well as material culture. These include *Cultural History and Material Culture* (1990) and *Victorian American: Transformations in Everyday Life, 1876–1915* (1991).

Dell Upton is Associate Professor of Architecture at University of California, Berkeley. His publications include *America's Architectural Roots* (1986), *Holy Things and Profane* (1986), and *Common Places*, with John Vlach (1986). He is currently working on a study of the urban cultural landscapes of early New Orleans and Philadelphia.

John Michael Vlach is Professor of American Civilization at The George Washington University, where he is Director of the Folklife Program and Chair of the American Studies Program. His major publications include *The Afro-American Tradition in Decorative Arts* (1978), *Charleston Blacksmith* (1981), *Common Places*, with Dell Upton (1986), *Plain Painters* (1988), and *By the Work of Their Hands* (1991).

Introduction

Gerald L. Pocius

In the early years of the twentieth century, North American cultural studies were in their infancy, and scholars interested in the nature of culture found themselves asking questions that had rarely or never been asked before. Researchers excitedly documented the cultural forms of peoples previously never studied. The results of this fieldwork challenged the dominant norms of modern Western life. Ethnographers often turned first to the cultures of native peoples, and scholars like Franz Boas carefully recorded their myths, rituals and artifacts. Boas—though based in the United States—spent much of his time working in Canada, studying the Kwakiutl of British Columbia and the Inuit of Baffin Island. Other fieldworkers documented the native traditions farther to the south in the United States. This small band of intellectuals with like-minded interests would often gather at one-day professional meetings to share their findings, and discuss what questions still needed to be asked. Students of language, belief, ritual, narrative, and artifacts would meet to argue how each cultural form related to others, and investigate the dynamics of the common cultural rules that ordered people's lives. At these small gatherings, scholars challenged one another on fundamental questions. Researchers from Canada and the United States could exchange ideas on the differences and similarities of their respective approaches to cultural research, which included the role of artifacts.

The joint meeting of the American Anthropological Association and the American Folklore Society in late 1913 was one of the first instances where dialogue between American and Canadian scholars directly influenced material culture scholarship. The American Museum of Natural History in New York, where Franz Boas had worked until 1905, hosted this joint meeting of the AAA and AFS, and a small number of scholars presented papers on a wide range of topics at the one-day gathering. During the break in sessions at West Assembly Hall, Boas had lunch with a young anthropologist from Québec, Marius Barbeau. Barbeau, like Boas, had an interest in native American traditions. During their conversations, however, Boas asked Barbeau about his own Francophone culture, and whether any of its traditions had been studied. Puzzled but curious, Barbeau went back to Québec with a new enthusiasm which soon led to research on his own Francophone culture, documenting narratives, beliefs — and artifacts.

This meeting of Boas and Barbeau serves as a microcosm for the varieties of North American material culture research that began early in this century. The infant discipline of anthropology extensively documented the material traditions of native peoples, as in Boas' work, but here and there, especially in continental Europe, culture-oriented folklife researchers (today known as ethnologists) began to turn their attention to European materials just as Barbeau was to do. This meeting between Boas and Barbeau also mirrors the intellectual contact that has typically existed between Canadian and American scholars in many disciplines. This communication at times has been considered beneficial, at times strained, with voices either complaining of academic imperialism or praising the virtues of international co-operation.

Material culture research in these early years was focused squarely on the cultural questions that artifacts could address. Drawing heavily on fieldwork, and with little concern for the boundaries of departments and disciplines, material culture scholars shared an interest in, finally, the reasons behind the objects. Objects were a means to an end, and that end was culture, be it historical or contemporary culture. Objects were not superorganic entities that spawned chronologies, or mere illustrations of past truths that had already been discovered through other sources, but actual manifestations of behaviour that could reveal basic meanings. Boas would work on primitive art as well as myths; Barbeau would document hooked rugs, as well as co-author a study of French-Canadian song with the linguist Edward Sapir, his superior at the National Museum. But as most of anthropology gradually moved into an academic framework by the 1930s, no longer grounded in a museum world where objects were the reasons for existence, anthropologists turned their back on the artifact. And as other researchers lapsed into antiquarianism, the questions that the artifact could answer were no longer considered important enough to be asked.

In the last twenty years material culture studies have witnessed a remarkable expansion in North America, often led by scholars whose disciplines have only recently discovered the artifact. An increase in publications and academic programs mirrors this interest in the object as a new source of information. The study of material culture, while not consolidating itself into a codified discipline, continues to become increasingly part of the academic landscape. Yet practical problems still exist. The study of objects continues in many ways to be hampered by a focus on disciplinary concerns. In spite of whatever claims for co-operation that are made, methodological constraints seem to insist that much artifact research take established academic paths. Archaeologists concentrate primarily on objects that are excavated and, therefore, are often concerned with problems of the archaeological record. Historians, in their focus on questions of the past, seldom involve themselves with interviewing and fieldwork. In their attention to artifact style as indicator of fundamental cultural values, art historians often focus more on the intentions of the creator than on the realities of everyday object use. Cultural geographers remain primarily interested in broad spatial studies of essentially large-scale units: houses, fields, fences—all exterior objects found on the landscape. These constraints of disciplinary methodologies often mean that when material culture research occurs within an academic subject, it by necessity follows certain agreed-upon avenues that are considered legitimate by the other experts in those fields.

These disciplinary constraints have meant that gatherings of scholars engaged in material culture research are rare. While anthologies and journals frequently assemble studies by a core of researchers, the scholars only meet infrequently, and rarely in large numbers. Yet, as the study of material culture begins to attempt to break disciplinary constraints, particular institutions have begun to take a lead in fostering increased contact. Over ten years have passed since the pioneering forum on "Canada's Material History" organized by the Canadian Museum of Civilization (the former National Museum of Man) in Ottawa (March 1979). While aimed largely at historians and the museum community, the forum was seen as a ground-breaking effort involving a wide range of disciplines. Winterthur Museum, as well, has become a centre for such cross-disciplinary work. In conjunction with the American Bicentennial celebration, a conference was held in 1975 to address broad issues of material culture and the study of American life from a number of diverse perspectives. More recently, with the establishment of a National Endowment for the Humanities Research program within its Office of Advanced Studies, Winterthur has brought researchers from various backgrounds together to exchange ideas on current research areas. In the past ten years, many of those who today are considered the leading material culture scholars in the United States have one way or another been connected with Winterthur, either as teachers, students, or NEH Research Fellows. This has facilitated co-operation and created a network of researchers who may have otherwise not been aware of one another's work.

While at Winterthur as a NEH Fellow in 1985, I felt the time had come for a conference that would again bring together people who normally did not get the chance to interact because of disciplinary loyalties. I used Winterthur's conference of 1975 and the National Museum's forum of 1979 as models. Yet I felt this meeting could be slightly broader in its geographic scope. Working in a Canadian institution, I have found that Canadians often know more about material culture research in the United States than they do about what is going on in their own country. Yet, ironically, theories being developed in the United States are not strictly applicable to the Canadian scene. While at Winterthur, I also realized—not surprisingly—that Americans know little about what is going on in Canada, though they are eager to learn. In short, I sensed a need for a forum where a broad range of North American material culture specialists could come together to assess the theoretical gains of the past two decades. I also felt that a meeting would be useful to develop some collective sense of the theoretical directions needed in the coming years. To these ends, I organized an international conference called "North American Material Culture Research: New Objectives, New Theories." This meeting, held in St. John's, Newfoundland, 19–22 June, 1986, brought together material culture theorists from both the United States and Canada. It was co-sponsored by Winterthur Museum and the Institute of Social and Economic Research at Memorial University.

This volume does not contain the full proceedings of the conference, but is rather a selection of revised essays that came from oral presentations. Constraints of space made it necessary to reduce the number of papers, as well as to reorganize them according to more general themes, in a plan somewhat different from the actual conference program. But this revision should not detract, finally, from the usefulness of this volume.

Two fundamental criteria were used in soliciting the papers. First, while each speaker would obviously draw on a body of data from his or her own region and time period, the major points of the essay had to be general enough so as to be useful for material culture specialists working in other genres and regions. Certainly these papers would not merely be presentations of the latest documentary or field data, but rather theoretical statements applicable to similar kinds of data no matter where it was compiled. Second, as the title of the conference implies, each presentation was to provide at least some suggestions for new approaches, new directions, new ways of looking at artifacts. While delineating a series of issues that I believed should be addressed, I was also interested in assembling a diverse group of researchers that would reflect the broad disciplinary perspectives common in current artifact research. I wanted a balanced mix of Canadian and American scholars, as well as representatives from different regions and institutions in each country. Constraints of time ultimately produced less than an ideal balance; more input from archaeologists and cultural geographers, for example, certainly would have been useful. Yet in the end I was satisfied that national and disciplinary representation was broad enough, and that the necessary voices would be heard.

The resulting papers do address a number of major themes. Material culture scholars have long engaged in ethnographic fieldwork, and some researchers maintain that interviewing and observation are more accurate ways of obtaining cultural information than through reading the artifact itself. In the first section, two essays suggest some of the current ways that fieldworkers have documented the world of artifacts within a particular culture. Ethnography may focus on the object in everyday life, how it is conceived of and used by a particular group. On the other hand, the question of artifact-related institutions as cultural worlds themselves is also raised. Objects have particular meanings for the public, whether within the institutional framework of a museum or government agency. Indeed, such institutions have influenced material culture theory through both the type of artifacts deemed collectable and the theories deemed appropriate for the organization's goals. Both regional and national issues often direct institutional methodologies, and careful ethnographies of public institutions that preserve and display artifacts are as important as fieldwork dealing with the original cultural meanings surrounding the object.

While material culturists have been quick to champion the artifact as a historic source, many historians have been reluctant to turn to this type of data. The essays in the second section confront the problem of whether, indeed, the artifact reveals anything of historical importance. Traditional historians might argue that we have been wasting our time arguing that objects are a rich source of alternative data. They sometimes claim that documents provide all the necessary data for most historical problems. These essays, however, counter that objects do provide information—social, cultural, historical—not available from such other sources as written documents or ethnographic interviews.

For many disciplines the aesthetic component of the object has been the focus of concern, yet in recent years the influences of semiotics, literary criticism, and structuralism have pushed this kind of analysis closer to the social sciences. Indeed, many studies now examine the interrelationship of personal identity, aesthetics, and the object within a specific cultural framework, an issue discussed in section three. An individual in part socially constructs the world through objects, and interacts with others through these objects. Some scholars have questioned whether the aesthetic and stylistic dimensions of the object really reflect meaningful forms of human behaviour; indeed some critics even claim that aesthetic analysis often borders on the idiosyncratic. Yet, art history and literary criticism can provide basic readings because of the recent reorientation of the aesthetic with cultural beliefs.

Many current artifact studies have attempted to examine how objects are used to maintain economic class and power, how they foster certain cultural ideologies. Section four contains essays that deal with the political and economic dimension of the object. Perhaps too much work has concentrated on the general notion of goods, rather than on case studies of specific objects. These essays link specific objects with evolving political and economic structures, moving beyond the simple assertion that goods equal power and class in most cultures.

The closing section deals with both current directions and perceived needs of material culture research. These essays examine the fundamental disciplinary frameworks of material culture research, looking at the current state of our work in the United States and Canada. Are there distinct theories that material culture specialists are developing, or are we simply in the business of borrowing ideas from recognized disciplines? Researchers have asked whether there is a theory of material culture. Do we have unique methodologies, or are there only approaches that fit neatly into existing disciplinary categories? Some have argued that the development of material culture theory and method is simply a professionalization of what were previously non-academic pursuits: antiquarian collecting and connoisseurship. Perhaps object enthusiasts are working on the fringes of disciplines like history or folkloristics in an attempt to gain respectability within the academic community. And, finally, where should we go from here? What is needed to refine both our theories and our methodologies, and what new questions need to be asked?

This collection, then, consists of essays by leading theorists in the study of North American material culture as well as some new and perhaps not so well known scholars. Some of the essays indicate that certain researchers have worked independently of colleagues in a neighbouring country, while others are aware of cross-border developments.

Rather than arriving at *the* definitive statement of what is new and necessary, this volume provides as much a sampling of state of the art research in North American material culture study at a critical stage in its development. Arguments continue as to what is important, but such diversity only confirms the increasing concern that so many disciplines have raised about the central role of objects in everyday life. The artifact can no longer be considered a simple illustration of a people's past or present, but a complex blend of competing expressive concerns that takes a unique three-dimensional form. A variety of emphases in the study of artifacts is evident from this collection of essays, as well as a number of suggestions for future material culture research. Yet, the purpose of this volume, as the conference that produced it, is to rekindle that spirit of exchange that Franz Boas and Marius Barbeau shared over lunch many years ago, an exchange that increased awareness of material traditions in both countries. These essays, then, are intended to advance the dialogue that will enable scholars, no matter what country or discipline, to interpret artifacts more carefully and meaningfully, and thus more fully understand the human beings who fashioned them.

Ethnography

The Meaning of Objects   1

The Poker

Jean-Claude Dupont

Even in isolation, the shape of a material object is significant. Within the context of its technological function and the circumstances of its use, the object takes on greater value as a figurative document and can thus further our knowledge of human behaviour. As a figurative document, in other words, it has meaning.

In order to uncover the way such meaning may work I have chosen to do a reading of a simple tool—the poker—as it was used in rural Québec from the seventeenth up to the mid-twentieth century. My approach gives priority to direct ethnological practice involving informants and objects collected in the field. Empirical study reveals that, in the initial stages, in order to shape an object like a poker, popular knowledge uses a simple conceptual system ordered by transmitted experimentation. The object is later successively modified, its shape adapted to an immediate milieu of technological use in accordance with the economic situations of its users. In folk society, the household tool becomes multi-functional, even used to perform tasks outside the home. It thus has secondary functions which, although foreign to its primary purpose, are devoted to sustaining the material life of the family. Moreover, the object acquires symbolic or ritualistic meanings sometimes imported from other regions. Such symbolic functions, considered useful or enriching for the individual, the family and the community, are practised when needed.

In what follows I will argue that the study of the poker can reveal several things: a reasoned conception behind the object; an adaptation of the object dependent on the milieu of technical function, which varies according to the economic conditions of the user; and, finally, the existence of secondary functions, some real, others magical or symbolic.

SHAPE AND CONCEPT

The poker is a tool used to keep a fire going. It falls within the category of "household equipment" since it is found within the home and is one of the objects on which domestic life relies. It is usually a metal rod with a handle at one end. The other end, which may be bent and pointed, is used to stir embers. This description, both functional (de Verville 1977) and formal, constitutes the first phase of a decoding of this tool. It presupposes that the poker is observed within the context of its usage. The poker, then, must be located within a conceptual "family," and placed in turn within a "system" or milieu of material life. It must be identified in relation to objects that are "poker-shaped" but that have been made for other purposes. Thus, in order to contextualize an object, it is necessary to discover first to which "family" it belongs. This is possible only if most of the similarly shaped specimens to be identified have already been the object of direct study in the field.

Conceptual analysis of the poker requires an understanding of its formal structure, its functional dynamics (a combination of the forces at work) (Leroi-Gourhan 1971), its uses (typological adherence), its genre (designation) and its specificity (particularity) (Figure 1). To consider only one aspect can result in confusion. Thus, an object which has all the dynamic components of a poker is not necessarily a poker. A poker can be described as an instrument of immobilization or as a hand tool for displacement. Yet the former description could also be applied to a small bar or latch or a support; the latter could be applied to a gripping tool or a percussion tool or a lever. The small bar or latch, for instance is an object of immobilization used to prevent another object from being pulled or pushed; examples of this type are door hooks in monastic buildings of the eighteenth and nineteenth centuries or on mid twentieth century double cellar doors of rural houses. Supports are instruments that hold objects in variable fixed positions: different types of angle-irons or struts used up to the 1950s; poles or shafts of a hay press (which set the drum in motion); moving boards of the floor of the sack-lift in flour mills; reversible mould-boards of a plough used for tilling in

FIGURE 1: CONCEPTUAL ANALYSIS

SHAPE	DYNAMICS	FUNCTION	GENRE	SPECIFICITY
FAMILY	CATEGORY	TYPOLOGY	DESIGNATION	PARTICULARITY
Hooks	Implements for immobilization	Bar or latch for locking into position	Hook 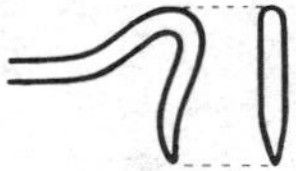	- of convent doors - of cellar doors
		Support for holding in fixed varying positions	Angle-iron 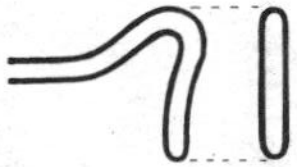	- of pole of a hay press - of sack-lift - of mould-boards of a plough - of sluice-gate
	Hand tool for displacement	Prehension	Poker 	- of open fire - of stove - of boiler
		Maintained percussion	Hand 	- of roller in mechanized pulp mills - of cold press
		Lever	Key 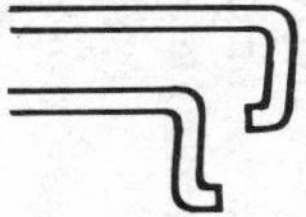	- of grave-digger - of manhole cover

one direction (on a hillside); or sluice-gates or slides for ferrying objects.

Certain kinds of pokers (for open fires, stoves, and boilers) are gripping tools. Others are levers, similar to the grave-digger's key used to undo the straps holding a coffin once it has been lowered into the ground. Some are simple keys, such as the key for manhole covers. Finally, certain kinds are similar to set percussion tools (such as are used to separate the pulp into sheets formed on the flannel in paper mills, or the metal rod of a cold press such as is still used in the aluminum factory at Cap-de-la-Madeleine). Such levers, keys, or percussion tools are identical in shape to the large pokers used for open fires or box stoves.

These similarities point to the need for becoming acquainted with the material milieu in the field in order to discover the basic concept which underlies the existence of an object, that is to say its family, so that one can then correctly attribute the function of that specific object. An object taken to be a poker at first sight could in reality be one of many other implements. Christian Bromberger maintains that "to analyse the significance or meaning of a technical object is first of all to discover and hierarchize the contextual demands it fulfills and to bring to light the processes by which the form has adapted to the functions assigned to it by culture" (Bromberger 1979:108). Henry Glassie stresses the inadvisability of studying objects on museum walls and emphasizes the need for recovering these objects as documents in their original historical context (Glassie 1982a:125).

SHAPE AND TECHNOLOGICAL CONTEXT

In material culture, objects studied diachronically must also be studied synchronically in relation to elements with which they are associated at particular moments in time. In French Canada, the poker must be seen in relation to different kinds of fires (Figure 2).

In the open fires and large fireplaces of the seventeenth and eighteenth centuries, food was cooked in vessels usually hung on a bracket, pot-hanger, trammel, or hinge-pin. Logs were placed across the width of the fireplace. The long poker then in use had a bent extremity shaped like the blade of an adze. One could move the logs and break the burning blocks of wood along the grain (which made the fire burn better), as well as more easily rake together the scattered live coals. In this period of colonial history, however, other specialized fire tools were also found in the homes of the rural middle class and in convents: the fire-rake, used to ventilate the fire, to break the cap covering the coals and to lift the fire to see the state

FIGURE 2: SHAPE AND TECHNOLOGICAL CONTEXT

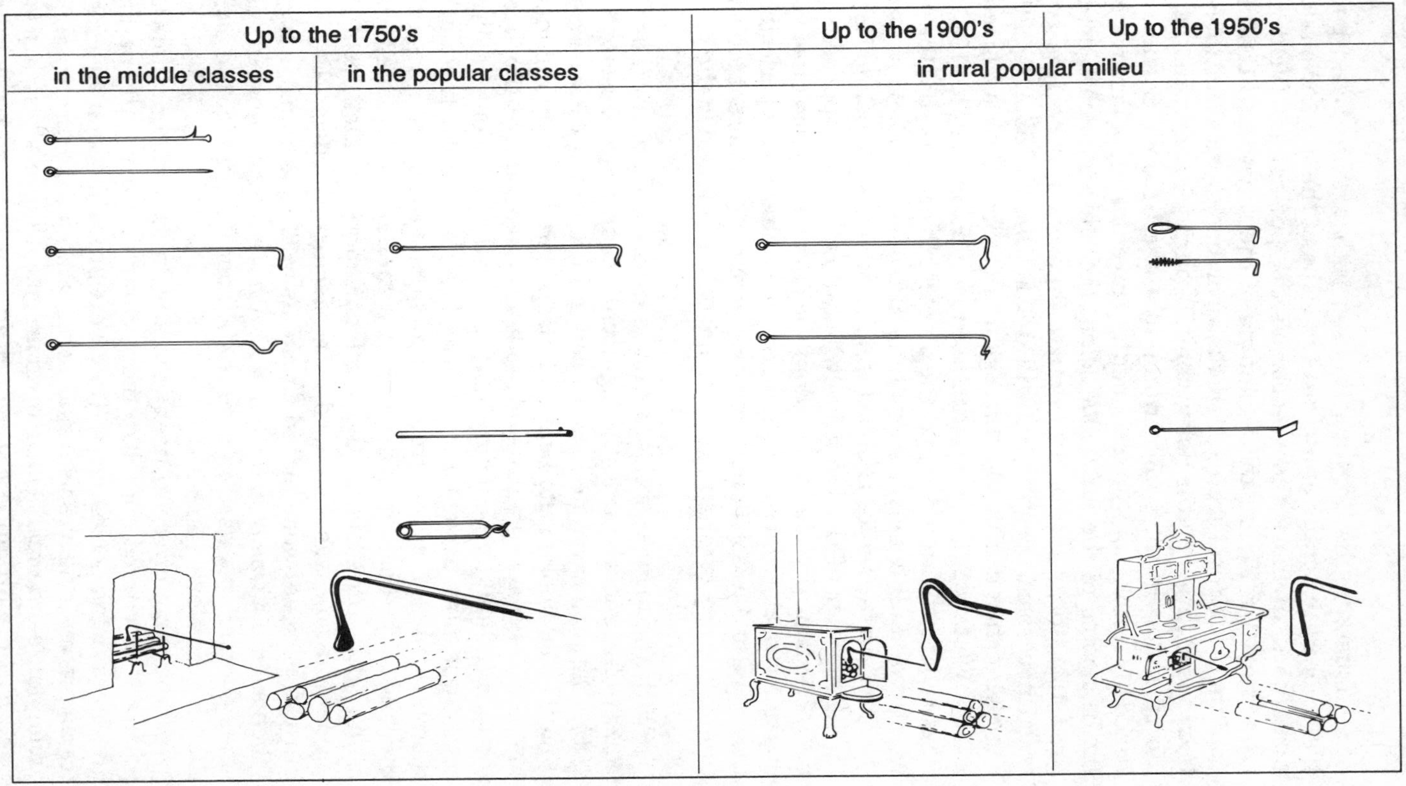

	Up to the 1750's		Up to the 1900's	Up to the 1950's
	in the middle classes	in the popular classes	in rural popular milieu	

of combustion; the fire-iron, a chisel with a curved and pointed blade, used to scrape and clean the walls of the fireplace; and the hook used to move the vessels on the pot-hanger (Velder and Lamothe 1976:21). At the beginning of the nineteenth century in working-class rural French Canada, all of these specialized tools had been fused into one: the poker, a multi-purpose tool used in all the aforementioned ways. According to Robert-Lionel Séguin, who based his conclusions on testamentary inventories, pokers were rare in the homes of the *habitants* before the late eighteenth century; fire-tongs, tools used to manoeuvre firebrands, served as pokers when necessary (Séguin 1972:12–14; Mathieu 1983:216–220). In the eighteenth century in the region of Québec City, an inventory lists "a wretched old gun barrel used as a poker" (Audet 1981:75). It was not until the very end of the nineteenth century that the poker was used in all homes. By this time, the poker had borrowed from the fire-iron the semi-flat chisel which now formed a pointed end lip in the manner of the fire-rake (which now had disappeared from use). The bent portion would adopt the curve of the hook used to lift cooking vessels from the pot-hanger. These alterations perfected the the shape of the tool for reasons of economy; four different tools were united into one to form the traditional poker as found in the popular milieu of Québec.

With the arrival of closed fires (stoves with one, two, or three boxes)—in general use in the eighteenth century (Moussette 1983:198)—the poker was no longer used to lift cooking vessels; consequently, the hook on its bent end disappeared. The lip diminished in width; it became pointed and gradually changed direction becoming longitudinal to the handle (like the cutting-edge of an axe). The poker was now used parallel to the logs, and while it could still readily displace them, it was also used to split the burning logs along the grain. (The position of the end lip, it should be mentioned, varies from region to region.) In the nineteenth and twentieth centuries, the large poker was also used with basement furnaces that often burned blocks of wood placed on end as well as, at times, sawdust. When sawdust was burned, a poker with a blade or, more simply, a small scraper was used to remove the soot from under the oven of the cooking stove.

In the twentieth century one can still find in lumber camps large pokers with curved ends like those common during the period of fireplaces using pot-hangers. They were probably used as levers to transport cooking vessels since the camp cooks prepared "ash bread" (or "sand bread") in an open fire like a smith's hearth; the fire was heaped with embers in which an iron pot was buried (like a

Dutch oven) and from which the pot was removed by means of a lever (Archives de folklore, Université Laval, Collection G. Landry, Recording 37).

Another poker that did not follow the evolution of the stove poker is the one used in sugar cabins. This special poker, which is over five feet long, almost always has part of its handle made of wood to make it lighter. Its bent end has remained curved and it has a massive tip which enables the user to strike the end of the large blocks of wood and push them to the back of the boiler.

With the arrival of cooking ranges or cookstoves with fire chambers four times smaller than those of box stoves, the poker was modified further; it was shortened from approximately four feet in length to a foot and a half. Its shaft lost more than half of its diameter and its elbow-shaped section straightened out along its length to permit it to be used when necessary in the shaker or to remove ashes blocking the grates. Moreover, the ring-end (used to hang the poker on the wall) became a handgrip that encircled the hand or a coil, since a firm hold on the poker was necessary to operate the grate.

CONSTRUCTION AND VALUE

The large poker for open fires had a good market value. It was often an assemblage of pieces of iron, usually scrap (material was scarce until the Saint-Maurice Ironworks started to produce bar iron on a fairly wide scale). Worked in this way, the tool testifies to the output of energy and the time spent in its making by the blacksmith. This increased its value because forging different pieces of old iron hammered on an anvil required numerous stages of assembly.

The end ring used to hang the poker offers clues as to the way in which it was made. In the nineteenth century, this ring was the shape most quickly executed, since the blacksmith did not have to cut out a piece of iron to form a "rat's tail," but had only to weld a piece of the desired thickness (at that time, iron came in bars of different thicknesses) (Dupont 1979:62). By about 1900 the different stages of the work had further diminished; the smith now had machine-tools at his disposal—the drill to make the opening for the eye and the emery-wheel to shape the outer form. This technological evolution in drilling the eye occurred only for pokers in traditional rural dwellings. In middle-class residences, the poker was still shaped in the old-fashioned way to maintain its aesthetic aspects. The poker for large city fireplaces needed to be attractive, for it was hung in a prominent place. The poker used for closed country stoves was not kept in a visible place and thus had no decorative function.

By the first quarter of the twentieth century, the poker had diminished in size to adapt to the cooking range (models such as the McClary, Bélanger, l'Islet and Légar)) and by then had a radically diminished market value. It came with the purchase of a stove and was replaced on demand. In rural areas the poker began to play an ornamental role and was kept on a ledge along the edge of the stove. It was no longer made of iron and forged or cold-hammered but was nickel-plated rolled steel. The shiny appearance of the material implied wealth and was more important than an aesthetically worked form.

SHAPE AND SECONDARY USES

A reading of the object (based on direct field observation) regarding its secondary uses shows a rich ethnological practice. In a less affluent milieu a tool is adapted for a variety of non-specific uses. Other than to keep a fire going, the poker was used for many secondary purposes, mostly as a striking tool.

It was used, for instance as a beater to strike the sides of the pan to unstick bread. Pokers were also used to hit the outside of the stovepipe to loosen the soot. When banged on the tin fire shield (nailed to the wall behind the stove), the poker was a means of communication. This hammering, usually in the mornings, let those who slept in the rooms above know that it was time to get up.

Acadians in Louisiana use a triangle to give rhythm to their music; sometimes a poker is substituted for the small rod to strike the instrument. In the sugar refineries of the southern regions of Québec, night workers in the sugar cabins communicate with each other by means of a traditional sound code; when they do not have a biounne (a tin trumpet five feet long), they beat on an old sugar pan with the poker.

In the winter, when sacks of food for pigs were kept in the summer kitchen adjacent to the house, the poker could be used as a tool to reach out and mix and moisten the feed in the dish water. Women used pokers as levers to lift wool spindles out of dye. They also used them in springtime when boiling fleece.

A farmer might use a poker to manipulate an object in a stove (e.g., when removing a damaged piece of wood from the metallic hand-grip of a tool) or when doing simple blacksmithing. A poker was used as a lever to work the heat grates in the ceiling and floor above the basement furnace.

It was not uncommon, especially in summer when humidity spread through the unheated house, to use the poker to open the swollen cellar trap-door. A poker was sometimes hung as a weight from the regulating key of the flue-pipe (which goes crazy in strong winds) to stabilize it and restore calm to the house.

The poker was used during butchering to clean out intestines used to make blood sausage; one had only to slide the bent part of the poker along the length of the intestine to remove its contents. The poker was used as an implement for scorching: it was heated to red-hot and used to burn off the hairs from the skin of the pork which was cut for grilled meat or to singe the down from a chicken to be roasted.

Outside the house, the main secondary use of the poker was branding. A red-hot poker was used to burn initials in logs to be taken to the sawmill so they could be identified when the time came to saw them into boards or timber. In the same way, cedar shingles were marked with roman numerals to indicate the class. And in the Gaspé peninsula, barrels of fish were marked before being dispatched to the market. In Beauce County, when men joined together to raise the frame of a building, the pieces of wood which had been previously cut and marked by branding were quickly assembled. To identify quarters of pork entrusted to the owner of a smokehouse, a tag with a hole cut out of a piece of cedar shingle and marked with a hot poker was attached to the piece of pork with an iron wire (which also served to hang the meat on a hook). In Eastern French Canada, especially among Maritimers and French-speaking Newfoundlanders, fishermen-farmers used to brand their livestock so that they could recognize them in the autumn when the animals returned from the common land. Instead of making a nick in the animals' ears, occasionally a mark was burnt by a hot poker. In these regions, unlike Québec and Western Canada, a branding iron does not seem to have been used.

SHAPE AND MAGICAL FUNCTIONS

Behaviours associated with the poker express an extraordinarily rich language of rites and symbols based on the relationship between iron tools and the elements of nature. These behaviours (still perceptible in the first half of the twentieth century) seek to ensure that destiny is well disposed towards the participants in popular practices and beliefs (Panoff and Perrin 1973:233).

The poker, an iron object, was invested with powers that worked on liquids, plants, the human body and spirit. It could also re-establish social order within the home. It was a magical and religious medium for maintaining biological, spiritual, and social harmony. "A sword on the land, a poker in the home," explains an old proverb. The masters of fire, once the alchemist, the blacksmith, and the potter, who made matter pass from one state to another, had at their disposal a force which could change the world (Eliade 1977:65).

In traditional Québec society, the person who had this power was usually the housewife. Popular superstition maintained that the young girl who did not know how to use a poker skilfully made a bad wife. The woman maintained the internal order of the home, keeping spirits as well as humans and domestic animals in line. For instance, she could use a poker to stop dancers from violating certain taboos (dancing too soon after being in mourning or after midnight on Shrove Tuesday); she had merely to shake the poker close to the ground, level with the feet of the dancers, in order to make them sit down. Here, the poker symbolized a desire for stability and a wish to banish possible dangers or curses. Similarly, a poker was used (like a dance baton) to strike the ceiling beam to start or stop dancing during a wedding celebration (Dupont 1977:237–238). Here it was not a question of rendering harmless an incurred malediction but rather of temporarily removing a taboo.

Part of the tradition of the charivari, still alive today, consists of striking different implements, including the poker, on old pots and pans to disturb a new couple. This was done when a couple failed to follow established tradition: either they had married at a forbidden time, or too soon after being widowed, or without a celebration, or with too great a difference in age between the partners. The resulting din was meant to avert maledictions which threatened those who may have allowed this upset in the established order.

The poker was also used as a side arm to menace any individual who violated the privacy of the home. A woman could brandish a poker to chase away a too insistent stranger, whether a pedlar or a beggar. She could use a poker to surprise and "change the minds of the young people" when arguments arose. To restore calm and order, she would strike the curved section of the poker sharply on the stove, a gesture which reminded children of the need for respect and obedience to parents.

A woman might flourish a poker to encourage her husband while trying his strength at a game of tug of war called *tirer au renard* (pulling the fox). Two men would face each other, on all fours on either side of an open cellar trap-door, attached by a rope passed behind their necks. A wife would stand behind her husband threatening to burn his buttocks with the poker if he did not win. This never failed to provoke laughter from those watching.

The poker played a menacing role as well when it was used to invoke fear, being thrust suddenly in a person's face to stop a nose bleed or the hiccups. Likewise, after attaching a string to an unwanted tooth, suddenly startling the patient with a poker caused the head to be thrown back with enough force to extract the tooth. As for dogs or cats who fought under the stove, they would waste no time getting out and running for the door when the woman of the house shook her poker at them or struck it against the legs of the stove.

The magic that has been attributed to iron objects lies outside functional contingencies when it is seen to facilitate the communication between heaven and earth and the forces that dwell there. In folk belief iron objects protect harvest and animals from inclement weather as well as from curses. Horseshoes nailed to the frame of the stable door and sickles stuck against the outside wall of the barn were considered beneficial. While harvesting, if a farmer lost the small anvil used to sharpen the blade of his scythe, he did not grieve overmuch since "that brought good luck."

"According to a primitive belief originating in alchemic ideology, mineral substances share the sacred character of Mother Earth, as do embryos, and collaborate with Nature helping her to produce in a shorter time; they change the form particular to a material" (Eliade 1977:7). Traces of agricultural fertility rituals can be discerned in the old practice of straightening out a poker and sticking it in the earth as a stake for an indoor or outdoor plant that lacks vigour.

In symbolic thought, an object is never merely itself; it is also a sign or receptacle of something else. The poker can become a sceptre, a symbol of supreme authority, in the hands of the children who use it, to trace in the spring soil the lines of the "game of heaven" (the delimitation of heaven, purgatory and hell).

The poker may also be used to "play sheep," a ritual of killing. This is how the game is played. A child, playing outdoors, suddenly runs into a house and comes back out with a poker in his hand. He squats down and lightly strikes the earth, hollowing out a small hole, while other children watch. Then the other players question him in a monotone;

What are you doing there?
I'm digging a hole.
What's that hole for?
To make a fire.
What's that fire for?
To heat some water.
What's that water for?
To whet my knife.
What's that knife for?
To cut my sheep's throat!

The others run away as fast as they can and the first child chases after them. When he finally catches one of the children, he pretends to cut his victim's throat. This player then takes the principal role and the game starts over.

In Québec tradition, as elsewhere, the poker played a role in folk medicine. After treating an animal by blood-letting, the farrier would then use a red-hot poker to cauterize the wound. A hot poker was also used to congeal the blood after removing the horns of the oxen in the spring and to treat horses inflicted with lampas.

A poker has also been used in the magic healing of humans. Sometimes an intermediary will merely touch the wart on a hand with a poker (not necessarily heated) or place the poker against the stove door saying "your wart will go into the fire."

A poker, as an iron instrument acting on nature through liquids, was heated and used as a catalyst to transform matter. The practice of dipping a heated poker in wine for new mothers was known throughout French Canada: most priests and midwives recommended it. It was generally the midwife (but at times the father) who placed the poker in red wine, usually Saint-Georges. The mother would begin drinking it after childbirth and would take a little each day until it was gone.

To induce or hasten the fermentation of domestic wine (usually made with wheat), the master of the house would shake a poker, early in the morning, in the batch of wine left to ferment behind the stove. The container, almost always a stone jar, rested on two blocks of wood and was covered with a piece of linen. After using the poker, he would from time to time press his ear to the jug; if he did not hear it fermenting "to his taste," he would blame the yeast, the grapes or the wheat, claiming they were of poor quality, so strong was his faith in the poker. The custom was still practised at the end of the 1970s on the Ile d'Orléans where it was used in fermenting domestic beer (Cyr and Chouinard 1976:77). In Beauce County, a similar practice was carried out in the preparation of human urine as a pigment to dye cloth.

Even though the poker gives protection, it must not be handled carelessly for it also has the power of upsetting established order. It must never be laid down flat. Because of this taboo the woman of the house would hasten to hang up the poker when an uninformed person laid it on the top of the stove or a child threw it down. This reaction was as natural as hurrying to stop a child from turning a knife on the table, climbing up on the parents' bed, or playing with a rosary. Walking over a poker lying on the ground was as unlucky as passing over two planks laid down in the form of a cross on entering a house under construction. This taboo is still respected in European tradition (Varenne 1980:73). If the poker is inadvertently dropped, an unwanted visitor will arrive or a disagreement will arise. There is a common element in all of these examples of superstition: when it is not in its appointed place, the poker can disrupt natural laws and bring about misfortune. The poker must remain upright oriented vertically from the earth to the sky.

SHAPE AND VERBAL EXPRESSIONS

Even though by virtue of its magical and religious qualities the poker may command the respect of the social order in the community and be seen to govern certain aspects of nature, it is above all, in popular language, the symbol of the male sex organ because of its shape and characteristic uses for prodding enclosed, heated spaces. Through its shape which is like that of a key, suggesting the power to open and close, it constitutes a means of access to that which is hidden (Tondriau 1964:177). This meaning has been perpetuated through the ages, reinforced by the fact that in Indo-European culture, the source of French traditions, tools are said to be sexed (Eliade 1977:65).

In French Canada, the folk schema of thought develops around practical actions and daily activities are governed by certain taboos. For instance, when speaking of parts of the body or the act of procreation people will often refer to the "poker" and its actions. Thus a man wishing to have sexual intercourse with his wife will ask "shall we heat up the poker?" or say "Let's use the poker" (Dupont 1974:68–69). These expressions can be replaced by others more closely related to an immediate material concern.

Farmers in Beauce County, who have been sugar producers since their arrival in the region, will say instead "let's stir the sugar" or "the wooden spoon is sticky" to indicate their inclinations towards their wives (Dupont 1975:94). Technologically, the sugar is ready to be stirred when it is on the point of hardening and the "spoon" or perforated spatula is sticky when the taffy is ready to be poured into a container. The sexual aspect of these metaphors may be explained in part if fire is considered the result ("progeny") of a sexual union, born following a back and forth movement (similar to copulation) of a stick (representing the masculine element) in a cut in another piece of wood (the female element) (Eliade 1977:32).

The comparison of human work using fire (smithery, cooking) to the growth of an embryo in the womb has survived faintly in popular expression. In French Canada, when baking bread, a long poker was used to place the dough in the oven (a womb) which has an

"abdomen," a "heart," "cheeks," "feet," a "body," a "skeleton," a "face,"
a "forehead," a "backside," a "back" and a "mouth" (Dupont
1974:73). It is said that the bread "cries out" when taken out of the
oven and that if it turns out well it has "eyes." All of these images
taken from human existence make the oven a living being similar to
a woman who gives birth. It is interesting to recall here that a midwife
was often nicknamed *pelle-à-feu*, or fire shovel, and *fourgon*, or
fire-rake (Dupont 1974:74). The latter term is still used in popular
language to designate a poker (Lavoie, Bergeron, Côté 1985), and it
is most often defined in dictionaries as "an iron bar, hooked or not,
used to poke the fire or stir the embers in the oven."

Oral literature conveys human situations in which the poker
plays a particular role. In folktales, the poker appears most often in
stories about blacksmiths. In one group of tales, the poker is used
to overcome intruders, often the devil, or to chase from his hiding
place a wife's lover come to cuckold the blacksmith in his own forge.
In the second group of tales the smith uses his poker in his
endeavours to recreate life or to rejuvenate and make an old woman
beautiful again (perhaps to let her experience sexual pleasure, if we
interpret the actions of the poker in this way).

One version of the first type describes the blacksmith's attempts
to catch his evil visitor. When Satan takes refuge in a tree, the
blacksmith discovers no better way to make him come down than
to burn his behind with a red-hot poker (Dupont 1979:270).

Another story in which the poker is used for defence tells of a
foolish and jealous blacksmith who is married to a "big beautiful
woman." His wife has the effrontery to be unfaithful to her husband
in a room above the forge while he hammers iron down below. She
even asks her husband to carry on his back the stoneware jar or
wooden chest in which her lover has hidden. The smith discovers
the ruse and smashes the container with his poker.

In the second group of tales, Christ, in the guise of an iron-
master, is accompanied by an arrogant blacksmith who tries to
imitate his master. The Lord throws an ugly and decrepit old woman
into the smith's hearth. He stirs her in the fire with a poker and then
reshapes her on the anvil. She turns into a beautiful young woman.
The smith tries to rejuvenate another old woman but fails completely. He claims that he "quenched her too brittle" (Archives de folklore,
Université Laval, Collection "J-C Dupont," recording 178). Often the
description of the smith's actions with the poker parodies copulation.

Here is an excerpt of an Acadian version of this tale in which
Christ rejuvenates the princess:

Telephone the king and tell him I can make his princess young again, as if she were fifteen again.

...Yes, tell the king I want a room sixteen feet square, a furnace with a cord of hardwood in it in one corner, and in the other corner tell him to have the princess there on a beautiful white bed....Oh and a shovel near the furnace and a poker.

...Well, then, after they had been sitting down for a bit...he got up and went over to the furnace. He took out a match and lit the furnace. God, did that ever heat up, that really dry wood! But the furnace was too open, it was making the floor shake. He went and lowered all the openings in the furnace, he closed them so that it would draw better. Once it was really burning well, lots of hot embers....Then he took his shovel and his poker. He pressed a pedal down below to open the furnace doors. He went and packed down the embers with his shovel and poker.

He went over to the bed then. He slid his hands under her backside and shoulders and picked up the princess and went and threw her in the furnace. She burned as quickly as a candle. Ooo-woup! A little gust of wind and it was all over....He went and shook out the ashes and bones on the bed. All at once, there's the princess like she was at age fifteen! She's sitting there on the bed, on the edge of the bed and she's trilling "turlute." Goodness, was she a beautiful girl! (Dupont and Mathieu 1986:222–223).

A poker also figures in some legends, usually related to the sudden appearance of a ghost or Satan. The ghosts are relatives or friends who visit humans to warn them of impending danger, to give advice or to seek their help to enter heaven. These spirits appear in human form in a place they frequented during their lifetime and carry out actions which they used to do there. Thus the male or female ghost will be seen poking the fire in the stove in the home, in the boiler in the sugar cabin or in the large tin stove in the lumber camp. At times, the poker appears alone and stirs the embers in the stove by itself. For instance, "in 1858, at Saint-Ferdinand, in the presbytery...the priest saw a poker entering the door of the stove" (Fréchette 1909:258–261).

Usually the ghost, male or female, who appears in the family home with a poker in its hand does not speak. However, the ghost who appears in the sugar cabin and who is generally the father or neighbour of the sugar producer, asks to be freed from a debt so that he might enter heaven. In the lumber camp, the ghost is an old lumberjack who used to curse and who had stopped practising his religion. He comes back to tell his fellow workers that he has gone to hell and to warn them to change their ways and give up their bad habits if they do not want to undergo the same fate.

In each case when the ghost with the poker appears, the outcome is beneficial. The lumberjacks go to confession in the nearest village; the sugar producer repays the debt, and a mass and prayers are said for the ghost who visited the family home.

Legends in which a poker is used to chase the devil away are less widespread. In one tale a mother who is at home alone with her children hears a knock on the door and tells whoever is there to come in. Her visitor turns out to be the devil. He tells the frightened mother that there are two ways of keeping him from entering homes. The first is to never say "come in" when someone knocks on the door but always "open" and the second is to burn a cross with the poker on the door frame to frighten him away. This last motif, heard around 1950 in the Rivière-du-Loup region, recalls the uses of a hot poker in branding wood.

CONCLUSION

We have seen that in the particular milieu of certain social and economic conditions—the seventeenth and eighteenth centuries, the period of settlement in French Canada—a tool may play several related roles in folk society and take the place of several tools then in use in the middle classes. It also changes shape as the context of its use evolves. Moreover, the tool reaches the stage where it performs a group of secondary technical activities for which it was not originally destined and these additional functions differ according to the occupations of the users (Figure 3). Since material life is so closely linked to spiritual culture, the meaning of the object takes on added special significance when one examines its presence in the rituals of life and its uses as a signifier in popular language.

The comparison of technical and magical functions shows that the elements transformed by the handling of the poker operate on two levels, the material and the social/spiritual. The first material practice relates to production and consumption in domestic life, whereas the social/spiritual practice relates to socialization and personalization. When you consider the poker in the material sphere, the real functions of the poker outnumber what might be termed the "imaginary" functions by a factor of two. In terms of the social/spiritual spheres, however, the imaginary functions are almost four times more numerous than the real functions (Figure 3). The material survival of humans (food, heat, shelter, clothing, and medication) and the different aspects of production (stockbreeding, agriculture, and crafts) depend primarily on technological practices, whereas social and spiritual behaviours depend more on ritual and symbolic practices.

FIGURE 3: GESTUAL FINALITY OF SECONDARY FUNCTIONS

FIELDS OF IMPACT		REAL FUNCTIONS	IMAGINARY FUNCTIONS	
		TECHNIQUES	RITUAL	SYMBOLIC
MATERIAL FUNCTIONS	CONSUMMATION heating	4	1	
	clothing	2	2	
	food	5	4	
	medication			
	shelter	1		
	PRODUCTION stock producing	2	3	
	agriculture		1	
	fishing	1		
	crafts	6		
SOCIAL AND SPIRITUAL FINALITY	SOCIALIZATION family	2	4	3
	community		2	
	PERSONALIZATION sexuality		6	4
	physical well-being			3
	religion		1	4
	entertainment	4		
Total cases studied: 65		27	24	14

Ritual practices and symbolic verbal expressions in Québec perpetuate archaic forms whose prototypes originate in the agrarian civilization of French Europe. Yet once these practices and expressions are resituated in rural Québec they develop according to economic conditions. Thus, when the substance and shape of the tool are altered, the change causes the disappearance of ritual or symbolic practice. For instance, when a poker is made of steel and can no longer be straightened or bent, the tradition of using a poker to add iron to wine dies out. The presence of nickel on the tool likewise makes it unsuitable for this custom.

The sphere of the technical is grounded in actual practice; it is evident that the main concern of Québeckers when using the poker was to maintain domestic life and to produce economic goods. Yet when uses are meant to enrich family and community behaviour or to confer individual values, the practice falls within the sphere of magic behaviour.

This analysis is limited to an object consisting only of a single part. Yet some of the procedures I have presented may well be applied to other objects. Indeed, a very rewarding study is already being carried out on a much more complex structure, the house. Undertaken in collaboration with Marcel Moussette, a specialist in historic archaeology, our project intends to analyse a number of houses in relation to domestic activities concerning shelter, heating, clothing, rest and food. On an even grander and more complex scale than the simple poker, it has already revealed a great deal about rural and urban life.

Negotiated Realities 2

Towards an Ethnography of Museums

Jeanne Cannizzo

Martin Luther King, Jr., died on the second floor balcony of the Lorraine Motel in Memphis, Tennessee, in 1968. After his murder the motel gradually declined, used mostly by prostitutes and their johns. Now it is to be transformed (by 1991) into a high profile civil rights museum, the brainchild of a former activist. But the community is divided. Shouldn't the money be used for affordable housing, for furthering The Dream? Will the use of the murder site highlight the violent racism Dr. King's movement sought to combat, rather than his explicitly non-violent methods? And what of the plans to use a laser beam as a display showing the bullet's last trajectory?

That these questions are so anxiously raised and passionately debated suggests that museums are not only or just expressive and reflective institutions, but also instrumental ones. For as archaeologist Mark Leone reminds us, "reading, writing, telling, presenting and performing history are *active* and form modern opinion, modern nationality, modern identity, class interests and social positions" (1983:41).

And this is why, over the last twelve years or so, I have been looking at museums and their collections as forms of visual ideologies, as cultural texts. This form of analysis is particularly appropriate when we question the meaning of objects to the public. For museums are symbolic structures that render visible our public

myths. Museums, their collections, and the exhibits they put together from these objects, reveal the categories we create when we
carve up the universe in our attempts to make manageable our
collective reality and exact some measure of control over our collective experience. It is, however, both physically and imaginatively
impossible for any museum, even a national collection, to collect all
the artifacts which constitute a people's past or display all those
objects which constitute its cultural and artistic heritage. So
museums conserve, research, and exhibit only "the selective tradition" or "the significant past" (Williams 1973:7).

There is nothing in this sense natural about our museums, their
collections, or the ways in which those objects are presented to us.
For museums are always fictional in that they are always created or
constructed by us in a particular set of social and historical circumstances; they are negotiated realities. As such, museums are
some of our most interesting forms of visual ideology. Ideology, as it
is used here, is not some form of political extremism or polemic, but
it is a cultural system, one among many. Composed of ideas, values,
and beliefs, it is generated as we go about our ordinary political and
economic business, but also as we take part in our religious or moral
and aesthetic lives. So symbols and styles, tastes and trends are
part of ideology as well (Hadjinicolaou 1978).

Social scientists, as well as art historians like Hadjinicolaou,
have looked at the cultural manifestations and social functions of
ideologies. One of America's most distinguished anthropologists has
concluded that "ideologies are important in defining (or obscuring)
social categories; stabilizing (or upsetting) social expectations;
maintaining (or undermining) social norms; strengthening (or
weakening) social consensus; and relieving (or exacerbating) social
tensions" (Geertz 1973a:203). So an ideology is a kind of map which
allows us to find our way, or at least a way, through the dense and
difficult terrain of reality.

Museums and collections are full of such maps. We might begin
with the idea of the personal collection, a museum of one's own as
it were. One of my favourites is that of the rather eccentric squire
Charles Waterton (1782–1865). A naturalist, traveller, and, of
course, collector, he made a large natural history collection during
a trip to the tropical forests of Guyana in 1820. While there he
captured a crocodile for his collection by jumping on its back and
riding it rather like a cowboy at a rodeo. Ever the scientist, Waterton
also spent several nights with his big toe sticking out of his tent,
hoping to attract a vampire. When he got home to England he not
only preserved these specimens, using a secret method, but also

invented many new animals with the leftover parts generated by his unusual taxidermy.

This personal collection or museum, really a memorial to a particular person, is inconceivable in other societies. I want to contrast such an individual collection with a more collective museum, this one in Havana, Cuba. The old Presidential Palace is now the Museum of the Revolution. Physically, it remains the same. It is a golden white pseudo-baroque tropical sort of place, slightly pockmarked by bullet holes. But the ideology it houses and objectifies in its collections is different.

This difference is apparent even from the outside. The yacht *Granma*, in which Fidel and his followers sailed from Mexico to Cuba in 1956 to launch the Revolution, is now permanently anchored in the former palace gardens. Nearby is an old, red, parcel post van advertising "fast delivery"; it was riddled with rifle fire when used in an attack on the Presidential Palace in 1957. A Russian T-34 tank in which Fidel rode during the Bay of Pigs invasion completes this trilogy of the engines of revolution.

We might begin our tour of the inside with the brochure. Besides offering the usual information on opening hours, it clearly spells out what museologists call the mission statement:

> Valuable historic relics, such as articles, photographs, and documents make up a compound synthesis expressing the history of more than 100 years of struggle of our people, which are divided in three main chronological stages: Colony, Puppet Republic and Revolution.

> The first stage shows a sight of our aboriginal past and the evolution of the Cuban nationality, from the Discovery to the wars for independence and the U.S. Intervention.

This last reference is to what Americans know as the Spanish-American War at the end of the last century. The brochure continues:

> The halls dedicated to the Puppet Republic show the different periods of the state of exploitation and misery under which Cuba was subjected by the national oligarchy and the country's rulers.

> The Revolution area begins with the armed actions of 26 July 1953 led by Fidel Castro against the Moncado garrison in Santiago de Cuba. There are samples of the revolutionary struggle carried out by the people in mountains, cities and plains.

> There is a brief panorama gathering the main victories of the working people in the creation of a new socialist society, without exploiters or exploited. Also shown are aspects of the imperialist aggression and the invasion of Giron Beach.

This is what Cubans call the Bay of Pigs invasion. The museum guide finishes off with:

The Halls of the former Presidential Palace today house a brief account of the history of a humble people that fights and works.

While visiting the museum you, dear visitor, will be able to better understand our historic roots and our profound will to build the beautiful reality of the First Socialist state in the American continent.

This mission statement is materialized in the museum. At the entrance is a big white marble staircase. It is lined with alabaster busts of the great nineteenth-century liberators: Bolívar, Martí, Juárez and Abraham Lincoln. Then comes the palace's grand ballroom, which is empty, and Batista's cabinet room which has its original green leather armchairs but nothing else. This is all part of the creation of new messages. Here there is a suggestion that the present Cuban government is the legitimate heir of the past century's heroes of independence and emancipation, in contrast to the empty illegitimacy of Batista and the rule of the oligarchs.

But some of the most interesting and moving exhibitions are the hundreds of photographs, used very self-consciously and effectively, of dead revolutionaries, all of whom seem very young. Each person's picture is accompanied by a brief description of his or her contribution "in the struggle." There is a paucity of actual objects or artifacts: a pair of jeans worn by Raoul Castro when he was imprisoned on the Isle of Pines, some medical instruments and a beret which belonged to Che Guevara and a typewriter used by Fidel during his jail sentence. What we see at work here is the transformation of a functional object, for example, the typewriter, first into artifact and then "relic."

But the most striking things are the tiny collections made up of the personal possessions of much less famous people, sometimes just an old Zippo cigarette lighter, or an ordinary cheap shirt, or some small crudely made black shoes which someone was wearing when he was assassinated. There are several dog-eared, hand-written diaries and many pencils and ballpoint pens.

Here the objects themselves are being altered—even having their existence extended by the museum process. For in the normal course of events, the shoes would have worn out, the diary would have disintegrated, and the plastic pens broken and thrown away.

But, more importantly, all of these things are very carefully collected symbols. They have a huge emotional appeal for a people whose pre-Revolutionary history was one of material deprivation, of landless poverty, and of illiteracy. So the diaries, shoes, and pens are all easily recognizable collective representations of the most important achievements of the Revolution.

These collective symbols are in a kind of code, one which is easily shared and deciphered by everyone. A very different code, as revealed by Carol Duncan and Alan Wallach, is found in the Museum of Modern Art in New York. Its collections are a tribute to individualism, embodied in its most extreme form in abstract expressionism which has no shared symbolism or collective code. The museum itself they describe as a piece of "late capitalist ritual" and they remind us that, like churches in the past, our museums play a unique ideological role; through their objects and the context they provide for them, museums transform ideology in the abstract into living belief (1978; see also Horne 1984).

The Museum of Modern Art in New York is as much an expression of American or capitalist ideology as the Cuban Museum of the Revolution is an expression of a socialist state. But what of museums in non-industrial societies, in states neither capitalist nor communist?

Sierra Leone is a tiny, "underdeveloped" country on the West African coast with some three million people. The term "White Man's Grave" was coined here because of the high mortality of British governors. This, along with its equatorial ecology which was unsuitable for either large plantation agriculture or family farms, ensured that the European population was always small. As the homeland for numerous social experiments involving the settling of freed slaves, Sierra Leone was always of some interest in British intellectual life. But it was, and remains today, an insignificant place in international terms. However, the great powers and their client states conduct a propaganda war for the hearts and minds of the determinedly non-aligned politicians and peoples of Sierra Leone. This propaganda is disguised as foreign aid and public gifts from various world governments. The Israelis gave one of the earliest gifts, a parliament building, and Israel was rumoured to have provided advisors for the security services. In 1976–1977 when I was there, Cuba was said to provide the same services. The Chinese ran experimental rice farms, very useful in a country which regularly has a hungry season when it cannot feed its own people. But the Chinese were disliked for their alleged disinclination to mix with Africans.

All of these gifts, controversial or even resented, made an impact. The same cannot be said of a gift from the United States which, I was told, was totally ignored by its recipients. It was a new museum, built in an up-country "bush town," as it is described in the capital.

Although there was a real attempt to involve the community by using local labour in construction, and to take into account the latest thinking from curatorial circles, the people for whom the museum was built stayed away in droves. The winners of the propaganda wars that year were the North Koreans who built a football or soccer stadium. Soccer is a national passion in Sierra Leone and the sports pages attract some of her most gifted and highly-paid journalists, all of whom mentioned the generosity of the North Koreans every time a game was played.

But why was the museum such a flop? Because, what we might call a museum mentality is not universal, it is not a cross-cultural phenomenon. This is not to say that aesthetic criticism, the accumulation of objects and occasionally their active preservation, does not occur in Africa, merely that such activities in the pre-colonial period have not been part of a museum. Rather, they have occurred as part of shrines, ancestral memorials, or masking associations.

Museums are very peculiar and singular institutions. They are the product of certain periods in history, and of certain mentalities, associated with particular kinds of worldviews, social structures, and economies.

As Philip Fisher, writing of "The Future's Past," has suggested, "The presentation of images without belief, loyalty, or memory would be as unthinkable before the museum age as for a contemporary man to carry pictures of someone else's children in his wallet because the photographs he had of his own weren't artistic enough" (1975:592).

But images are *not* presented without belief or memory in our collections, they are only presented without their *original* loyalties. We regularly invent new loyalties, and indeed new categories which reveal as much about the collectors and curators as about the original creators of the objects.

When we put a Bundu or Sande mask, made for use in the masquerades of the women's secret society of Sierra Leone, into a museum of primitive art, we transform a ritual object into an art form. This is art "by metamorphosis" and can be contrasted with art "by designation," such as an abstract expressionist painting, which has been made especially to hang on the walls of a museum or gallery (Maquet 1979). In our society, museums and galleries are common, full of art by designation and art by metamorphosis. In Sierra Leone, museums are rare, the national museum is a colonial legacy, and art by designation exists only in elite circles educated abroad or produced by pop artists inspired by movie posters and magazines from the wider world. What we carefully preserve as masterpieces of primitive art are masks and sculptures intimately related to social structure and cosmological complexities, never meant to be displayed, contemplated and deprived of their contextual reality. And it is this sort of paradox which makes the study of museums as cultural artifacts so intriguing and the life history of individual objects so revealing.

As an example let us consider two pieces which appeared in an exhibition I curated in 1989. In exploring these objects and discovering the history of their collection, we can glimpse not only African but also European sensibilities, and in doing so begin to answer the questions of what such collections mean and what they represent. One of the objects is a splendid gold necklace from Ghana. Described in the catalogues as a piece of "barbaric jewellery once belonging to the kings of Ashanti," it was probably the property of a subchief or court functionary. It was transformed from an African object into a war trophy and eventually a museum specimen by the intervention of General Sir Garnet Wolseley. This necklace was part of the personal spoils of war taken by Wolseley after the siege of Kumase, in 1874. A potted life history of the Asante necklace reveals the accidental nature of the objects in many museum collections, as well as how the contextualization of an object significantly alters and thereby determines not only the function but also the meaning of the object. The transformational powers of museums are unique.

The other object is of equal historical and cultural interest, although of little monetary value. It is a Basotho "nosecleaner" from South Africa and is now in an ethnographic collection because of the Boer War. The Canadian contingent sent out to chase the Boers over the veldt was accompanied by a war correspondent for the *Toronto Globe*, Lt. Frederick Hamilton. When he wasn't filing his dispatches from the front or visiting the sick in their hospital beds, he was busy collecting a few objects on behalf of the Royal Ontario Museum. From his diary of 26 May 1900:

> Bought today at a Kraal near Wonderpan, the 'Kaffir Handkerchief' from an old Basuto woman which is used for picking the nose. The natives regarded my desire to own this as a huge joke.... The old woman who was the owner was reluctant to give it up, but found 3 shillings enough to induce her to part with it.

Not surprisingly, the small collection he managed to assemble is as fragmentary as his journal entries. The light that his note throws on the process of collecting, however, enhances the historical and ethnological value of the objects. It also, of course, illuminates some of what now strikes us as the absurdities of the British Empire.

The imperial sentiments of Anglophone Canadians were highly aroused by the outbreak of the Boer War in 1899. For, it should be remembered, when Lt. Hamilton collected his nosepicker, at the end of the nineteenth century, "there was no exact dividing line between a Canadian Briton and a British Briton ....The excitement of the New Imperialism was almost as intense in Toronto as it was in London" (Morris 1979:391).

That intensity of feeling for the New Imperialism is now of course gone from Canadian political life. And indeed even the memory of it has disappeared as Canadian history has become part of a nationalist discourse rather than a coda to imperial derring-do the world over. In the recession of our recent past, we have even lost the knowledge of the context in which those events were played out. And with that knowledge has gone the explanation for the development and growth of some of our most enduring public institutions, which, particularly in North America, were at least partially the product of that age. Indeed, the later part of Victoria's reign has been described as the museum age; it was also the age of liberal laissez-faire capitalism and it witnessed the birth of some of our most important civic institutions—not only the public museum, but also the public zoo, the public garden, and the department store.

Michael Brawne, writing over twenty years ago now, in his analysis of museum architecture, felt the museum was the cultural counterpart of the Victorian department store (Brawne 1965). However, there is more here than just an accumulation of material goods and their display and consumption which suggest the comparison. The prophet of pop culture, Andy Warhol, described Bloomingdale's as the "new kind of museum for the 80s"; so perhaps it is time for a political economy of collecting.

Surely it is no accident that a show of African art at the Michael Rockefeller wing of the Metropolitan Museum of Art was criticized for displaying its objects as though they were on sale in a store with only the price tags missing; the objects were presented without any contextual material. Allegations of "cultural imperialism," intellectual vandalism, and lack of meaning frequent the exhibition halls when "primitive art" is on display.

But this loss of context is inherent in the democratization of the museum. If these works are to be gathered together for the moral or cultural or aesthetic benefit of the people of London, New York, or St. John's, they must be, by necessity, removed from their original functions, their original settings, and their previous owners. As John Updike writes in his story *Museums and Women*, "We turn a corner in the Louvre and meet the head of the Egyptian Sphinx whose body is displayed in Boston" (1972:12).

But this decontextualization is where the great power of the museum lies. Precisely because of their own history, because they are the products of disruptive and sometimes violent social forces, museums are full of decontextualized things—fragments of other lives, other pasts, other cultures. This breaking down of context means that we, the museum visitor and worker, can fill in the gaps, bringing to bear our own personal, cultural and ideological frames as we interpret the original meaning of the artifact *and* its functions as a museum object.

The museum is an important and distinctive institution because it is a wonderful place for the manufacture of metaphors. Metaphor is usually thought of as a literary device, a way of transferring sense from one semantic field to another. Yet metaphors are not necessarily verbal. Anything we invent or create can be read as metaphor. The shifting of context provides the grounds for a fresh reading. Thus objects, whether shells or weather vanes, cradle boards or gold necklaces, can be decontextualized and juxtaposed in new categories to generate contrasts, oppositions, and unexpected conjunctions in turn giving ideologically rich significations to the objects.

An example of the wonderful power of museums and their collections in the manufacture of metaphors is found in V.S. Naipaul's, *A Bend in the River*. It concerns a Catholic priest's collection of African masks. Father Huismans collects only copies that he feels to have magical power. Though he is very knowledgeable about and indeed excited by his masks, he is curiously unconcerned with anything else about Africa or Africans. This is because he believes the real Africa is disappearing. In this scene he agrees to let the narrator, a much younger man, into the gun room of the old lycée where the masks are stored.

> When Father Huismans first opened the door of that room for me, and I got the warm smell of grass and earth and old fat, and had a confused impression of masks lying in rows on shelves, I thought "This world is dead." That was the effect of those masks lying flat on the shelves, looking up not at forest or sky but at the underside of other shelves. They were masks that had been laid low and had lost their power.

> That was the impression only of a moment, though. Because in that dark, hot room, with the mask smells growing stronger, my own feeling of awe grew, my sense of what lay all around us outside. It was like being on the river at night. The bush was full of spirits; in the bush hovered all the protecting presence of a man's ancestors; and in this room all the spirits of those dead masks, the powers

they invoked, all the religious dread of simple men, seemed to have been concentrated.

The masks and carvings looked old. They could have been any age, a hundred years old, a thousand years old. But they were dated; Father Huismans had dated them. They were all quite new. I thought, "But this one's only 1940. I was born that year" (1980:70).

Museum-going and the collecting of objects are creative, reflexive activities in which we can discover or invent for ourselves what Kierkegaard called, very simply, the meaning of life and the nature of things. Museums, and the metaphors they allow us to create within their walls, describe and reveal both the mundane and the greater truths of our collective lives.

History

The Objects of Discourse   3

Evidence and Method in Material Culture Study and Agricultural History*

Bernard L. Herman

Does the artifact reveal anything new? This is a curious question, one that presents us with a number of biases inherent in the methods we employ to study historic and contemporary cultures. The question betrays a sense of primacy in the range of evidence available to researchers. Indeed, it embodies an unfortunate assumption that people habitually record in words what is important to them in their ordinary and extraordinary life experiences. The question suggests that all meaningful communication is oral or written. That such a question might be asked ignores established data-gathering and analytical methods in such fields as archaeology, art history, and geography. The question posits the belief that the function of historical evidence, written or material, is to provide concrete answers; this position denies the importance of data which poses questions. Why do so few individuals ask another closely related question: does the *document* reveal anything new? Obviously artifacts speak to us, and provide us with a unique communication of a culture. Why is it, then, that we find ourselves reiterating established arguments aimed at demonstrating the validity of material culture study as an indispensable element in fields such as social and cultural history, folklore, decorative arts, industrial archaeology, and historical ethnography?

Does the artifact reveal anything new? The answer apparently depends upon the nature of evidence and the questions asked. The primary research obstacles to more comprehensive and compelling ethnographic object- or document-based historical inquiries are centred on historical survival and the process of reification. Survival defines the types of records that have come down to us from the past in terms of their content, completeness, and social represent-ativeness. Researchers who have worked with historic documents in the United States know, for example, that regarding authorship and subject matter, written records generally pinpoint the concerns of propertied white males. Underscoring a parallel deficiency limit-ing the success of comprehensive social historical inquiry is the phenomenon of reification—the process "whereby a culture's struc-ture of everyday life becomes so taken-for-granted, so naturalized, that members of that society do not even think about the reasons for their actions, norms, beliefs, or artifacts" (Handsman 1983: 69). Survival and reification—the lost and unspoken—are factors in all historical and material culture investigations.

Does the artifact reveal anything new? This question may best be answered by example rather than by recourse to bold or mislead-ing theoretical pronouncements. What I propose to offer here is a case study of farming practices identified in rural Delaware from 1770 to 1830. My principal source materials for the following observations are drawn from farm buildings—specifically barns—first, as they are described in Delaware's county orphans court records, and second, as objects standing in the landscape. I choose to begin with documents because I believe they are significantly limited in how much they can actually tell us. Artifacts, by contrast, considerably broaden our ability to interpret the past. The point I wish to demonstrate is that the assumption of evidential primacy—the belief in a hierarchy of historical sources defined by medium rather than content—will always thwart meaningful interpretations of historic processes. Thus, research strategies premised on the integration of information from systemically related sources will invariably be the most revealing.

For an introduction to the Delaware landscape, we can turn to agriculturalist James Tilton's answer to an inquiry concerning the State of Delaware and published in the *Columbia Magazine* in 1789 (Figure 1):

> The Delaware State lies between 38° 30' and 38 47' north lat. is
> about 40 miles wide on the sea coast, and extending from cape
> Henlopen up the bay of Delaware about 100 miles in length,
> terminates in a twelve-mile circle, eight miles above Wilmington:
> the mean distance across, about 24 miles. The length of the winter
> is about three months. The rivers generally freeze up before

Figure 1: Map of Delaware showing its position in the Middle Atlantic Region of the eastern United States.

Christmas, and the trees begin to bud and blossom before April. The mercury has been known to descend below 0; but, in ordinary, the extreme degrees of cold and heat are about 5° in winter, and 96° in summer, by Fahrenheit's scale. The general temperature of the air is moderate, though liable to frequent and sudden changes.

The nature of the soil is very fertile. The mold or vegetable earth, may every where be made deep. There are few stones, except on the hills of the Brandywine, in the upper extremity of the state. In the upper county of New-castle, the soil consists of a strong clay; in the middle county of Kent, of a sandy loam; in the lower county of Sussex, of a loamy sand ... .

There are various methods of cultivation, and no settled standard ... (Tilton 1789:156).

Tilton, an early proponent of agricultural reform, went on to outline the principal crops (corn and wheat), husbandry (milk cows, beef cattle, and sheep), crop rotation, adversities (blight, vermin, and drought), and such basic farm practices as plowing and threshing. While Tilton's description provides a useful introduction to the basic characteristics of Delaware's climate, topography, and agricultural produce, his exposition does not assess the range or significance of varied agricultural practices he observed throughout the state.

In 1850, sixty-one years after Tilton's essay, Delaware was composed of four primary agricultural regions: the northern dairy region, the central grain region, the south-central mixed farming region, and the southern home manufactures region (Michel 1985; Schwartz, Michel, and Herman, 1986). The characteristics separating the four regions have been compiled through the quantitative analysis of agricultural and population census returns, the reading of farm ledgers and agricultural correspondence, and the field survey and recording of rural architecture. The result of this recent research on mid-nineteenth-century Delaware is the opening of a window in time through which we may study rural economy, the sociology of capitalism and agricultural reform, and the physical settings designed for the organization of work and the presentation of self within one's community (Michel 1985; Herman 1987).

The cultural and agricultural regions of Delaware in 1850 were, however, already established when Tilton wrote in 1789. Although detailed agricultural census materials do not survive for Delaware during the early national period, other sources do assess how farming worked. Two of these are in different senses architectural. One is the period description of rural architecture contained in court ordered assessments intended to value and protect the property rights of orphaned minor children. The other is the buildings that have survived to the present day. As we shall see, neither documentary nor material source is without its biases and limitations. Information in the written record is defined by the legal obligation to maintain the productive value of real property for minor children inheriting an estate. The descriptions made by the appraisers are consequently most concerned with the preservation of capital improvements and the productive stewardship of agricultural lands. Surviving buildings are rare. That they do survive is the result of a number of variables such as their suitability to changing methods of agricultural production and their durability of construction.

When the orphans court appraisers visited the Sussex County farm of Thomas Hinds in 1774 they found among the other buildings "the Barn being weather boarded with Inch Plank set up Right with small nails many are now Loose and some Dropt off and Lost we therefore think it necessary that eight pound of small Spike Nails be got and One or More be Drove in each Plank with a few Plank Put on where they are lost of[f]" (Siders and Herman 1986:14). The barn on Dr. David Thompson's New Castle County estate in 1795 was the object of extensive alterations with directions that it "be clapboarded and sufficiently supported by pillars of brick; a cellar to be dug under the barn and converted into a stable for horses; a shed to be erected over the front part of the same, ten feet by the length of the barn, for the purpose of sheltering horned cattle" (Siders and Herman 1985: 48). And, in Kent County court-appointed visitors recommended in 1802 on behalf of Benjamin and James Blackiston that "a new frame Barn 24 feet in length and 20 feet in breadth be built & roofed and weather boarded with oak Clapboards and ceiled inside to a sufficient height to hold wheat and other grain" (Nelson, *et al.* 1983:10).

These three descriptions are exceptional in the detail they contain. The overwhelming majority of the orphans court descriptions contain the name of the building (a barn), the building materials (log, frame, stone), physical condition (good, middling, sorry), and, in some locales, overall dimensions. A typical entry would run "one log Barn in bad repair." If we take all the descriptions found in geographically defined locales and code them for all the information they contain on building types, materials, condition, dimensions, orchards, directives for repair, etc., we can begin to evaluate rural architecture as an index to economic and cultural preferences in agricultural production. Thus, on the basis of 1,100 cases representing fifteen of Delaware's twenty-four pre-1830 hundreds (the state's equivalent to townships), we can begin to determine distribution patterns for agricultural building types.

Barns historically were not the most common type of farm building in Delaware. While they were a preferred form in some areas, in others they were a distinct minority of the agricultural building stock. Plotting distribution frequencies derived from orphans court property valuations onto maps showing hundreds, we can offer certain generalizations regarding building density, condition, relation to farm size (farm size is architecturally defined here in terms of types and numbers of buildings), and comparison to similar information derived from the orphans court for other agricultural structures.

Barns, as noted by the county courts from 1770 through 1830, were most common in the north of the state and in Dover Hundred located in the south central region of the state; they were recorded most infrequently in the southern hundreds (Figure 2). Until around 1800, barns throughout the state were of log or frame construction, with frame predominant in the south and log in the north. The typical farmstead in the north was composed of the dwelling, a domestic service building such as a smokehouse, and a single agricultural building—most often a barn. Farms in the central region of the state tended to be architecturally dense with a complement of varied household and farm-related buildings in addition to the dwelling. Forty percent of the southern farmsteads possessed no farm buildings; for the remaining percent, the favoured building was a small corn house. The way in which barns fit into these varied landscapes is best discussed on a region by region basis.

Barns in the hilly northern region were after 1800 increasingly built of stone (Figure 3). This shift to stone is reflected in the description of barns which, after 1800, are more frequently designated as being in "good" condition. "Good" was applied to buildings that were generally new or unusually well maintained. "Bad" denoted buildings that were poorly maintained or constructed. The northern hundreds, where "good" buildings were concentrated, was also the scene of a transformation to better building materials in the early 1800s (Jicha and Cesna 1986). Here barns represented the greatest percentage of all agricultural buildings including corn houses, stables, and granaries; they were present on 85 percent of the steadings where the court's representatives recorded only a single agricultural building and on 91 percent of the estates with multiple farm buildings.

The barns of the south provide sharp contrast. These southern barns number only a third of the northern totals. These buildings were twice as likely to be in bad condition—in some instances lacking roofs or beyond repair. All the appraised barns in the south

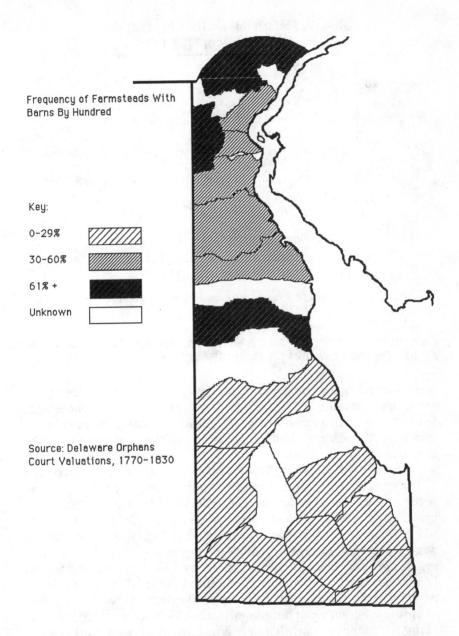

Frequency of Farmsteads With
Barns By Hundred

Key:

0-29%

30-60%

61% +

Unknown

Source: Delaware Orphans
Court Valuations, 1770-1830

Figure 2: Statistical map showing the frequency of farmsteads with barns identified
in the Delaware orphans courts from 1770 to 1830.

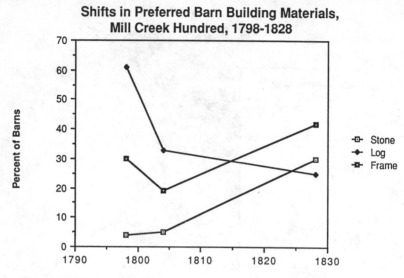

Figure 3: Table reflecting the shift in preferred barn building materials in Delaware's northern Piedmont zone from 1796 to 1816. (After Jicha and Cesna, 1986)

were of frame or log construction and often no larger than the typical dwelling, averaging 360 square feet on the ground floor. There were fewer barns than corn houses and stables. Barns were present on less than 30 percent of all valued farms in the south compared to over 61 percent in the north.

The barns throughout the central hundreds, with the exception of Dover Hundred, fall in a middle range. Barns were listed on 39 percent of all assessed farms. These barns of the central hundreds typically wanted significant repairs as in St. Georges Hundred, where 60 percent of the barns were listed as bad. Where dimensions were provided, they appear to have averaged around 700 square feet on the ground floor. Although there were a few masonry-walled barns recorded, the majority remained built of wood. Over 50 percent of the farmsteads in the central hundreds were composed of multiple agricultural buildings. Barns stood in ranges and courts along with stables, corn houses, granaries, and combination work and storage buildings. The tendency toward architecturally dense farmsteads in the central hundreds suggests that these barns were used for a more limited range of activities than in the north but, unlike the south, farms still required a substantial investment in work and storage buildings.

In our documentary evaluation of the historical significance of Delaware barns, we must consider the relation of barns to other architectural and agricultural structures. Following the geographic divisions already established, we see that in the northern hundreds the preferred farm buildings, in descending order, are: *barn*, stable, corn crib/house, combination building, miscellaneous farm structure, and granary (Figure 4). In the central hundreds the pattern is: corn crib/house, stable, *barn*, miscellaneous farm structure, combination building, and granary. In the southern hundreds the order runs: corn crib/house, miscellaneous farm structure, stable, *barn*, granary, and combination building.

Figure 4: Major Agricultural Building Types in Order of Preference, Delaware, 1770–1830

Northern Hundreds	Central Hundreds	Southern Hundreds
BARN	corn crib/house	corn crib/house
stable	stable	miscellaneous farm structure
corn crib/house	**BARN**	stable
combination building	miscellaneous farm structure	**BARN**
miscellaneous farm structure	combination building	granary
granary	granary	combination building

Source: Delaware Orphans Court Valuations, 1770–1830

At this juncture we can summarize what we have learned about barns from the quantitative analysis of the orphans court property valuations. First, barns were the leading agricultural building type in the north, but ranked third in the central hundreds and fourth in the south. Second, in the southern and central hundreds where barn dimensions were often recorded, we observe that the southern barns are generally smaller in overall size and square footage. Third, the barns in the north were typically in better condition than in the central and southern hundreds. Fourth, barns in the north represented the only group with significant numbers raised with masonry walling. Fifth, barns in multiple building farm complexes throughout the state were most likely to be paired with corn houses and stables. Sixth, while the high incidence of barns in good condition separates the north from the south, they are akin in their general lack of stables, granaries, and multiple farm building steads.

We have now established the general statistical outline of barn structures as they were assessed in reports from 1770 to 1830. Individual property valuations can fill out details about methods and materials of construction. Yet these details—neither general nor particular—yield little information about how the buildings were actually used. And here is a larger problem. We can deduce certain relationships between building types and agriculture on the basis of the documents. The hundreds characterized by relatively large numbers of stables, for example, suggest the presence of significant numbers of horses (Figure 5). The horse, capable of plowing twice the acreage in a day as an ox, is the animal of the early rural industrial revolution. The horse required greater investments in feeds and shelter than the ox (Michel 1985; Herman 1987). A greater frequency of granaries, corn houses, and combination grain-processing and storage buildings in the central hundreds indicates that barns too are part of an extensive grain market. Corn houses, the most common farm building type in the south (42 percent of all assessed farm structures) are recorded on only one half of all farmsteads, thus implying markedly less intensive overall grain cultivation and more of a subsistence farm economy.

Yet the documents do not help us get beyond broad generalizations. When we begin to compare surviving barns from the period with their documentary equivalents, though, we immediately see some very interesting inconsistencies. For one thing, the word "barn" conveyed radically different meanings and images from place to place throughout the state. Furthermore, we can read in buildings a range of functions and meanings far broader than conveyed by the written record. Buildings are objects of design, and in the measure and disposition of architectural space and finish, we can discern the dynamic of work (Glassie 1974; Glassie 1975a). Few barns survive from the 1770 to 1830 period, and naturally those structures which still stand are generally better built and somewhat larger than the average barn recorded by the orphans court (Figure 6). Even so, these remaining barns tend to parallel the patterns revealed in the quantitative documentary analysis.

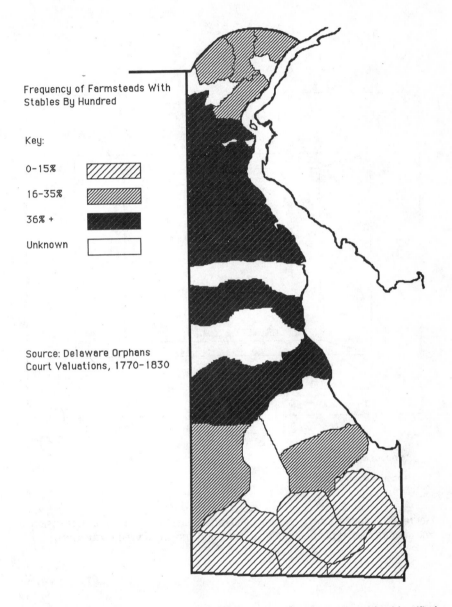

Frequency of Farmsteads With
Stables By Hundred

Key:

0-15%

16-35%

36% +

Unknown

Source: Delaware Orphans
Court Valuations, 1770-1830

Figure 5: Statistical map showing the frequency of farmsteads with stables identified
in the Delaware orphans courts from 1770 to 1830.

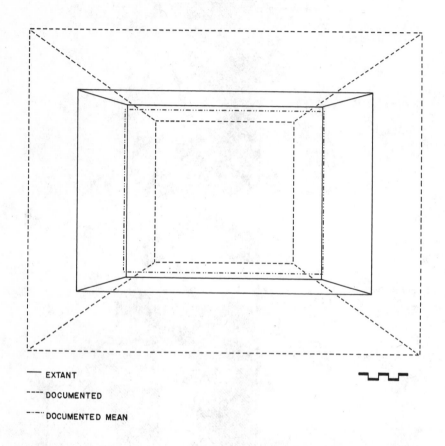

EXTANT

DOCUMENTED

DOCUMENTED MEAN

Figure 6: Relative barn sizes in southern Delaware by external dimension as reflected through orphans court valuations and known surviving structures.

At least a dozen barns dating from the study period have survived in the southern hundreds. Although the buildings range in proportion from nearly square to rectangular, they are all organized around a central runway or threshing floor flanked by storage areas. At the Martin Barn (c. 1790–1810) the barn was originally raised on brick piers or wood blocks, floored with plank, and provided with side bays vertically subdivided at a height of six feet (Figure 7). The resulting vertically and horizontally partitioned plan, along with evidence of scribed bushel counts on the walls, define a pattern of use where the central aisle and the area outside the door were used for threshing, the interior lower levels for keeping unthreshed cereals and other crops awaiting processing, and the loft for storing hay and fodder. Corn in the ear was contained in a small framed corn house standing nearby.

Despite differences in appearance, the same functional layout was employed in two Sussex County barns: the Marsh Barn (1820–1840) and possibly at the Hardscrabble Barn (1800–1820) (Figures 8 and 9). Both of these buildings were more rectangular in shape than the Martin Barn, but both also contain the same basic internal divisions. There appear, however, to be key functional distinctions between the two buildings. Corn storage in the Marsh Barn was contained in an original shed crib built against one gable end, and the floor of the Hardscrabble Barn may have been earth, suggesting the possibility of animal shelter as well as crop storage. When other standing barns in the southern hundreds are compared to these two examples, we find a great deal of diversity within a shared architectural concept. A barn here could be for the storage and processing of feed or cereals, for work space, for animal shelter, or for a combination of tasks. What the buildings reveal—and the documents do not—is notable variability in the spatial organization of a rural economy concentrated on subsistence agriculture.

If the barns of the southern hundreds describe a varied and somewhat marginal farm economy, those of the north reveal a very different pattern. The surviving barn type associated with the Piedmont hundreds is the English-style bank barn built into an embankment with a lower story for horses and cattle and an upper floor for hay storage, threshing, and grain storage (Figure 10). As a group they are large buildings (often containing in excess of a thousand square feet on a floor) and spatially complex with their interior spaces subdivided according to a variety of specific functional criteria. The Peters Barn (1800–1820) contains an upper level composed of a central runway, threshing floor, and hay mows (Figure 11). The lower or basement level provided space for shelter-

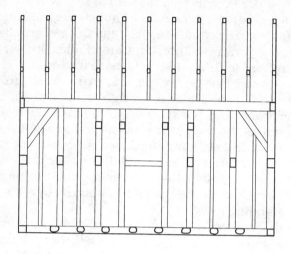

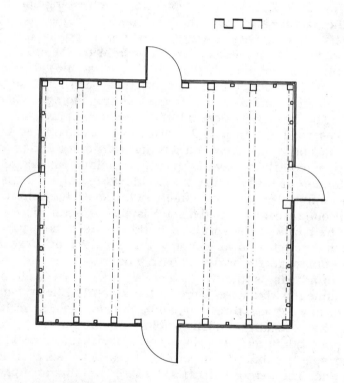

Figure 7: Martin Barn, Cool Spring Vicinity, Indian River Hundred, Sussex County, Delaware. Plan and Frame Section.

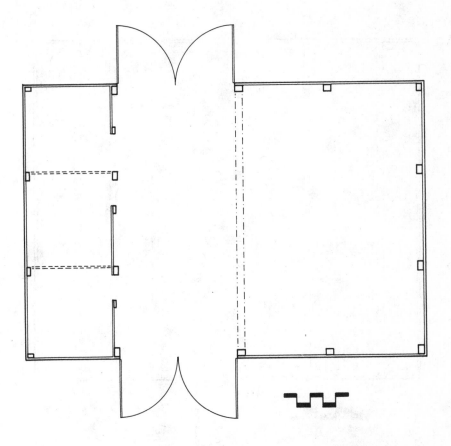

Figure 8: Marsh Barn, Angola vicinity, Indian River Hundred, Sussex County,

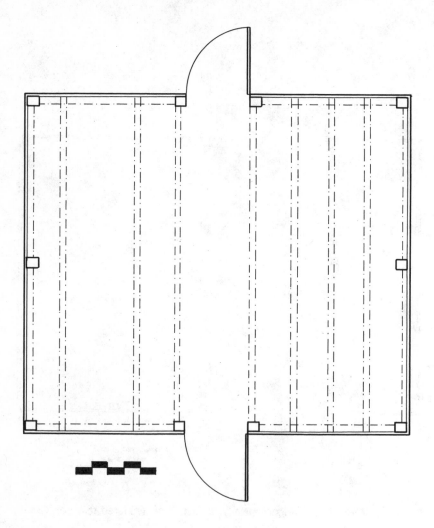

Figure 9: Barn, Hardscrabble vicinity, Broad Creek Hundred, Sussex County, Delaware. Plan.

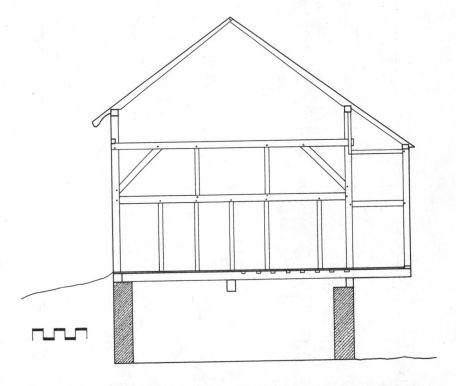

Figure 10: Bank barn section, Hockessin vicinity, Mill Creek Hundred, New Castle County, Delaware. (Drawing: M. Mulrooney)

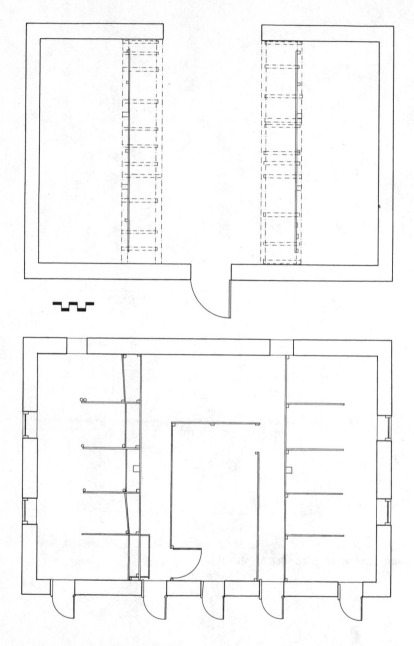

Figure 11: Peters Barn, Newark vicinity, Mill Creek Hundred, New Castle County, Delaware Basement and threshing floor plans. (After drawings by Stewart Dixon)

ing horses, cows, and other livestock. Whether built in frame or stone, the bank barns throughout the area contain evidence for nearly identical patterns of use. Showing us what documents cannot, the buildings indicate a pattern of agriculture organized according to a collective concern for the consolidation (and thus the streamlining) of farm work and storage. Here agriculture has assumed a distinctly modern tone describing the intensive utilization of architectural space—and of the land itself.

Finally, the central regions of the state present us with a third pattern of farm usage which is ultimately made clear by barns. Here the barns of the 1770 to 1830 period survive with the lowest overall frequency measured against their known historical density. No more than six standing barns are currently known to date from this period. The survivors, like the now departed Davies Barn (1810–1830; Figures 12a and b), are all remarkably alike in design, construction, and size. Rectangular, three-bay buildings averaging 25 by 40 feet, the barns of the central hundreds are raised on full foundations, have provisions for temporary upper level hay mows, and possess evidence for lower level partitions suggestive of storage areas for special feeds and cereals awaiting processing. As in the Retirement Barn (c. 1800; Figure 13), they typically lack provision for animal housing. The single known barn with livestock housing is the Mount Pleasant Barn (c. 1810) in northern Kent County. While the plan and construction of this 24 by 36 foot building are nearly identical to the other barns, it was clearly used in a different way. Evidence for opposed entries leading to now vanished stalls and the original absence of floor joists in the structure's east bay indicate that one end of the barn housed cattle while the opposite end contained hay. The runway between the two bays was both a feeding aisle and crop processing work space.

Of all the barns in Delaware, those in the middle region of the state exhibit the least variability in layout and contain the most limited working functions—primarily threshing and hay storage. As historical sources, these barns describe an agricultural economy focused on the cultivation of wheat and feed; the most common related building types are designed for stabling and grain storage. What the buildings describe is an agricultural economy designed in accordance with the segmented organization of very specific farm tasks. Multiple buildings with limited individual uses describe a high degree of specificity in the allocation and segregation of working space. An examination of other period sources reveals that domestic and occupational separation is also reflected in increasingly compli-

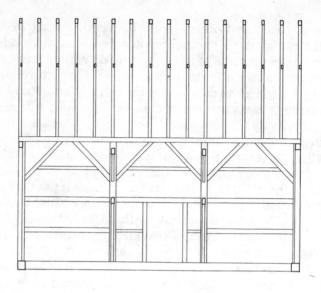

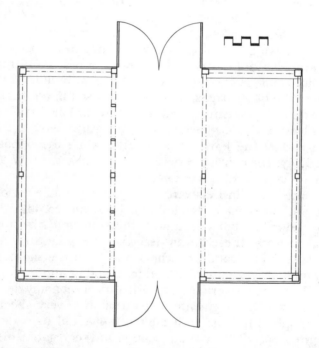

Figure 12a: Davies Barn, Little Creek vicinity, Little Creek Hundred, Kent County, Delaware. Plan and framing section.

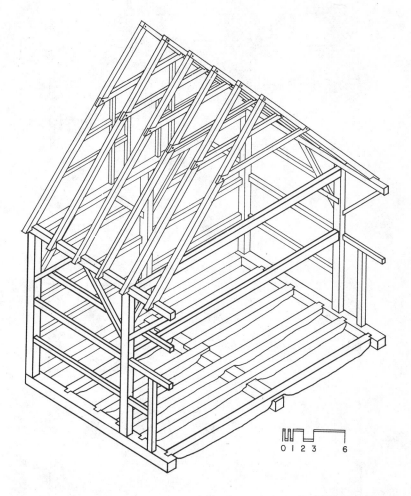

Figure 12b: Davies Barn, Little Creek vicinity, Little Creek Hundred, Kent County, Delaware. Sectioned framing isometric.

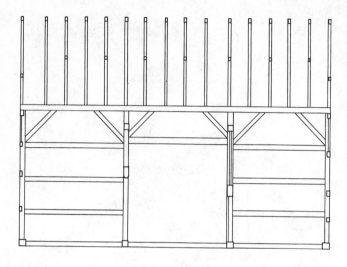

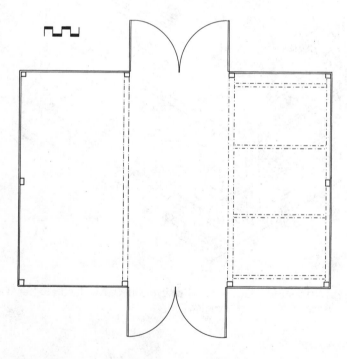

Figure 13: Retirement Barn, Port Penn vicinity, St. Georges Hundred, New Castle County, Delaware. Plan and framing section.

cated house plans, systems for maintaining farm accounts, and even field patterns (Herman 1987).

The physical structure of the barns, like the orphans court valuations, provide us with some provocative information about the particulars of the statewide organization of agriculture from 1770 to 1830 and more generally about regionalism and cultural process. Agricultural building design in the northern Piedmont region reflects a uniform concern for the consolidation of multiple farming functions within a single building. The barns in the central regions of the state suggest a preference for functional specificity. These buildings seem to have been conceived of, and built with, a very limited range of functions in mind. In the southern hundreds, barns were more varied in shape and use than anywhere else in the state. The pattern of variability found in the objects reveals a diversified agricultural economy without narrowly defined categories of market crops and animal products. In other words, the buildings describe a dual pattern of agricultural diversification. The late eighteenth- and early nineteenth-century middle Atlantic region was not characterized by uniform types of crops. There were, within a greater landscape geared toward grain and dairy production, other economic alternatives based on activities like lumbering and home textile production. The model of "modern" agriculture promoted and prized diversification within categories. Thus, cereal cultivation included not only wheat and corn, but also rye, buckwheat, and oats.

We could expand our observations dramatically by turning our efforts to other parallel and complementary bodies of historic information. Probate inventories (the often detailed listings of personal estates) yield information on the types, quantity, and value of farm implements and machinery, livestock, and crops. By collecting inventories made throughout the year, we can deduce seasonal aspects of sowing, cultivation, harvest, and processing. The study of the actual tools coupled with archaeologically recovered floral, faunal, and architectural remains presents us with information on the quality, textures, and physical mechanics of agricultural production. When we begin to relate barns to other building types and historic trends in architecture identified throughout rural Delaware and the surrounding region, our vision of the past becomes even richer. Simply stated, to interpret meaningfully the complex realities of past cultures we must marshal and evaluate all sources of historical evidence.

What have we learned from the objects and the documents in this limited exercise? We know something more about the nature of agriculture in Delaware in the decades between 1770 and 1830. More profoundly, we may have gained some knowledge about the structure of historic evidence. Barns and period descriptions of farm buildings are two elements in a rich expressive culture. But what is the internal cultural reasoning behind their respective expressive content? While both sources tell us something about the ecology of middle-Atlantic agriculture, they do so with very different intentions. The orphans court valuations were taken as a function of the court to monitor and preserve the property rights of minor children. The document protects wealth and the legal governance of property. Buildings, by contrast, delimit aspects of a cultural environment composed of customary and innovative relationships observed in rural society. Although barns were commissioned to shelter the labours and contain the fruits of agriculture, their utility also included a vital symbolic component. We can read in the fabric and spaces of barns the elements of interaction between the individual, the community, the agrarian economy, and the land itself. Taken together, the barns and the property descriptions—the objects and the documents—begin to speak to us about an unbroken historic whole.

Note

*   The fieldwork required for this essay was funded in part by the Bureau of Archaeology and Historic Preservation, Delaware Division of Historical and Cultural Affairs. A generous grant from the University of Delaware's General University Research Fund enabled me to collect and compile orphans court property descriptions (1770–1830) for Delaware. I am indebted to Rebecca Siders for her work on the statistical analysis of the orphans court valuations. For help in the field, thanks are extended to Bert Jicha, Dean Nelson, Richard Carter, and David Ames. Meg Mulrooney produced the finished inked drawings used in the text. My appreciation is also extended to Mary Helen Callahan, Barbara Ward, and Henry Glassie for their comments on earlier drafts of this paper.

Artifacts and Documents in the History of Quebec Textiles* {#sec-4}

Artifacts and Documents in the History of Quebec Textiles*   **4**

Adrienne D. Hood and David-Thiery Ruddel

Despite the potential of textiles as rich sources of information, few historians use them as evidence because they require such specialized technical training to decipher. In this paper we explore several issues relating to Quebec history and show how textiles can offer a wide range of historical insights. Indeed, textiles may indicate status and class; they may provide an understanding of craft-production and the technological sophistication of a society; and they may also illuminate more general political and economic realities. They can be used, for instance, to help explain important historiographical issues such as the relevance of gender in the production of Quebec fabrics and the impact of British colonialism on textile manufacture in Lower Canada. Not only do they yield information otherwise unavailable from documents but, perhaps more important, they also suggest new avenues of research. Artifacts test knowledge gleaned from more traditional sources and are invaluable in the way they illustrate the reality of daily life.

    E. McClung Fleming's and Jules Prown's models for material culture studies serve as a useful springboard for establishing a method of textile analysis (Fleming 1974:153–173; Prown 1982:1–19). Following is a brief outline of the steps we have taken in analyzing textiles as historical evidence.

ARTIFACT ANALYSIS

The first step is *fiber analysis* which identifies the raw material from which a textile was made. Prior to the twentieth century this raw material was restricted to plant and animal fibers. Flax (which becomes linen when processed) or hemp (a fiber similar to flax) are labor-intensive to produce and after the early decades of the nineteenth century were supplanted in most areas of Canada by comparatively inexpensive factory-spun cotton. The cotton was usually obtained from the United States or Britain until later in the century when imported raw cotton was spun in Canadian mills. Another fiber was wool, necessary for warmth, yet difficult to produce high quality (without a lot of care, sheep are difficult to raise and the wool produced is often very coarse). Wool was therefore often mixed with other materials such as cotton. Silk from silkworms was not produced in Canada but was imported as sewing thread and luxury fabric, principally for the garments and household furnishings of the upper levels of society.

The next step is *yarn analysis* which examines the twist or spin of yarn and whether it is plied together. This analysis can assist in dating a piece since yarn spun or plied mechanically can look quite different from handspun yarn. When *dye analysis* is done scientifically, it can determine whether a dye is of vegetable or man-made origin and possibly what it is, thereby helping to situate it in time and place.

Then follows the *technical analysis* which includes how the basic textile was made. With woven fabrics this includes a *weave structure analysis* which, despite its complexity, can be further explained with the help of diagrams (Burnham 1980). Technical analysis can also indicate what type of loom was used, its degree of complexity, and suggest the methods used as well as the location of a weaver's training.[1] Although more difficult to find than textiles, extant looms can help to verify the information suggested by the technical analysis.

Of great importance are the *overall design elements*, which include color, texture, and pattern. Besides giving insights into the artistic sensibilities of the makers and users, design can also help us to understand ethnic or cultural influences in a society. Moreover, when analyzed in terms of similar artifacts produced over time or by people in another culture, we can begin to assess how a society is changing.

Next is an analysis of the *function* of a fabric. In Quebec, and in North America in general, the majority of extant material consists of bedding, other household textiles, and, to a lesser degree, clothing.

Fiber, yarn, dye, weave structure, design and function analysis help to *authenticate* a textile, rendering it valid as historical evidence. North American handweaving does not enjoy the high market value of prestigious oriental carpets, for instance; thus it is not likely that forgeries will be made to dupe collectors. Even so, historic sites produce reproduction costume and textiles and independent weavers make them for use in restored homes; some of these could in time find their way into museum collections. As a result, there always remains the need to verify the authenticity of these artifacts.

Above all, to use textiles as evidence, one must understand the *collecting history* behind them, especially since many handwoven textiles are now in museum collections and not in the field. It is crucial to try to determine who collected the artifacts—where, from whom, when and why. Are the textiles nonrepresentative because they survived at all? Are they typical of local fabric production in general? Or do they simply reflect a particular collector's taste or interests? Furthermore, no one place in North America was completely self-sufficient in cloth production; one must ask what sources, other than local ones, could have provided textiles.

Just as documentary evidence is constantly tested by historians in order to ascertain its objectivity and validity, textiles (indeed artifacts in general) must withstand a similar rigorous scrutiny. They should be used along with other sources in order that their value as historical documents be fully realized.

DOCUMENTARY SOURCES

Quebec, like France, possesses rich notarial records which can be analyzed to describe the structure and evolution of society. These records contain two sources which Jean-Pierre Hardy and David-Thiery Ruddel have used extensively: labor contracts between apprentices, journeymen and masters, and post-mortem inventories. Labor contracts are important because they reveal working conditions and labor relations. Of the more than 3,000 contracts they analyzed for the rural and urban areas of the Quebec City region between 1660 and 1830, Hardy and Ruddel found references to numerous artisans related to the clothing industry, such as tailors, seamstresses, milliners and mantua-makers, but none to apprentice or journeymen weavers (Hardy and Ruddel 1977).

In an article on Quebec textiles, Ruddel published the results of an initial analysis of over 400 post-mortem inventories that revealed the amounts of both imported and homespun fabric present in urban and rural dwellings (Ruddel 1983:95–125). When these results are combined with the study of other sources such as census returns, commercial and government reports, and newspapers, they provide the basis for drawing conclusions, not only concerning colonial textile production, but also about the lifestyles and *mentalités* of the colonial population. Ruddel's article is a starting point for a number of the questions we here re-examine. Of course, it should be understood that since the analysis of the household inventories and labor contracts has not yet been completed for the Montreal area, the documentary findings are still incomplete.

WOMEN AND PROFESSIONAL WEAVERS

Although women did most of the weaving in Lower Canada, many of the weavers in eighteenth-century Pennsylvania and in most of nineteenth-century Ontario were men (Hood 1988:112–174; Burnham and Burnham 1972:11). However, other records also indicate that women wove in nineteenth-century New England, and in the last half of nineteenth-century Ontario, but this usually occurred when the craft of handweaving was in transition or when the settlements consisted of people who had not emigrated from those areas of Britain or Europe with well-developed textile industries (Cott 1977:27–28; Burnham and Burnham 1972:11).

Because of the discrepancies between Lower Canada and other regions, we decided to re-examine the documentary sources in combination with artifact analysis to help shed more light on the roles of women and the varying levels of professionalism found in nonmechanized North American textile production.

Although sources for the Quebec City area suggest the absence of trained male weavers, documentary information shows that these artisans did indeed exist in the Montreal region. According to census returns, professional weavers worked near Montreal as early as 1665 (1665–1666 Census of New France in *Censuses of Canada, 1665 to 1871* IV:4). Because there was a hiatus in the practice of identifying weavers for census returns between the late seventeenth and the early nineteenth centuries, information concerning them for those years must be found in other primary sources such as newspapers. According to an advertisement in the *Montreal Gazette* (6 June 1796) for a professional weaver, a textile establishment existed at Coteau du Lac, 47 miles from Montreal in the late eighteenth century. In 1810, trained weavers were plying their trade in at least five villages in the Montreal area (*La Bibliothèque Canadienne* February 1826:93–94). The earliest woollen mills in

Lower Canada were built in the Eastern Townships in the 1820s: for example, a wool factory existed at Memphremagog Lake in 1826 (*British Colonist* and *St. Francis Gazette* 11 May 1826) and at Sherbrooke in 1832. This being said, it is interesting to explore the reasons for the absence of trained weavers in the Quebec City region.

Because the documentary evidence suggested so strongly that women did the majority of weaving in the area around Quebec City, we examined the textiles to see if they could shed further light on the levels of skill of the French-Canadian weavers.[2] We compared the Quebec textiles with a body of weaving from British and German communities in Canada, both of which contained a number of highly skilled, professionally trained male weavers. The material, drawn from the Royal Ontario Museum collections, demonstrates some very distinctive differences. Some of the features particular to the Quebec textiles in Figure 1 are the eight-pointed star as a design motif; the predominant use of the most basic weave structure, tabby, which can be woven by anyone with rudimentary skills, but which allows more design flexibility than some of the more complex structures; the use of locally grown and processed linen well into the twentieth century; and the use of recycled and slightly unusual materials such as cow hair and reprocessed wool—a fact not easily apparent from the photograph, but one on which we will elaborate later.

British Canadian textiles (Figure 2) largely from Ontario and Nova Scotia, are very different from the Quebec examples. The majority were woven on looms ranging from four to sixteen shafts, with some being produced on complex jacquard looms which use a series of punched cards to create patterns. Many of the weavers were trained professionally, probably in Britain, and continued their work after their arrival in Canada. The materials utilized were predominantly wool, cotton, or a combination of the two; linen was used most frequently in the early decades of the nineteenth century. Recycled material, usually found in rag rugs, only appeared in any quantity in British-Canadian weaving later in the nineteenth century when handweaving was declining.

The surviving textiles made by people of German descent (Figure 3) in Ontario suggest that their work was more complex than that produced by either French- or British-Canadians. In fact, most of the thirty known Canadian jacquard weavers were of German origin (the others were British). The materials, like those used by the British, were generally linen in the early years of the nineteenth century, wool, imported cotton or a combination of wool and cotton.

Figure 1: Examples of 19th and early 20th century Quebec handwoven textiles from the exhibit, "Canada's Handwoven Heritage," ROM, 1986 (photo: Bill Robertson)

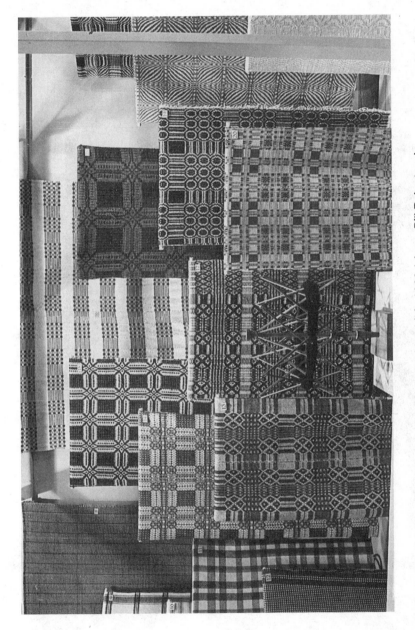

Figure 2: Examples of British-Canadian handweaving. ROM exhibit, 1986 (photo: Bill Robertson)

Figure 3: Examples of German-Canadian handweaving. ROM exhibit, 1986 (photo: Bill Robertson)

The comparative examination of French, British and German-Canadian textiles suggests that there were, indeed, differences in the level of skill of the weavers in each group. Much of the British and German material could only have been woven by well-trained professionals. In seventeenth- and eighteenth-century Britain, where cloth production was a large scale industry, weavers were men unless a widow of a weaver took over her husband's tools after his death (Wetherill 1986:145–8). The German immigrants also came from a male-dominated professional weaving tradition. Quebec fabrics, which were comparatively less technically complex probably represent the work of women who did not receive the long apprenticeship needed to weave many of the complex pieces made by people of British and German descent.

A number of extant Quebec looms are four shaft and capable of weaving more complex fabrics than the majority of surviving Quebec textiles would suggest.[3] The looms may be substantially older than the fabrics woven on them, suggesting the presence of professionally trained weavers (male and/or female) in the eighteenth or early nineteenth centuries. As the nineteenth century progressed, perhaps an increase in the number of women, possibly unmarried, in the rural areas provided workers for the labor-intensive tasks of cloth manufacture. Large numbers of nineteenth-century British and German immigrants, many of whom were professional weavers, settled in Ontario where they continued to practise their craft; this did not occur in French-speaking areas of Quebec. Growing economic necessity in rural Quebec may have required that the weavers receive only rudimentary training with which to make simple, yet serviceable, cloth with little capital outlay, on looms often inherited from another generation of more skilled weavers. In order to test these hypotheses, it is necessary to do more demographic, immigration and economic studies, with particular reference to subsistence farming.

LINEN AND SUBSISTENCE FARMING

Possible reasons for the existence of large amounts of linen in Quebec and of hand weaving far into the nineteenth century are numerous; one of the more important was the role of textile production in subsistence farming. The domestic textile industry provided the rural family with some of its own clothing and household linen when money was low and complemented its income at other times. The domestic work did not, however, remove the desire or need to obtain imported textiles. Although 63 to 83 percent of rural homes had spinning wheels and 31 to 42 percent had looms during the

1792–1835 period, almost every country household possessed some type of imported clothing (Ruddel 1983:102–106).

Some rural families sold wool and linen cloth to their neighbors as well as to members of urban laboring groups. It is unlikely, however, that this practice led to the establishment of dynamic local or national textile markets. Although urban worker families bought quantities of household linen from rural producers, the biggest consumers of cloth, the families of urban merchants and professionals, acquired only negligible amounts (Ruddel 1983:111).[4] Clothing worn by urbanites was either made to order by tailors or seamstresses, bought ready-made, or constructed within a family using imported cloth and patterns.

The increasing number of spinning wheels and looms found in household inventories in the early nineteenth century suggests that domestic production was growing, but newspaper writers continued to note that it was insufficient to meet the farming families' clothing needs. In 1819, a writer in the *Quebec Gazette* (2 August) exhorted farmers to produce more flax and raise more sheep to clothe themselves during periods of low grain prices in the British market. Other reasons given by local commentators for the necessity of increasing the production of domestic textiles included diminishing revenues from the exportation of raw resources and rising prices for imported goods (*Quebec Gazette* 18 October 1821 and *Journals of the Legislative Assembly of Lower Canada*, 1826 App. E). Because comparative statistics for domestic production in other countries are often lacking, it is difficult to evaluate the significance of the Lower Canadian figures. According to a study of domestic textile production in the United States, farming families in 1810 made approximately ten yards of cloth per inhabitant (Tryon 1917:166). Lower Canadian production came close to the 1810 American output only once, in 1827 when it reached 8.3 yards per person, falling thereafter to 3.2 yards in 1842 and 2.7 in 1851 (*Censuses of Canada*, 1665 to 1871, IV).

Lower Canadian farmers continued to produce linen when American and Ontario farming families were abandoning this time-consuming practice. Like their American counterparts, Upper Canadians replaced domestically produced linen cloth with cheap, factory-woven cotton fabric. In 1851, only 14,711 yards of linen were made in Ontario, compared to over 900,000 in Quebec (*Censuses of Canada*). Between 1851 and 1870, the Ontario production of cloth continued to decline, while that of Quebec rose by over 50 percent (McCallum 1980:88). By 1870, Quebec farming families were producing four times the amount of cloth made by their Ontario counterparts. Thus, the fabrication of linen was an essential part of the farming family tasks throughout most of the nineteenth century.

The textile artifacts underline the reality of subsistence farming suggested by the above on several levels: the use of linen yarns well into the twentieth century; the extensive use of recycled and other unusual materials; and the excessive wear and patching of many of the textiles. The late use of linen suggests that in parts of rural Quebec, not only weaving, but the processing of a fiber requiring a lot of labor to produce but no capital outlay, occurred due to economic necessity.[5] This is further supported by a survey of other Quebec handweaving. A coverlet detail (Figure 4), possibly from about 1830, illustrates the use of recycled cloth or rags combined with handspun wool and cotton which was likely spun in a mill, to produce an attractive bedcovering. Made about 1900, another coverlet (Figure 5), combines factory-spun cotton with rags, but it also uses a variety of other fibers such as handspun wool, linen, and jute. The weaver of an 1880 coverlet (Figure 6) used a mill-spun cotton warp and a combination of cotton and wool yarns in the weft in order to complete it. When it wore thin it was patched and kept in service, probably until it was collected in the 1930s. Another coverlet (Figure 7), woven using a commercial cotton warp and handspun wool weft was used long after the design was no longer very visible. When it tore across the center the owner carefully mended it and when the ends wore out she pieced scraps of cloth together in order to obtain sufficient material with which to repair them. A blanket in the collection of the Royal Ontario Museum (Accession 966.211.22) demonstrates a practice documented in Quebec (*La fabrication artisanale des tissus* 1974:95). Wool from an old textile would be unravelled, washed, recarded, respun, and then rewoven (or knit) to create a new product. Finally, again a phenomenon which shows up mainly in surviving Quebec textiles was the use of cow hair, obtained by the weaver from a local tannery, to supplement a scarce wool supply. In Figure 8, brown cow hair was combined with pink wool to create an attractive blanket that was used and mended until it was almost beyond repair.

Examples such as the above, although often embellished with attractive designs, were probably made from a variety of materials because the weaver lacked the financial ability to buy raw wool or commercial yarns and/or the farmers lacked the resources needed to produce enough material with which to make a complete product. By further supplementing this practice with recycled materials and cow hair in addition to using fabrics until they were completely worn

Figure 4: Detail of Quebec coverlet made of recycled cloth, handspun wool and possibly factory-produced cotton, probably about 1830. Note the use of strips of recycled cloth in the weft. ROM 970.90.5.

Figure 5: Quebec coverlet, about 1900, illustrating use of a variety of fibers including handspun wool, linen, jute and mill-spun cotton. ROM 971.83. (Photo: Bill Robertson).

Figure 6: Quebec coverlet, 1880, showing use of a variety of available materials and excessive wear and patching. ROM 970.90.3.

Figure 7: Well-used Quebec coverlet, 19th century. ROM 970.90.2.

Figure 8: Quebec cow hair and wool blanket, about 1900. ROM 970.90.16.

out, it was possible for subsistence rural householders to meet some of their cloth needs.

Most textiles in museum collections are bedding. Given the worn condition of many of them, it is probable that a variety of pieces did not survive. However, it is unlikely that even the poorest household or community made all their own textiles. In the past, collectors concentrated on documenting local weaving, so we must look at documentary evidence for clues about what alternative sources of cloth might have been available to a community.

MERCANTILISM

The mercantilistic policies of the French in New France and the British in the Thirteen Colonies were similar to those transferred to Lower Canada by the British after they conquered the French territory in 1759–60. Simply stated, this complex system attempted to encourage the colonial production of raw materials as well as the consumption of manufactured goods from the mother country, making it more convenient and profitable for the colonists to devote themselves to acquiring British-made objects rather than develop their own manufacturers. This system ran into serious problems in the Thirteen Colonies for a number of reasons, including the existence of a strong current of economic nationalism.[6]

In New France, patriotism was not as forceful as in the Thirteen Colonies, and did not have a significant impact in Lower Canada before the 1820s. Although some colonial administrators during the French regime deplored the lack of manufacturing establishments and suggested that livestock be increased to provide more wool and leather for the production of clothing and footwear, the Crown refused to send weavers to the colony (Renaud 1928:395; Dechêne 1974:302). In spite of a number of encouraging initiatives, neither domestic nor professional weaving developed to any significant degree in New France.

In general, imperial and colonial governments provided little support for local manufacture. One of the reasons the colonial government was so ineffectual in promoting industry in both New France and, for long periods in Lower Canada, was the fact that imperial policy discouraged the establishment of elected governing bodies at the local level.[7] Important economic strategies in Lower Canada, therefore, were largely left to imperial representatives in Great Britain whose goal was to encourage the importation of manufactured goods to Quebec rather than encourage local industry.[8] Thus, although British authorities in Quebec did not prevent Canadians from producing their own clothing, they discouraged the establishment of colonial competition to imperial manufacturing.

Combined with the reduction in commercial relations between France and Canada following the British takeover of the colony, was the difficulty francophone tailors and merchants had in trading with anglophone textile suppliers. This resulted in the disappearance of many French-speaking merchants and artisans in Quebec and the almost immediate domination of the import and retail trades by the British. For example, in Quebec City during the 1760s, 110 British merchants were competing with 80 to 90 Canadian merchants. Ultimately anglophones not only controlled the import trade, including the acquisition and shipment of goods, they also owned most of the wharves. By the end of the eighteenth century, over 90 percent of textile merchants were anglophones while francophones were largely relegated to the secondary position of retailers or shopkeepers. Scots dominated the trade: between 1765 and 1800, approximately 45 percent of the importers and retailers were of Scottish origin, 34 percent were English, and 21 percent were Canadian (Ruddel 1987:60).

During his research Ruddel came across a published illustration of a shawl (Figure 9) maintained to be homewoven in early nineteenth-century Quebec (Burnham and Burnham 1972:79). This assertion is problematic because although French-speaking women might have made imitation Scottish shawls, that these garments were being imported from Scotland to Lower Canada in large quantities by Scottish merchants in Quebec and Montreal suggests this particular one was not domestically produced.

We therefore decided to re-examine the shawl (Figure 10 is a detail) using the analytical framework outlined above. The fiber is long-stapled wool of a quality difficult to produce in North America in the early nineteenth century because it required well fed and cared for sheep.[9] Long-stapled wool is more suitable to spin the "worsted" yarn used to weave this shawl, as opposed to the "woolen" yarn found in most surviving nineteenth century, North American-made, wool fabrics. Worsted yarn was combed by highly skilled wool combers, while woollen yarn was carded using brush-like implements; carding requires less skill than combing and can be used to process even low quality wool. Not only were sheep difficult to look after in this period, there was little demand for the skills of a wool comber when carding could be done easily within a family or by sending the wool to a carding mill.[10] Because worsted production was minimal in Canada and given that Britain had a major worsted

Figure 9: Woman's shawl, probably used in early 19th century Quebec. ROM 961.112.1.

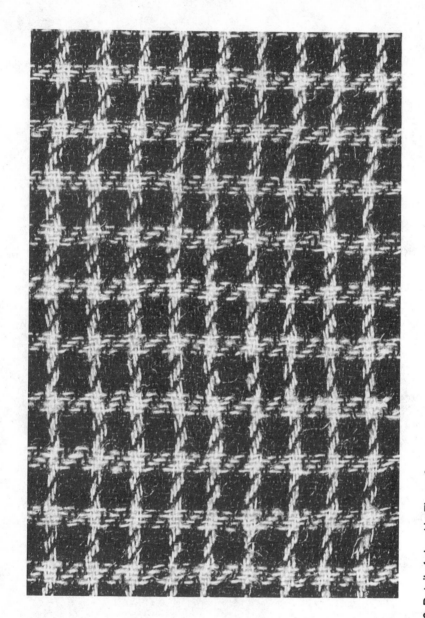

Figure 10: Detail of shawl in Figure 9.

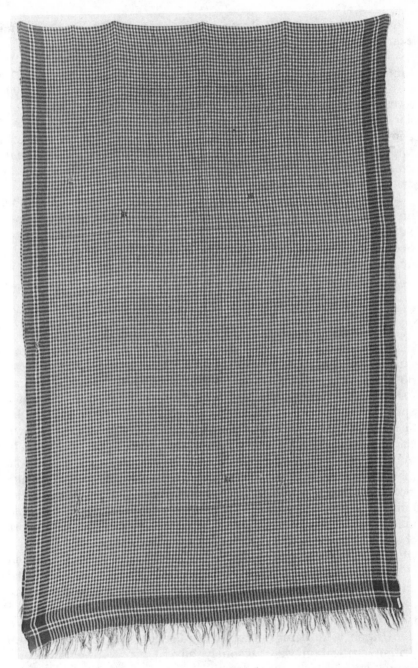

Figure 11: Man's shawl woven in the Scottish tradition, mid-19th century. ROM 948.5.1.

industry, it is most likely that the shawl was made there and exported to Quebec (Coleman 1969:417–429).

The weave of this artifact is twill which is more complex than the tabby weave structure found in most extant Quebec textiles. The design, a blue and white check, is typical of many Scottish shawls as can be seen when it is compared with a Scottish man's shawl with a very similar overall appearance (Figure 11). The collecting history shows the woman's shawl was donated to the Royal Ontario Museum by a person who said it was woven by her great-great-grandmother. However, this type of oral history, like other forms of evidence, needs to be carefully evaluated.

The dating of the shawl could well be 1810, but both the artifact analysis and the documentary evidence relating to the activities of Scottish merchants strongly suggest that it was imported from Scotland to Lower Canada where it was purchased for use by a family, probably related to the donor, living near Quebec City in the early nineteenth century.

COLONIALISM

As discussed earlier, British economic domination also spread to related textile making activities such as tailoring. Anglophones quickly established themselves in this trade; for example, by 1840, 86 percent of Quebec City tailors were English-speaking tradesmen using British techniques and patterns. In effect, this supremacy spread to most economic spheres, affecting both common and highly specialized crafts (Ruddel 1987). By 1820, British influence in Lower Canada had become so pervasive that a writer in the local gazette maintained that everything in Quebec City was British. Tools, institutional buildings, private dwellings, and the latest clothing fashions—all reflected current British styles. Even the English language began to appear in documents written in French. With the massive importation of British goods came English-speaking merchants, artisans, troops, sailors and waves of immigrants, all of whom altered the socio-cultural composition of Lower Canadian cities. For example, if one considers the floating population of British origin in Quebec City in the 1830s, anglophones made up about 54 percent of the people in this former French capital (Ruddel 1987). It is not surprising, then, to discover that some of the daily habits of the British were being promoted by French-speaking merchants. British civilization was obviously having a profound impact on French culture.

With this strong British influence in mind, we began re-examining textiles, especially in the collections of the Royal Ontario

Museum, the Canadian Museum of Civilization, and the National Gallery of Canada. Some of the textiles woven in rural Quebec reflect the transferal and assimilation of British socio-cultural symbols. Among the strongest examples of this are the coverlets woven in tabby embellished with a weft loop design, known in Quebec as *boutonné*. Figure 12 is a Quebec example woven about 1830. But coverlets using weft-loop patterning were also produced in a large-scale cottage industry in Bolton, a weaving town in the cotton manufacturing area of Lancashire, England. Many of the Bolton coverlets were exported to North America where they were in vogue throughout the late eighteenth and nineteenth centuries; Figure 13, dated 1804 and Figures 14 and Figure 16 are other examples of Bolton designs made during the nineteenth century.

If we compare the nineteenth-century Bolton coverlets with those made in Quebec, it is clear how strongly local weavers were influenced by the imported British bedcoverings. This is illustrated in the series of photographs which compare Bolton coverlets with those made in Quebec. In particular, one should note the central medallion seen in Figures 14 and 15 which often contains a large eight-pointed star. As well, there are a variety of stylized flowers and pine tree-like motifs evident in Figures 16 and 17. But there are also some major differences. The Bolton pieces were woven in a single width on a wide loom but in Quebec the use of a narrow loom necessitated a center seam (Figure 17); and the Bolton coverlets were always woven in cotton, while those from Quebec were made of linen.

The designs in these artifacts imply that country people, unable to afford fashionable Bolton coverlets, knew what they were, how they looked and that they were in vogue. Perhaps because they could not purchase an original, they wove bed coverings which closely resembled those made in England.

Boutonné coverlets continued to be woven in Quebec throughout the nineteenth and well into the twentieth centuries. But as Figures 18 through 21 illustrate, they were no longer direct copies of the Bolton coverlets. The textile illustrated in Figure 18 contains elements of the designs found in the early Quebec *boutonné* pieces—the zigzag borders and checkerboard horizontal banding—but they have added the eight-pointed star and stylized pine tree common in the Bolton copies. Gradually, the designs became more free-form as in the artifacts which still combined the star and tree motifs, but demonstrate that the weaver's imagination had begun to exert its influence. For example, in Figure 19 a tail has been added to the star in commemoration of the 1882 viewing of the Great Comet. Although the ubiquitous star is the major motif in Figures 20 and

Figure 12: Quebec *boutonné* coverlet, probably about 1830. NGC 9617 (photo: ROM).

Figure 13: Bolton coverlet made in England and dated 1804. ROM 969.3.2 (photo: Bill Robertson)

Figure 14: British coverlet about 1840. ROM 970.284 (photo: Bill Robertson)

Figure 15: Quebec linen *boutonné* coverlet, about 1860. ROM 970.90.6.

Figure 16: Bolton coverlet made of cotton, English, 19th century. Note similarity of motifs between this and Figure 17. ROM 943.24.16 (photo: Bill Robertson)

Figure 17: Detail of a mid 19th-century, Quebec linen coverlet showing center seam. Note also similarity of motifs with those in Figure 16. ROM 963.88.

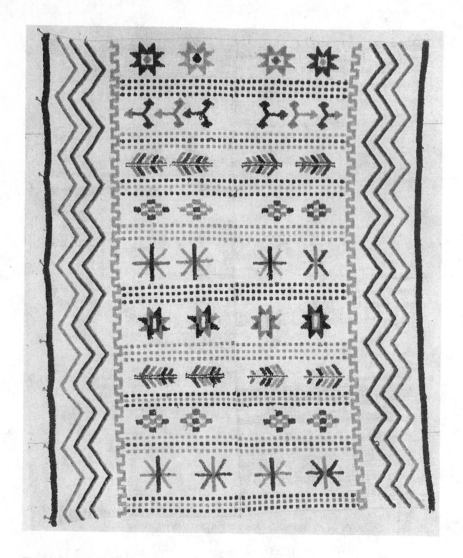

Figure 18: Quebec *boutonné* coverlet, 1870–75, with zigzag borders seen on earlier pieces (e.g. Figure 12) but also now incorporating Bolton-like designs. NGC 9614 (photo: ROM)

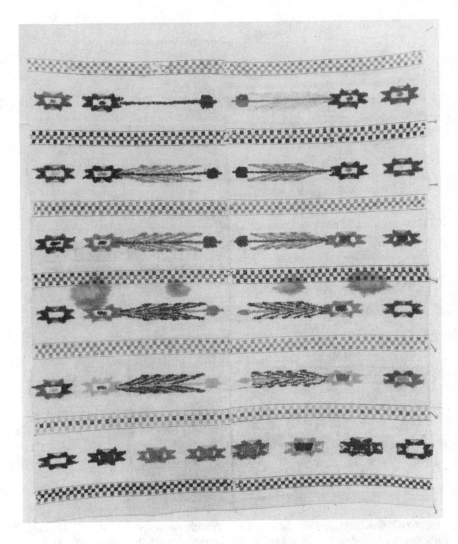

Figure 19: Quebec coverlet, about 1880, which shows the 8-pointed star with a tail added to commemorate the viewing of Halley's comet. NGC 9619 (photo: ROM)

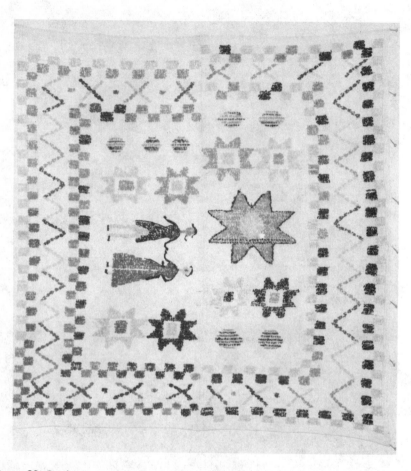

Figure 20: Quebec coverlet, about 1870. Although the 8-pointed star still dominates the design, the weaver added the folk-art-like elements of the human figures. NGC 9625 (photo: ROM)

Figure 21: Quebec coverlet, about 1870. Heart motifs appear in this piece, along with the more usual pine trees and stars.

21, there is the addition of other more folk-art-like designs such as human figures and hearts.

The eight-pointed star and pine tree motifs have become synonymous with Quebec handweaving. Yet the preceding analysis sheds light on the evolution of this supposedly "pure" folk art, from an artifact of British origin which was copied and gradually modified and embellished by Quebec weavers to acquire the appearance of a traditional design. The importance of the British origins of this folk art form has been lost. One possible reason was the twentieth-century revival of Quebec weaving to create a needed cottage industry; at that time many of the so called "traditional" Quebec textile motifs and techniques were collected and printed as weaving manuals, thereby freezing in time an evolving design (Bériau 1943:22).

Textile researcher Harold Burnham was the first to notice the strong similarity between the Bolton coverlets and those produced in Quebec, as well as others likely made in the United States, but he was unable to do detailed research on the subject (Burnham 1971:22–29; unpublished notes and correspondence in Royal Ontario Museum). Indeed, there is very little in secondary sources on the diffusion of Bolton coverlets, but our work suggests that products of the British textile industry affected nineteenth-century North American consumption and production patterns.

CONCLUSION

This analysis of artifacts and documents has stimulated additional research by each of us. In order to further refine this kind of dynamic exchange a number of avenues are worth pursuing. It is apparent to us that the methods of studying material objects, in particular the textile samples here considered, warrant more work. Methods concerning theories of history and artifact analysis need to be tested on specific categories of objects by teams of specialists from a variety of disciplines.

The strong bias towards a "homespun" or romanticized interpretation of our past (which has so affected museum collecting policies and exhibits) has made some social scientists leery of using objects in their studies. Their wariness has been compounded by several factors. The artifacts, and often exhibits growing out of them, have not been collected, analyzed, or presented with the same rigour as documents. The relative inaccessibility of many artifact collections makes the artifacts difficult to study. And there is a dearth of historical objects dating from the colonial periods.

Consider the following situation. The History Division of the Canadian Museum of Civilization has about 300 artifacts dating from 1600 to 1850, or an average of just one object per year; most of these artifacts are poorly documented and come from the upper echelons of society. If you set this artifact base against even a modest collection of documents you can see how large the discrepancies can be. For instance, the sampling of post-mortem inventories we used in this paper yielded over 1100 documents, or more than 55 per year, with a data base of over 500,000 items touching all facets of peoples' daily lives. These figures may sound impressive when compared to the artifacts, but when other sources are added the documentary base is even more substantial.

Documents from the colonial periods tend to be more numerous than objects found in museum collections, thus the former provide a more readily available tool for studying the society and culture of that period than the latter. Even so, we are not arguing for the primacy of the document over the artifact. What we have been struggling with is the attempt to find a just balance between these two sources.

Approaches that combine an analysis of documents and artifacts tend to be overlooked in many studies of "material" culture. Moreover, many researchers studying the cultural past find terms like "material history" and "material culture" convenient because such terms help explain the use of objects, and because they legitimize a field of endeavour. We know, however, that culture—as the anthropologists remind us—is not material. And many ethnologists and historians analyzing objects often use more documents than artifacts in their studies of cultural change. Yet both documents and artifacts are clearly useful in analyzing a culture. What is important, therefore, is not to argue about the primacy of one or the other, but to use them as complementary sources.

Despite the problems inherent in using textiles as historical evidence, the type of complementary analysis of documents and artifacts demonstrated in this paper is well worth doing. For example, on the one hand, it would have been impossible to trace the influence of British designs on Quebec textiles solely through documentary material. On the other hand, documentary research on goods imported to Quebec made it possible to identify a shawl as an item probably made in Scotland, not locally. Taken further this may help in reclassifying other artifacts in museum collections. Technological analysis of the Quebec textiles, as compared with those made by British and German Canadians, reinforced what Quebec historians knew from documentary sources—that women wove. But it also suggested that francophone women lacked the professional training of the male artisans found in areas of Canada populated by people of British and German descent. Finally, more than any document could possibly illustrate, the blanket incorporating very hairy cow hair in its manufacture and used until it was in shreds, and the worn, repaired and patched coverlet give us a *sensory* perception of the reality of the life of nineteenth-century rural French Canadians.

Notes

* The use of the artifactual material in this paper was made possible by the labors of an earlier generation of researchers who collected and catalogued many of the textiles incorporated into this analysis. Special acknowledgment must go to Marius Barbeau who originally collected and documented most of the Quebec pieces; to Harold Burnham and Dorothy Burnham who catalogued and photographed the artifacts from a variety of collections and left their detailed notes for the use of future generations; and to Robert-Lionel Séguin who was one of the first researchers in Quebec to base an analysis of textile history on post-mortem inventories.

1. Sometimes idiosyncrasies in the set up of a loom are based on local tradition, but this would not be apparent in the pattern of a textile. These details can provide clues as to cultural diffusion.

2. It should be noted that the majority of surviving Quebec textiles found in museums come from the Quebec City region.

3. Although the four shaft Quebec looms are capable of producing textiles with a more complex weave structure than the simple, two shaft tabby weave found in most surviving French-Canadian textiles, they are not as complex as the multi-shaft looms used to weave some of the textiles with a British- or German-Canadian attribution. For a more detailed discussion of textile structures and terminology see Burnham (1980).

4. The amount of homespun used by urban artisan and laboring families grew from 25 percent of their household linen in 1800 to 42 percent in 1825 (Ruddel 1987:95).

5. Linen production is labor-intensive. About a year and a half elapses from the time of planting the flax seed until the yarn is spun and ready to be woven into cloth; during this time, the flax undergoes at least ten different operations. In seventeenth-, eighteenth-, and much of nineteenth-century North America labor was in short supply; thus even in the early years of settlement it was often cheaper to buy imported cloth than make it (Hood 1988). Although in the nineteenth century people still wove cloth, many purchased some or all of their yarns, and cotton, spun first in the New England mills, and later, more locally, supplanted linen. As a result, linen yarn was rarely used in handwoven textiles after about 1830, and it was almost never used after mid-century.

6. At the same time that British legislators were attempting to suppress the manufacture of colonial homespun, indigenous politicians were equally busy legislating conditions which would free them from imperial restraints. Most colonies passed laws to encourage the manufacture of linen, woollen, and cotton cloth (Tryon 1917:15–61). When the British attempted to enforce restrictive policies, especially in the 1760s, colonists responded with an even greater effort to stimulate domestic production. After American independence from Great Britain, economic nationalists continued to stimulate both domestic and industrial production. In 1790 President Washington delivered his message to Congress clad in a broadcloth suit made of Connecticut homespun. One of the results of the President's demand that Congress promote indigenous industries was the establishment of an elaborate customs policy on imports, as well as financial support for local manufactures (Rossiter 1967:29).

7. This was true of New France and of the Province of Quebec until 1791, when a constitutional government was allowed. Thus, between the date of the British takeover of New France in 1760–1761, and 1791, no elected representatives existed on the provincial (or colonial) level and between 1760–1832 and 1835–40, no municipal governments were allowed. While granting a constitutional government in 1791, the British decided not to allow the existence of municipal governing bodies because of the role they had played in the American Revolution.

8. At the beginning of the British regime in Quebec (1763), the imperial government made it clear that Governor Murray was not to assent to the establishment of any manufacture harmful to British trade (Copy of instructions for James Murray, 7 December 1763, in Lambert:12; and *Documents Relating to the Constitutional History of Canada, 1765–1791*, 1914:200 and 609). Five years later, Lord Hillsborough instructed Governor Carleton to discourage the production of linen by encouraging other industries less prejudicial to British manufactures. Carleton responded that the cultivation of flax and hemp would provide habitants with money they could use to purchase English clothing.

9. In his article "Wool Supply and the Woollen Industry," P.J. Bowden argues that an underfed sheep in a cold climate will be small and grow a fine, dense fleece suitable for producing woollen (or carded) yarn. The same sheep fed well would be much larger and produce a longer, coarser wool used to spin worsted (or combed yarn) (Bowden 1956–7:45). In England this change took place because of the enclosure of fields. Generally, in North America, labor was too limited to provide the care needed to produce long-stapled wool. In addition, the quality and length of the wool fiber gradually decreased throughout the eighteenth century due to restrictions placed on exporting sheep from Britain and indifferent breeding practices in North America (Hood 1988:81–96).

10. This area of research needs more work. It should be noted that we are not claiming that wool combing was not done in Quebec, just that it occurred far less frequently than carding.

The Celestial World of Jonathan Odell

Symbolic Unities within a Disparate Artifact Collection

Ann Gorman Condon

The historical artifacts belonging to Jonathan Odell form the most elegant, most élite collection of Loyalist personal objects in the province of New Brunswick. They include a striking pair of globes—one celestial and one terrestrial—mounted in mahogany casings and marked with Newtonian symbols and classical references; a set of jewelled buckles for dancing shoes; a case of inlaid brass optical instruments from France; almost 300 books, an imposing library of classical and modern authors; a pianoforte given to Odell's daughter Mary by Governor Thomas Carleton (in tribute, no doubt, to her father's long service to the Carleton family); and a few slightly more utilitarian objects such as his seals of office as Provincial Secretary, a silver drinking tankard, a tea caddy, and a technologically innovative reading lamp designed by his friend Benjamin Thompson, Count Rumford. And there are also the more public and more famous items—poems, letters, sermons, a house, the remains of a church.

Although the objects in this collection are not sufficiently grand or rare to be classified as fine art, they do convey a sense of elegance, rationality, and leisure. They conjure up images of refinement and order—the detached Augustan world of an eighteenth-century colonial gentleman, a pious cleric, an amateur scientist, and a widely-read man of letters. They are uniformly pleasant and worth having, but they do not seem exciting to our twentieth-century sensibilities. There is a passivity, a remoteness, an almost other-worldly quality about these objects. They convey no emotional energy, no internal dynamism or sense of conflict. Instead, Odell's objects tend to confirm our received notions of the Loyalist governing class as being privileged and cultivated but ultimately peripheral—reactionary in their own times and utterly anachronistic in ours. Although these objects continue to be revered, they are not perceived as relevant, as containing a historical force of enduring significance. Odell himself remains a stereotype, a caricature—a slightly absurd Dr. Syntax—the quintessential example of an elegant but super-cilious Tory who busied himself writing classical poetry while the American Revolution whirled about him and then, neglecting his Loyalist comrades' harsh struggle with the wilderness, retired to New Brunswick to build a little island of privilege. Generations of historians and literary critics have dismissed Odell as ineffectual.[1] Even some of his contemporaries mocked his preoccupation with religious ritual and the life of the mind, calling him a snob, a "quack tutor," "a high priest on the order of Melchisedec," a "Dr. Touchy" (Davies 1987; Glenie 1800; Condon 1983:180; Condon 1986:125). Both the man and the artifacts in his collection are not perceived as vital evidence of a past culture, but as clichés (Figure 1).

Yet the larger historical record tells us that these impressions are an illusion. Odell's life was not marked by privilege and haughty indifference, but by unremitting, soul-searing controversy, from his birth into a "New Light" family during the Great Awakening through his service as a propagandist and spy during the American Revolution to his final years as a lonely, deprived exile in the New Brunswick wilderness. The challenge for the historian is to reconcile the known facts of such a turbulent life with the puzzling as-semblage of artifacts Odell left to his heirs and to history as his final statement: the monuments, poems, sermons, library, and private tokens of intellect and civility. The scholar's task is to break though the accumulated layers of cliché, piety, and prejudice that encumber our understanding of Odell and relocate him in the particular community, tradition, and living current of thought which con-stituted his historical universe. Only by examining these artifacts afresh, by identifying their content and style and reestablishing their contemporary meaning in Odell's life, will it become possible to probe their relationship to the larger issues of that historical mo-ment—the war over power and truth and beauty which shaped Odell's life in such cataclysmic ways.

Following the example of that inspired historian of the eight-eenth century, Carl Becker, I have described Odell's world as a

Figure 1: Jonathan Odell. Artist unknown. Detail. Watercolour on ivory. Collection of the New Brunswick Museum.

"celestial" one. In part the reference is to the distinctive pair of globes which form the physical centerpiece of the Odell collection. More significantly for my purposes, the term celestial refers to the rarified nature of the vision Odell brought to New Brunswick and expressed not only in his object choices but in his deeds and his poetry. This essay will explore the historical basis of Odell's vision by comparing the objects he chose during his New Brunswick years with the distinctly different kinds of objects which dominated his youthful, prerevolutionary years. By juxtaposing the stylistic evidence offered by these two sets of objects, it will become apparent that the artifacts from Odell's New Brunswick years provide material documentation of a complex cultural commitment, amounting to a civil religion, which he and other élite Loyalists hoped to establish in British North America. This cultural commitment emphasized traditional British forms of expression and contrasted sharply with the republican style of the new American nation. Odell and his colleagues deliberately used the objects to shape the official culture of their young colony. The aesthetic and ideological implications of these objects lead to the conclusion that the Odell collection of artifacts is an important, representative example of the Loyalist contribution to nascent Canadian culture.

Before proceeding to an examination of these historical objects, it will be necessary to explain the emphasis on material evidence in the analysis and to describe the methodological procedures used to disclose the historical significance of the Odell collection.

METHODOLOGY

In seeking to restore meaningful context to the Odell collection, the material history approach is extraordinarily useful. Man-made objects are more securely anchored in time and place than texts or ideas or values. They are concrete and time-bounded: they were made at a particular place, by identifiable people, with ascertainable materials. Usually they are sold for a specific price and bought for a specific reason, be it ideological, sensuous, or utilitarian. The processes which accompanied the life of the artifact—fabrication, transactions, trade routes—can also be traced. All these expressions and bits of empirical data, these minutiae of everyday life are levers which help to pry open a specific historical universe. They enable us to overcome the distance and strangeness of the past by giving us a palpable, detailed sense of how specific human beings, living in a given natural environment, come together to create "a human dwelling place" out of their material circumstances, their needs, and their aspirations.[2]

Ultimately of course the objects, products of human hands, must be related to the accompanying texts, deeds, and larger historical context. This requires the development of a research technique that does not stop with data on the surface characteristics of objects—maker, materials, dimensions, value, use, etc.—but which goes on to explore the deeper historical issues, the intellectual and stylistic properties of these objects which led to their making, acquisition, and preservation. Thus the researcher must not only explore the external evidence presented by an artifact, but must interpret its importance for its makers and users, must "read" its internal content so as to identify its role within the particular historical circumstances. Through this process of interpretation, in which the full meaning of an object within a culture is brought to light, the object itself becomes an analogue which can then be compared to other types of data—literary texts, chronological events, personal choices—so that the totality of evidence for a given historical universe can be understood. Admittedly, this interpretive task raises subtle and complex questions: how to read the internal meaning of objects? how to establish legitimate correspondences between objects, texts, and deeds? And so forth. Such questions fall within the domain of modern critical theory, which works to articulate both the superficial and latent meaning of all categories of human expression so as to recover their full significance. In this sense, critical theory can aid the historical investigator in the common search for verifiable, comprehensive methods of interpreting disparate kinds of evidence.

Put simply, critical theory—whether taken from linguistics, sociology, anthropology, or biblical exegesis—assumes with Buffon that "le style c'est l'homme même." Beneath the manifold varieties of human expression there exists an underlying pattern, a network of affiliations—be they economic priorities, political loyalties, aesthetic values, neurotic needs, or spiritual ideals—that provides a basic unity to a person or a culture. Ever since Vico and Voltaire issued their separate calls for a "new history," students of the human past have searched for the interpretive key that would unlock the enigma of a personality or culture and reveal its full meaning. For the past two hundred years a dazzling, inventive series of theories and methods has been put forward to ferret out this deeper significance. While none of these theoretical approaches are scientific in the mathematical sense, they have enriched our descriptive capacities and our ability to identify the unities and differences which characterize a particular culture at a particular moment in time. This allows us to read texts, objects, and actions as a series of comparable expressions. One of the most lucid and fertile modern contributors to this field is Paul Ricoeur, the French philosopher and semanticist, whose published writings include works of scriptural analysis, substantive studies of the writings of Sigmund Freud and Edmund Husserl, and a wide-ranging series of shorter comments on developments in psychology, linguistics, and structural anthropology.[3] Ricoeur's primary interest is hermeneutics, the theory of rules which preside over the interpretation of symbols. He defines symbols as cultural instruments that have a "double meaning" or "a complex signification where another meaning is both given and hidden in an immediate meaning" (Ricoeur 1970:7).[4] Although most of his own work is confined to literary texts, Ricoeur recognizes that these symbolic expressions occur in "diverse modalities" including "the great cosmic symbols brought to light by a phenomenology of religion...with all its equivalents in folklore, legends, proverbs, and myths; the verbal creations of the poet, following the guidelines of sensory, visual, acoustic, or other images or following the guidelines of space and time" (Ricoeur 1974:13).

Ricoeur seeks to establish the theoretical basis of the rules which govern the interpretation of a particular text or of a group of signs that may be viewed as a text. The merit of his approach is that it combines the positive strengths of nineteenth-century textual criticism with the subsequent insights of three much more skeptical analysts—Karl Marx, Sigmund Freud, and Friedrich Nietzsche—who exposed the elements of illusion and distortion in both cultural and personal expressions (Ricoeur 1970:20–36). The richness of Ricoeur's analysis can only be appreciated, of course, by reading him first-hand. All that is possible here is to outline, in skeletal form, his investigatory techniques so as to use them to penetrate the stereotypes surrounding the Odell collection and to restore its contemporary meaning.

Ricoeur first distinguishes between simple and complex cultural phenomena. Simple, "univocal" expressions are those bits of evidence which contain only a single message, where the surface meaning constitutes the entire meaning. Ricoeur does not propose interpretive guidelines for this category, since the direct, apparent evidence is sufficient. Rather he confines his attention to cultural expressions which have a double meaning—variously termed "equivocal," "ambiguous," or "plurivocal" expressions. Only such double-meaning expressions qualify as symbols, or cultural instruments, in his lexicon. Ricoeur's second, more ambitious, and more original contribution is to propose a three-stage mode of analysis to decipher both the apparent and the latent meaning of symbols in order to recover their full significance. Reduced to its essence, his interpretive investigation would proceed as follows:

1. The "hermeneutics of recollection" is the first stage, in which the literal, immediate, intentional, or surface meaning of the symbol is recorded as fully as the evidence permits.

2. The "hermeneutics of suspicion" constitutes the second stage, in which the hidden, unconscious, indirect, or obverse contents of the symbol, those meanings for which the surface meaning is an illusion or mask, are pursued. Ricoeur insists on the importance of penetrating such denials or suppressions, although he acknowledges that evidence for these hidden meanings can only be arrived at inductively. The critical tools developed by psychology, sociology, and symbolic logic in uncovering false consciousness, ideological masks, and disguised will to power are the primary means of deciphering hidden meaning.

3. Finally, Ricoeur's third stage consists of "reflection" on the correspondences within the first two equivocal sets of meaning so as to apprehend their full philosophical richness and arrive at a new interpretation of the symbol's meaning, a new sense of its total significance. Ricoeur admits that this third stage is speculative, but he insists that "symbols themselves demand this speculative reflection" and that the work of the first two stages will guide and discipline the reflective process of the third stage, making it as concrete as the contingent nature of cultural phenomena permit (Ricoeur 1970:40–42).

I have elected to apply Ricoeur's procedures in this analysis of the Odell collection because they seem compatible with the historian's traditional preoccupation with context. The virtue of Ricoeur's approach, viewed in terms of the disciplinary concerns of historians, is that it does not posit an *a priori* interpretive model, but is designed rather to extend the researcher's descriptive capabilities by exploring fully both the positive and negative implications of cultural symbols. In order to proceed with the analysis, it will be necessary first to separate out those Odell artifacts which have only a single meaning from those whose meaning is more ambiguous. Into the first "univocal" category, I have placed all the personal and professional items which a man of Odell's position—his wealth, his status as an Anglican cleric and member of the governing élite, his training as a medical doctor—could be expected to own. Thus, the tankard, dancing buckles, tea caddy, optical case, seals of office, and even the Rumford lamp seem to be predictable items for a man of Odell's background.[5] In addition, the Odell house in Fredericton appears to be a simple, univocal artifact whose size and stylistic properties conform with conventional historical interpretation. In a fine summary statement on "Loyalist Architecture in British North America," Stuart Allen Smith describes the design principles which the Loyalists brought from colonial America and which they sought to replicate in their new communities in colonial Canada, subject of course to the modifications imposed by the wilderness. Odell's house is, in fact, one of the examples Smith uses to illustrate typical Loyalist architectural conceptions (Figure 2). Odell yielded to the immediate need to shelter his family against the New Brunswick environment by buying and building upon a house erected a few years before his arrival in Fredericton. The older portions eventually were used as kitchens and servants' quarters, while the new portion was for family use and reflected the eighteenth-century principles of balance and symmetry so prized by the Loyalists. Yet even in this new portion, Odell had to trim his notions to fit the physical circumstances of his property and, as a result, to move the entrance of the house to the gable end. The resulting house is proportional and spacious as were most of the homes of the Loyalist élite in New Brunswick (Smith 1981). It is, however, by no means as grand as the house built by Anglican minister East Apthorp in Cambridge, Massachusetts in 1760 nor, most probably, as imposing as the vicarage which Odell himself lived in before the American Revolution in Burlington, New Jersey.[6] Thus in both its positive qualities and its limitations, the Odell house seems fully representative of Loyalist élite style and contains no special features requiring further investigation.

By this process of elimination, the nonliterary items in the Odell collection have been reduced to two three-dimensional objects whose intentions are not immediately comprehensible, whose style and surface characteristics are not fully explained by our conventional knowledge of the Loyalist élite. These are the set of globes and the Anglican church in Fredericton. Both of these objects have features which seem "inappropriate" for a backwoods élite in greatly reduced circumstances. There is something too grand, too novel about these objects. They depart too radically from our knowledge of the American background and from the survival challenge which the Loyalists faced during the early settlement period in New Brunswick. The globes in particular are simply too elegant: too finely crafted, too showy in their mahogany casings. Likewise, certain features of the church are unfamiliar. The double-storey, the raised steeple, and the enlarged scale all arouse skepticism. A deeper

Figure 2: Odell House, Fredericton. Reproduced courtesy of the New Brunswick Public Archives.

explanation of these features is required: how did they get to New Brunswick? and what role did they play there? It is this enigmatic element, this arousal of the investigator's skepticism by surface features whose meaning is not readily apparent, that suggests that these objects are proper candidates for further inquiry, using Ricoeur's three stages of hermeneutical or interpretive investigation. Whether these objects do contain a deeper, symbolic meaning cannot, of course, be ascertained until the investigation is completed.

FIRST STAGE—HERMENEUTICS OF RECOLLECTION

The first stage of the research process is designed to recover from the surface appearance of the objects all the positive, intentional meanings which they contain. In the case of the matched pair of globes, their twin surfaces are literally filled with intellectual and aesthetic messages (Figures 3 and 4). The tripod mahogany stands, with their compressed base and snake feet, are clearly inspired by

Figure 3: Celestial Globe. H. 57.15 cm. Mkr: Adams, Dudley. Mfg: London, England.
Odell Collection of the New Brunswick Museum.

Figure 4: Terrestrial Globe. H 57.15 cm. Mkr: Adams, Dudley. Mfg: London, England. Odell Collection of the New Brunswick Museum.

Figure 5: Surface, Celestial Globe. Odell Collection of the New Brunswick Museum.

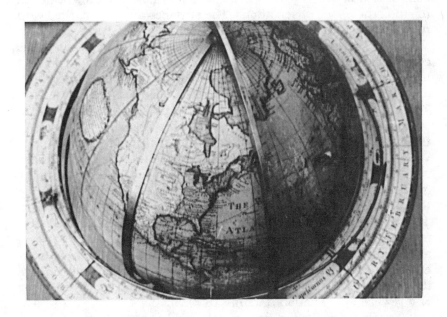

Figure 6: Surface, Terrestrial Globe. Odell Collection of the New Brunswick Museum.

Figure 7: Globe Feet and Compass. Odell Collection of the New Brunswick Museum.

the designs of Thomas Chippendale. They provide a classical frame for the bright patina of the spheres which are further highlighted by complementary color schemes and a series of metal bands designed to guide the user's observations. The surfaces are also marked with numerous astronomical notations and classical references (Figures 5 and 6). Two compasses have been placed below the globes in the center of the stands to add to the effect of scientific precision, making it clear that these globes were designed with informed knowledge and intended for active use in some kind of technical exercise (Figure 7). A direct clue to their origin is the insignia of their maker emblazoned on each globe: "Dudley Adams, Instrument Maker to the King and His Majesty's Ordinary Optician to H.R.H. Prince of Wales." A search for this craftsman confirms that these are indeed very special globes. Their prototypes were originally designed in the mid-eighteenth century by George Adams, the father of Dudley, for the instruction of the children of the royal family (Chaldecott 1951:5). They were accompanied, moreover, by a four hundred page text written by the elder Adams which is in fact a school book on astronomy explaining the Newtonian system and containing exercises to be used in conjunction with the globes which would "engage the attention of the young and may be used to encourage diligence and reward appreciation" (Adams 1800:vii).

Jonathan Odell must have purchased his set of globes between 1795 and 1800, the period when Dudley took over his father's business in Fleet Street, London. These dates coincide with the first grant from the New Brunswick Assembly to the struggling academy or "college" in Fredericton, an institution which convened originally on Odell's property and which he had nurtured in a variety of ways. Thus the evidence clearly suggests that Odell imported these exceptionally fine instructional globes to help launch the college, and that they eventually became part of his personal artifact collection by default, owing to the fitful, financially troubled history of the college in its early years. Odell's purchases for his library in these years support this conclusion: he departed from his customary pattern of choice to acquire introductory texts on chemistry and natural history, geometry, geography, algebra, and techniques of memorization. Although no college records exist for this early period, it seems clear that Odell, who had several tutoring posts in his early career, played an active role in setting up the program of instruction and that the globes were part of this effort. However, given the extraordinary financial difficulties of getting the college underway—the institution was opposed by many groups in the province and the legislature provided only one grant of £100 before the year 1800—it is still unclear why Odell would have invested in such sumptuous "royal" globes for use in this shaky educational venture (Condon 1983:194–5).[7]

The design and building history of Christ Church in Fredericton presents a similar note of unexpected extravagance. The church was one of four churches funded by a donation from the Society for the Propagation of the Gospel (SPG) in London to provide places of Anglican worship in New Brunswick for the incoming Loyalist refugees. A sum of £500 was allotted to each church, and it was clear from the SPG instructions that they were to be simple missionary churches in keeping with the indigent state of most of the refugees. Odell played a key role in the design and construction of the church, as a member of the management committee, on-site supervisor of construction, and longtime friend and close colleague of the rector, Rev. Samuel Cooke.[8] From the very start, the local committee exceeded their instructions and set out to build a grander edifice than the Society intended. As Cooke explained, the committee first decided not to divert any funds for a parsonage house, on the blithe assumption that once the church was built, pew rent would easily produce £30 per annum to cover the rector's housing needs. Two building plans were then debated, and the committee opted unanimously for the larger structure, "larger perhaps than at present is necessary, but we were willing to look forward with hope and expectation that time might provide a congregation to fill it" (SPG 16 October 1787).

The hope and expectation of the committee was not recompensed by wilderness New Brunswick. Building began on a double-storied structure, 72 feet long and 52 feet wide, with a full cellar, pillars under the roof for support, and two tiers of windows, "so that galleries may be erected, should time make them necessary, without any ill-convenience to the look of the Church." Within the year, the £500 had all been spent, the church was still not enclosed, and, as Cooke sorrowfully reported to the SPG "the desk, pulpit, chancel, pews ... and plaistering ... are still wanting, and I am afraid likely to continue so some time." Even the handsome gift of £150 from Governor Carleton was not sufficient to complete the business, and the local congregation proved to be so dispersed and short of cash that the distressed rector had to beg the Society to "look with charity" upon his work in the new colony (SPG 2 September 1788 and 7 July 1789). When Bishop Charles Inglis visited Fredericton in 1792 he noted the "mismanagement" of the still unfinished church and severely censured the grandiose dreams of its sponsors: "Portland Chapel in London was absurdly taken for a model to build this Church" (Inglis Typescripts, Harriet Irving Library Archives, University of New Brunswick 20 July 1792).[9]

The written records for this church are mainly illegible, and the only two extant views of it are nineteenth-century watercolors painted long after its completion (Figure 8).[10] In these sketches, the twin sets of windows and the elaborate bell-tower are the only visible details which stand out, but Bishop Inglis's reference to Portland Chapel provides an important additional clue to the intentions of the builders. As in the case of the globes, the choice of a royal chapel in London as an appropriate model for their church points to the determination of Odell and his colleague Cooke to transplant exalted imperial standards of style and achievement to their new homes. The fact that their plans ran into financial difficulties seems less remarkable than that they were attempted at all.

A subsequent comment on these plans by Cooke in 1791 hints at the basis of their hopes. In a jubilant letter to the SPG he announced that the arrival of a new regiment had created increased demands upon his church, and even though the original structure was still not completed, he had begun to draw up plans for four galleries to accommodate the "military and civil people" in hopes that some "unexpected assistance" might be forthcoming (SPG 29 June 1791). This vague reference suggests that both in planning the curriculum for their college and projecting the necessary scale of

Figure 8: Christ Church, Fredericton, New Brunswick, consecrated 1792. Woolford, John Elliott. Detail. Watercolour and gouache on panel. 1827. Collection of the New Brunswick Museum.

their church, neither Odell nor Cooke nor other like-minded members of the Loyalist élite were willing to confine their hopes to the backwoods circumstances of their immediate surroundings. In contrast to the simple Anglican structure chosen in Saint John and elsewhere, the élite clearly hoped that Fredericton's role as a military command post and center of provincial government would attract imperial patronage and enable them to cultivate standards more worthy of royalty (Figure 9).

The positive evidence presented by the globes and the church is exceedingly limited, but it does permit a tentative distinction to be made between the surviving public artifacts associated with Odell and the surviving private, personal items. The objects intended for public use are well-made, ostentatious, and royalist in their connotations, whereas the house and the more private objects are by comparison conventional and subdued. A brief survey of the literary portions of the Odell collection deepens this contrast. The most famous items in the literary collection are the political propaganda poems written during the American Revolution and the War of 1812. They are bitter, heavy-handed pieces—sarcastic, dogmatic, composed in antiquated verse forms and filled with obscure literary illusions. It is these poems which caused Moses Coit Tyler to label Odell "Toryissimus," and the image of an arch-reactionary has clung to him ever since. Yet the private portions of the literary remains convey an entirely different impression. His lyrical poems are delicate, introspective works which speak of domestic joys, the loneliness of war, and the need to accept life's vicissitudes with Christian fatalism.[11] His magnificent library—surely Odell's one form of personal self-indulgence—contains only two books on politics published before 1800, but numerous works of esoteric scholarship on poetry, the Bible, and the structure of language.[12] Indeed the books which Odell brought with him to New Brunswick, or imported from Great Britain while resident there, considerably challenge the traditional image of him as a political poet with a single *idée fixe*. Likewise, Odell's one sustained work of prose was a book on prosody—not politics—an analysis of the rhythmic structure and proper pronunciation of poetical texts (Odell 1805). It was this arcane subject which consumed most of his attention in his New Brunswick years and which he hoped would bring him lasting literary fame. Unfortunately his co-author Jonathan Boucher died before the text was ready, and Odell had to publish the book privately in 1805. It received some respectful reviews in Great Britain and brought Odell into correspondence with such leading British thinkers as John Thelwall and Richard Roe, as well as the

Figure 9: Trinity Church, Saint John, New Brunswick, consecrated 1792, burned 1877. Flewwelling, Charles. Wood engraving. Webster Collection of the New Brunswick Museum.

American Hebrew scholar, Clement C. Moore. This was a form of literary attention which Odell craved and it may have provided him some consolation for the years spent in his self-styled "frigid retreat" (Odell Family Papers, New Brunswick Museum 1802–1808).[13]

These intellectual and literary pursuits were clearly of tremendous importance to Odell. Even Governor Carleton complained that his "effusions to his muse" caused him to neglect his official duties as Provincial Secretary (Raymond 1901:528). While there is a deeply poignant aspect to this picture of a forlorn poet labouring for years in the forest to develop a systematic method of reading English poetry, these erudite pursuits of Odell rouse even more curiosity about the heavy didacticism of his public poems and sermons and the political pretensions of those objects he chose for public display, the globes and the Fredericton church. How does one reconcile the fastidious intellectual concerns of the private scholar with the ornate ritualism of the public man? To be sure, Odell felt the common Loyalist bitterness at the experience of defeat and exile. Yet most other members of the Loyalist élite were mainly bent on recovering their own personal comforts and privileges. Odell stands virtually alone in terms of the intensity of his determination to bring royal symbols to New Brunswick and to preserve the purity of traditional forms of thought and language. There was, it seems, a touch of fanaticism in Odell's gestures which was not manifested by his Loyalist colleagues. The details of the globes and the church provide tentative evidence of this; the poems and sermons, the library, and the book of prosody point much more clearly to a man who, although affable, yet somewhat ascetic in his private habits, was possessed of a crusader's zeal with respect to public ceremonies and traditional forms. Only by moving to the second stage of our analysis and examining alternative, contrasting artifacts in Odell's life can the significance of this discrepancy be assessed.

SECOND STAGE—HERMENEUTICS OF SUSPICION

Jonathan Odell's childhood and his student years were characterized by a way of life that was emotionally and aesthetically narrow to the point of severity. He grew up in a close family and was given unusually rich educational opportunities, but these benefits were secured in an atmosphere of sustained sensory deprivation. Odell was born in 1737 into a family closely identified with Protestant dissent, and he grew up in the storm center of the "Great Awakening" religious revival in the middle colonies. His father, Jonathan Odell, was a joiner from Connecticut, raised in the Congregational tradition of New England. His mother, Temperance Dickinson, was the daughter of Jonathan Dickinson, an eminent Presbyterian leader and first President of the College of New Jersey, the original name of Princeton University. This college was founded explicitly to train ministers to spread the gospel of "New Light" Presbyterianism and to save its young students from the "poisonous" liberalism being taught at Yale and Harvard. Odell was born in Elizabethtown, New Jersey, where his grandfather was both the local pastor and the head of the college, and he grew up in almost constant physical proximity to this dynamic evangelical movement. His grandfather died when he was ten and his father three years later, but the latter left instructions and just enough money in his will to ensure that Jonathan could "be kept to learning till he hath taken his degree at college" (MacLachlan *et al.* 1976:109–10).[14]

Five buildings stand out as especially significant structures during the formative period of Odell's life, and details on their size and style help to define the aesthetic parameters which shaped his young sensibilities. The first two were the Protestant churches in Elizabethtown, where Odell spent his boyhood, and in Newark, where the college moved under its second president, Aaron Burr, and where Odell studied for his A.B. degree. Since both buildings burned down before the end of the century, information on their configuration is inevitably sketchy. The first Presbyterian Church of Elizabethtown was built during the pastorate of Odell's grandfather. It measured 42 feet wide by 58 feet long and 24 feet high. It was made of wood, covered with shingles, and equipped with a partial gallery, a steeple, and bells. It was considered a "fine church" by Presbyterian standards and also served as a meeting place for general political assemblies and the colonial supreme court. It was thus a multipurpose building, with minimal religious decoration (*Architectural History* 1947). The second church to figure in Odell's life, the Newark Presbyterian Church, has been reproduced though an architectural reconstruction. As the sketch shows, it was a stone building, 40 feet square, built in the classic New England style with a receding roof leading up to a belfry (Figure 10). The curved windows and a "wine-cup" pulpit seem to have been the only decorative features ("Old First" Church, n.d.).

Classes for the college were held on the second floor of the County Court House in Elizabethtown. No overall description of the appearance of this building is available, but the Princeton architectural historian, Henry Littleton Savage, reports that classroom conditions were most unsatisfactory and cramped. The sole Recitation Hall was in a room directly over the jail, and expenditures on students were kept to a minimum in order to save money for a new college building (Savage 1956:8).

Figure 10: Newark Presbyterian Church, completed in 1724. From *"Old First" Church of Newark, New Jersey* (n.d.), Princeton University Libraries.

The fourth and doubtless the most important building in Odell's youth was Nassau Hall, erected at the college's third and final location at Princeton. A long, transatlantic fundraising campaign was conducted to finance this building during Odell's undergraduate years, and construction actually began in 1754, the year before he took his A.B. Odell would have been intimately aware of the building's progress because he stayed on at the college after graduation and served as a tutor at the Latin grammar school run by President Burr. He then took his A.M. in 1757 with the first class to graduate in the new building. Given the importance of Nassau Hall to the college itself and in the annals of North American architectural history, it seems fair to assume that it made a particularly strong impression on young Jonathan Odell (Savage 1956).

The building was hailed at the time as the largest single structure in North America, and its capacious size later made it the
meeting place for the Continental Congress. In the nineteenth
century, a series of fires enabled the trustees to add structural and
decorative embellishments, and in the twentieth century Nassau
Hall has become the central symbol of Princeton, with connotations
as both a center of international scholarship and as a paradisical
playground for the undergraduate heroes created by F. Scott
Fitzgerald. Yet however glamorous and historic Nassau Hall's image
today, the eighteenth-century reality experienced by Jonathan Odell
was very different. The original building was undeniably big, but it
was also made on the cheap and forbiddingly plain, in the spartan
tradition so carefully cultivated by New Light Presbyterians (Figure
11). The spirit of the college officials was expressed in their instructions to the builders: "That the College be built of Brick if good Brick
can be made at Princeton & if Sand can be got reasonably Cheap.
That it be three storey high & without any Cellar." In the end local
stone was used instead of brick, presumably to save money. Two
views of the early college survive from the 1760s, which historian
Savage describes as follows:

> There are three flat-arched doors on the north side giving access
> by a flight of steps on the three separate entries. At the center is a
> projection of five bays surmounted by a pediment with circular
> windows, and other decorations. The only ornamental feature
> above the cornice is the cupola, standing somewhat higher than
> the twelve fireplaces. Beyond these there are no features of distinc-
> tion.

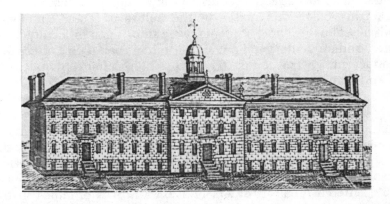

Figure 11: Nassau Hall, 1760. From Savage, Henry Littleton, *Nassau Hall 1756–
1956* (1956), Princeton University Libraries.

Even the cupola was simply copied from an eighteenth-century pattern book and had no special design features. The final effect, Savage concludes, expressed "much piety...but rather less of beauty," in fidelity to the college's commitment to religious austerity. Or, as President Burr put it at the time: "We do everything in the plainest and cheapest manner, as far as is consistent with Decency & Convenience, having no superfluous ornaments" (Savage 1956: 15–19).

The human environment at the college in Odell's years fully matched the sombreness of the physical surroundings. Nearly half the graduates in the first twenty years became clergymen, and almost all of these joined dissenting denominations. In Odell's class of 1754 the proportion was even higher, with 13 of the 19 students becoming dissenting clerics, mainly Presbyterians. The college was whiggish as well as evangelical: of the 279 graduates alive in 1775 only 8, or 3 percent of the total, became Loyalists, in sharp contrast to Harvard where 16 percent took the British side in the American Revolution. In fact, early Princeton produced the highest proportion of patriots of any colonial college (MacLachlan *et al.* 1976:xvii–xxii). The original curriculum placed heavy emphasis on the classics— Latin, Greek, and Hebrew texts plus rhetoric, logic, and astronomy—an intellectual orientation which Odell cherished all his life. The average entering student was sixteen years of age and student life, according to its most recent historian, was circum- scribed by a "brand of discipline more in keeping with a military barracks than an academic environment." Studies, meals, and prayers all took place within Nassau Hall, and the young students were forbidden: "'to intrude themselves upon superiors, to be absent from their rooms at stated hours without faculty permission, or to make any boisterous noises in the hallways.' Their chambers, normally housing three students, were to be open to faculty at all times, and students could not appear out of their rooms 'dress'd in an indecent, slovenly manner'....The prevailing atmosphere was one of repression and conformity" (Cohen and Gerlach 1974:71–2).

Jonathan Odell seems to have reacted viscerally against this early environment. In view of his grandfather's distinction, his own intellectual gifts, and his selection by President Burr to tutor at the classical academy, it is probable that Odell had been tipped by the Presbyterian elders for a career as a leader of the forces of clerical dissent in the middle colonies. Instead he joined the British army in 1757, entered Anglican orders in 1763 and was ordained in the "Chapel Royal" at St James's Palace, London, in 1767. He returned to America a zealous priest, deeply committed to the Church of

England's crusade to establish a bishop in the colonies and to "civilize" the narrow, sectarian Americans by introducing the enriched social and spiritual rituals of Anglican England. Indeed Odell became so closely identified with this "anglicizing" mission that his name was repeatedly mentioned as the likely "first bishop" for the American colonies.[15]

This was a remarkable turnabout, a religious conversion in the most fundamental sense. The impact on Odell was so profound that no mention of the dissenting members of his family, even his own parents, can be found in any of his poetry or personal correspondence, although he did write a celebratory poem entitled "My Pedigree" which exalted the seventeenth-century members of his family who supported the royalist cause in the English Civil War against the "raving Democrats" (Odell Family Papers, New Brunswick Museum). And of course he himself identified with the Loyalist cause in the American Revolution, in utter defiance of his Presbyterian and Princeton heritage. The material implications of this conversion experience can be best appreciated by comparing the four buildings described above with St. Mary's Church in Burlington, New Jersey where Odell became Anglican rector in 1767.

Burlington was the western capital and official residence of New Jersey's royal governor, William Franklin. The only son of Benjamin Franklin, William became a flamboyant Anglophile during his years with his father in England and particularly while a student at Oxford. He also married the heiress to a West Indian sugar fortune, the stylish Elizabeth Downes, and he and his wife took up their duties in New Jersey with elaborate pomp and ceremony. Mrs. Franklin in particular sought to assuage her loneliness for England by introducing aristocratic social forms—formal gardens, a deer park, Georgian furnishings, and elaborate entertainments—into the colony (Randall 1983:192–93, 223–24). Jonathan Odell had met Benjamin and William Franklin while a divinity student in London, and both father and son were impressed with his intellectual gifts and his flair for humorous poetry (Labaree 1959:5, 62).[16] Odell's appointment as rector at Burlington followed naturally, and after his arrival in 1767 he became the constant social companion of the Governor and his wife, as well as their religious representative. The couple could not have found a more willing or able collaborator in their efforts to endow New Jersey with an aristocratic veneer.

Odell's particular project was to renovate the old Burlington Church so that it was suitable for the more formal aspects of Anglican ritual and for the self-conscious dignity of the Governor and his wife. "The Church itself is very much out of repair," he reported to the SPG. Funds were found for the project from a special provincial lottery and from the generosity of the Franklin purse. The young cleric demonstrated his own zeal by declining to accept the customary local contribution to this salary—equivalent to an annual £19 sterling—until the debt for renovating the church was paid off six years after his arrival. By combining these monies, Odell was able to overhaul his church completely, extending the building westward and adding a gallery. In 1769 the SPG received the following report from their proud young missionary:

> The Society is informed by the Rev Mr Odell that the Church at Burlington is completed, and is not only a comfortable building, but an ornament to the place, being 63 feet by 33. Governor Franklin was very liberal on the occasion, and his lady has made them a present of the very rich and elegant furniture for the pulpit, desk, and table (Hills 1876:292, 301).

While no visual representation of this church is available, additional details of the renovations are contained in an unpublished manuscript in the Odell Papers at Princeton University. This source makes it clear that, besides lengthening the church, the changes made under Odell's direction significantly added to the interior embellishment:

> The old Church of St. Mary on Broad Street was surrounded by a wide area of unoccupied land. The one door at the west end opened to the long, narrow aisle on each side of which were the old-fashioned, high-backed pews. There was a narrow gallery at the west end, in the center of which was the organ gallery, enclosing a small but sweet-toned organ. On each side of the organ were seats for Sunday school children. The Governor's pew in the center of the Church was surmounted by a canopy. Rich damask hangings, the gift of Mrs. Franklin, adorned pulpit, reading desk, and communion table (Ford 1935).

The decorative features and regal ornaments of this fifth and final building in Odell's prerevolutionary environment provide a stunning contrast to the gloomy austerity of Nassau Hall and to the plain, puritanical structures in Elizabethtown and Newark. Likewise, the very phrases which Odell used to describe his renovated church—"not only a comfortable building but an ornament to the place... very rich and elegant furniture"—express an aesthetic philosophy diametrically opposite to the equally proud boast, quoted above, of Princeton's President Burr: "We do everything in the plainest and cheapest manner."

If material evidence can document a religious conversion, then surely the architectural details of these five buildings trace

Jonathan Odell's dramatic passage from Presbyterian piety to the highest forms of Anglican ritual ever realized in colonial America. The third stage of this analysis, the stage of reflection and interpretation, will consider the implications of this evidence for the artifacts which Odell chose in his New Brunswick years and for the nascent culture of colonial Canada.

THIRD STAGE — REFLECTION AND INTERPRETATION

In separate but complementary articles in the *Winterthur Portfolio*, Wendell Garrett and Jules Prown have argued that the philosophy of the American Revolution included specific attitudes toward art and pleasure which shaped the cultural policy of the new republic. Garrett uses the example of John Adams to illustrate the distinctive aesthetic orientation of the American Founding Fathers. He notes that although Adams was profoundly sensuous by nature and capable of responding powerfully to art and luxury, these feelings filled him with intense guilt and produced a lifelong fear of the effect of munificence and grandeur. Adams associated art and pleasure with decadence and frivolity, and feared they would corrupt the "hardy, manly virtues of the human heart." The triumph of republican ideology in America was accompanied by a stern attitude towards ornamentation and ritual in public life. As Adams put it, "I cannot help suspecting that the more elegance, the less virtue, in all times and all countries." The Founding Fathers recognized the need to encourage some forms of artistic expression in their new society, but they preferred mechanical and utilitarian forms and insisted that art should be didactic and controlled by reason. Both public and private ornament after the Revolution thus became noticeably more restrained and more intellectual. Roman forms were especially popular. Adams himself favored history paintings and inspirational medals, with their obvious educational content. By thus carefully controlling public exposure to beauty and luxury, the republican leaders hoped to avoid the "runaway effect" of art and make the world safe, as Prown puts it, for John Adams (Garrett 1964:242-55; Prown 1980:207-8).

Like John Adams, Jonathan Odell came from a stern, ascetic background, and he too responded powerfully to visual beauty and graceful public rituals. But he moved in the opposite direction. Odell rejected Puritan cultural values and wholeheartedly embraced the refining process by which art and hierarchic forms could transform life and expression in North America. He joined an Anglican crusade designed to expand American cultural life and introduce more complex values and more elaborate styles. The Burlington Church was the first and most successful example of his ideal at work. The artifacts he brought to New Brunswick were an extension and intensification of his determination to provide North America with an alternative to the Puritan way of life. In both Burlington and Fredericton, Odell sought to incorporate the experience of beauty and grandeur into social life by providing his community with ideal forms of thought and worship. In this paper I have termed this ideal "the celestial world of Jonathan Odell" with reference both to the Odell globes and to the rarified nature of his vision.

This essay has concentrated on artifactual evidence because — unlike the poetry, sermons, correspondence, or even the deeds — the surviving physical documentation spans Odell's entire lifetime and permits comparisons to be made between his experience as a young colonial American and his later expressions of Loyalist style. It is interesting to observe, in closing, that although Odell provides an extreme example of Loyalist mentality, he was by no means alone. Many other members of the New Brunswick élite — such as Edward Winslow and Mather Byles, to cite only the best known family names — were descended from Puritan stock. They too broke with the old ascetic tradition in the mid-eighteenth century and embraced the enlarged sensibilities and worldliness of traditional British forms. Their careers and their surviving artifacts provide ample evidence that, like Odell, these Loyalist leaders welcomed pleasure and sensory experience and sought to filter them through decorative art and ritual so as to create public forms that engaged the sympathies of the heart as well as the assent of the intellect. For example, in Saint John, the aging Ward Chipman encouraged the building of another historically notable Anglican church. Completed in 1824, the imposing tower of "Stone Church" is an early instance of Gothic architecture in North America (Figure 12). It arrived a full decade before John Keble launched the ecclesiological revival in England and demonstrates the unique bond which linked these New Brunswick Loyalists to the ancient heritage of the mother country. Similar examples could be drawn from the military uniforms which gave the struggling colony a bit of color and dash, or from the elaborate civil rituals which broke up the tedium of everyday life, or from the decorative motifs used to enhance the ceremonies of family life.

Fred Cogswell and Gwendolyn Davies have suggested that the enduring contribution of the original Loyalist generation was to develop structures and standards of taste for Canadian literature and Canadian education (Cogswell 1976:85–91; Davies 1987). This review of the Odell artifacts suggests that this insight must be

Figure 12: Saint John's Stone Church, Saint John, New Brunswick, consecrated
1824. Collection of the New Brunswick Museum.

Figure 13: Saint Paul's Church, Saint John, New Brunswick, consecrated 1871. A prime example of the wooden gothic tradition of architecture in New Brunswick. (Private Collection)

extended to the material basis of life. While the evidence of this single, limited collection must be supplemented by further research, Odell's object choices do suggest a need for scholars to view the American Revolution in terms of its stylistic implications for both republican America and colonial Canada. The ambitious church constructed by Odell and Samuel Cooke in Fredericton was not only the logical product of the Bishop's Cause and the Burlington Church, it was also the progenitor of Stone Church in Saint John (1824), Christ Church Cathedral in Fredericton (1853), "new" Trinity Church in Saint John (1883), and ultimately the series of "wooden gothic" churches which were such an important moment in the developing culture of the Maritime provinces (Figure 13). Odell and his colleagues brought the intense attachment to traditional British styles which laid the basis for Canada's imperial culture in the nineteenth century. Taken together, the monuments, rituals, and symbols which they used to express this attachment became the paraphernalia of a new civil religion, as ideologically significant to the Loyalists as were those parchment documents—the Declaration of Independence, the Constitution, and the Bill of Rights—to their revolutionary counterparts. This examination of Odell's material universe has permitted an isolated glimpse at the wealth of historical meanings contained in Loyalist cultural instruments. By probing more deeply into the significance of this particular collection, we gain understanding into the way objects present a man's spiritual dimension in terms of actual physical articulation.

Notes

1. The fullest and most sympathetic treatment of Odell's political poetry by an American critic is Tyler 1897:97–129. Yet even Tyler portrays Odell as a rigid partisan, "grim, scathing, absolutely implacable." Odell's most important revolutionary satires can be found in Sargent (ed.), 1860. Some additional early poems and a sensitive introduction appear in Edelberg 1983:45–70. The best appreciation of Odell's contribution to Canadian literature is found in Baker 1920:27–30. The major political poems written in New Brunswick are printed in Vincent 1978. Vincent (1980) also compiled a guide to the known works. Most Canadian literary critics have dismissed Odell as irrelevant. Fred Cogswell depicts him as representing a "now-dead tradition" and Desmond Pacey and Northrop Frye ignore him altogether in their comprehensive works. There are however some signs of new interest in Odell as witnessed by Vincent's work and an article by Gwendolyn Davies (1987). In a sweeping argument, Davies maintains that early Loyalist writers such as Odell played a definite, positive role in shaping the cultural foundations of colonial Canada.

2. For a rich exploration of the ways in which artifacts enable human societies to create a world that is distinctively human and far more durable than thoughts or deeds, see Arendt 1958, especially ch. 3 and 4.

3. Two anthologies suggest the range of Ricoeur's intellectual concerns: *The Conflict of Interpretations: Essays in Hermeneutics* (1974) and *Hermeneutics and the Human Sciences: Essays on Language, Action, and Interpretation* (1981). It must be stressed that Ricoeur's own studies are confined to literary texts, although throughout his work he acknowledges the pertinence of hermeneutical interpretation for other forms of human expression and behaviour. See for example, *Hermeneutics and the Human Sciences*, pp. 117, 203, 290.

4. Ricoeur's methodological procedures are described in fullest detail in the introductory chapter of *Freud and Philosophy: An Essay on Interpretation*, 1970, pp. 3–56.

5. Admittedly the Rumford lamp would require further analysis if Odell himself had been an inventor, but in this context it seems simply to be a gift from a Loyalist comrade. For a survey of the increasingly Anglophile culture of the colonial seaboard élite see Bushman (1984), pp. 345–83.

6. See Wendell Garrett (1960) for a full architectural and historical treatment of this important structure. Evidence on Odell's vicarage in Burlington is scant. Given the elaborate embellishment made by Odell to the Burlington Church, as described below, it seems likely that his additions to the vicarage participated in the same style.

7. Odell signed the charter for the proposed college and the original classrooms were in the lower end of his garden.

8. Odell and Cooke were longtime associates in New Jersey and during the American Revolution. Their families were later united through the marriage of Odell's son to Cooke's daughter. For Odell's direct involvement in the planning and construction of the original Christ Church (Fredericton), see S. Cooke to Dr. Morice, 16 October 1787 and 7 July 1789, Letters to the Society, SPG Records, vol. 22–24, Provincial Archives of New Brunswick microfilm 10007.

9. Details drawn from partially illegible letters of Cooke to Morice, in the SPG records and the Journals of Bishop Charles Inglis, University of New Brunswick typescripts. It is interesting to note by way of contrast that Inglis gave his full approval to the less ambitious church finished in Saint John in the same year, noting that although it was somewhat "defective" in the ornamentation, it was "a neat building and the work well executed." (Journal entry for 15 July 1792).

10. The watercolor by John Elliott Woolford is reproduced in the pamphlet by Watson (1984), p. 2. The painting by John-Charles Armytage can be found in Hachey (1980). See also Richardson (1966).

11. Odell's poems are part of the Odell Collection, New Brunswick Museum. For a typescript of these poems, see Anderson (1961).

12. Odell Collection, New Brunswick Museum.

13. After Odell's death, this essay was in fact included in the 1822–23 London edition of Jonathan Boucher, *Boucher's Glossary of Archaic and Provincial Words. A Supplement to the Dictionaries of the English Language, particularly those of Dr. Johnson and Dr. Webster* (edited by Joseph Hunter and Joseph Stevenson). Odell's softspoken but clearly painful description of his intellectual isolation occurs in a letter to Jonathan Boucher, 8 November 1802, Odell Family Papers, New Brunswick Museum.

14. The most useful biographical sketches of Odell are Bailey, 1983, pp. 628–31, and MacLachlan *et al.* (1976), pp. 109–12. See also a type-script of Whitfield Bell's sketch of Odell for the American Philosophical Society, deposited in the New Brunswick Museum. The most recent biography by Cynthia Edelberg (1987) is particularly strong on the literary aspects of Odell's work, but indifferent to the significance of his Loyalism. Princeton's early history is traced in Wertenbaker (1946), pp. 3–46.

15. The history of the Bishop's Cause is related in Bridenbaugh (1962), pp. 171–340. A fine monograph by Gerardi (1977–78), pp. 149–96, supplements Bridenbaugh's account and stresses the ideological intensity of the Anglican missionaries. Odell was probably too young to have been a serious contender for the bishopric. Nonetheless evidence that his candidacy was mooted can be found in Hills (1876), pp. 302–3, and in his poem "Tis Large Indeed," where he satirically compares his parole during the American Revolution to the circumference of a Bishop's ring (Odell Family Papers, New Brunswick Museum).

16. The poems which amused the Franklins are probably those recently uncovered by Edelberg (see note 1).

Art

The Case for Kitsch   **6**

Popular/Commercial Arts as a Reservoir of Traditional Culture and Humane Values

Alan Gowans

Two of the last major sequences of daily strips that were drawn by E.C. Segar, creator of *Thimble Theatre*, a.k.a. *Popeye the Sailor*, before his death from cancer in 1938 were *The Pool of Youth* (14 January to 20 April 1935) and *Popeye's Ark* (22 April 1935 to 10 April 1936). I have published them in full in *Prophetic Allegory: Popeye and the American Dream*, so that one illustration from them will do to demonstrate the content and style of Segar's art and thought—the daily strip of 11 July 1935 (Figure 1).[1] Popeye the Sailor, having built an "ark" with the goal of founding a new country where there would be no problems and everyone would be happy, discovers a new continent and addresses his "sheeps" rather in the style of John Winthrop on the *Arabella* or Lenin at the Finland Station. But the context is very different. There are no lofty sentiments about lights set on hilltops or new eras of socialist equality; instead, a passage that translated into regular English might well have been written by Samuel Johnson. In fact, in *Taxation No Tyranny*, the old Tory expressed himself in almost identical terms:

> All government is ultimately and essentially absolute. In sovereignty there are no gradations. There may be limited royalty, there may be limited consulship; but there can be no limited government. There must in every society be some power or other from which there is no appeal.

Figure 1: "A new nation is gettin' bornded" — discovery of Spinachova, 11 July 1935. The other character is Mr. Spink, millionaire misogynist who funded the new nation on condition there be no women in it (!)

Reproduced courtesy of Alan Gowans, *Prophetic Allegory: Popeye and the American Dream,* Watkins Glen, American Life Foundation 1983.

Several observations are pertinent about Segar's strip.

First, it is a satire on utopias, of a distinctive kind to be discussed later; *Popeye's Ark* and *The Pool of Youth* are by no means the only satires of this kind in Segar's work. There were half a dozen similar examples during the 1930s, though this was the most consistent and profound.

Second, it is a representation of a kind of folklore, that is, a tale growing out of the deep unconscious of a people. Segar was no intellectual; he was not a literary artist; he had no poses and no pretensions to be a Fine Artist; he spun allegories in the naive unselfconsciousness of a folktale spinner drawing on the collective infrastructure of attitudes and values traditional in his society.[2]

Third, it is, I am prepared to maintain, an example of the material culture (in the sense of that term used by material culture students) of our age.

Some time ago I participated in a conference in Oahu, Hawaii, and spoke on the definition and preservation of traditional material cultures. Some participants felt that, because there were now many artists trying to work in traditional techniques and themes, traditional cultures of the Pacific were alive and experiencing a renaissance, after their near-extermination by invading and settling Western European peoples. Others were more pessimistic and felt that the traditional Pacific cultures and folklife were not being reborn, only artificially maintained; their outward forms preserved but their inner essence gone. My contribution consisted of two propositions:

First, the way to tell a living culture from an artificially revived one is by social function: do the traditional arts now being practised again perform in present-day society those functions in and for society which they used to perform in and for traditional, historic, Pacific societies? If they do not, then their present state is an artful imitation, not the real thing. Not that such an imitation is without value; far from it. All sorts of people in the region are given a deeper sense of place and roots by means of these revived arts.

Second, artful revivals are not the only ways traditional culture is perpetuated to enrich present-day lives. Popular/commercial arts perform the same function also, on a larger scale. I pointed out that in Hawaii, McDonald's fast-food stands can be found shaped like traditional Polynesian huts and decorated with prints made by artists of Hawaiian descent celebrating traditional Hawaiian themes; that the Bank of Hawaii sponsors artists who work in many areas of traditional culture; that the Honolulu Chamber of Commerce sponsors exhibitions and otherwise promotes survival of traditional culture (admittedly in all these cases there is a self-serving element; but in Fine Art that is true also—the point is not the motives, but the perpetuation itself).

What happens in Hawaii happens elsewhere. Pennsylvania German culture is promoted and perpetuated (capitalized upon, if you like) in chains like Dutch Pantry restaurants. Popular/commercial promotions of what is alleged to be traditional New England culture supports a thriving tourist industry in the old Northeast, while in the Southwest and Mountain states an "Old West" culture is likewise perpetuated. In all of this, there are elements of folkloric material, of course; but the boundaries between folk art and popular/commercial art are always murky.

The central point is: popular/commercial arts are the arts of our time, in the traditional sense of the word "art." Popular/commercial arts are not, of course, art in the modern avant-garde sense of an activity which often seems to exist by itself quite apart from any social need or function and appears definable as the self-expression by persons called "artists" of their inner thoughts, ideas, and reactions—or as anything such persons may use for expressing themselves. Popular/commercial arts are art in the sense that they also perform in and for our society the kinds of functions historically done through the activity called art: imagery, illustration, beautification, conviction/persuasion.[3] Specifically in this case, popular/commercial arts, including here material culture, are the means by which traditional attitudes and values are transmitted from one generation to another.

Popular/commercial arts are an effective means of carrying on traditional culture. Certainly Modern arts do nothing of the sort; by definition they are dedicated to a revolutionary break with the past in a virtual "tradition of revolt," not merely (it has come to be) of one generation against the next, but of an individual artist's newest work against an earlier piece. Nor will Postmodernism pass on the traditional culture until it overcomes its present obsession with obeying the dictates of *Zeitgeist*, which it inherited from Modernism: arts, according to the new doctrines, *must* express the spirit of their own time, hence Postmodern buildings must display endless quirks and quotes and quips to make sure everybody understands they are products of the 1980s and not, God forbid, something Academic or Revivalist.

Furthermore popular/commercial arts carry on traditional culture of many kinds on every level of society. How is a sense of the past in general transmitted today, for instance? In part through historical museums; but far more through movies and television plays, period furniture, Disneylands and the like, not excluding displays in department stores (which have influenced museum techniques a good deal). Folk culture of the older sort and new sorts of folk culture alike are promoted by Santa Claus parades, Easter-bunny egg hunts, Thanksgiving football games, and their impact is heightened by all sorts of cross-references.[4] Commercialized rituals, one may say? To be sure they are; but is there really a choice?

Given this demonstrable role of popular/commercial arts in our society the obvious next step, surely, would be to give them something like the kind of serious attention we pay to the historic arts whose functions in and for society they now serve. We might expect to find scholars busy making *catalogues raisonnés* of major popular/commercial art forms, collecting data on major figures, assembling archives of important works, as they have been compiling since the 1860s on Renaissance painting, since the 1880s on Byzantine, and so forth. But for all intents and purposes very little of this sort is going on.

The *Thimble Theatre* illustration here (Figure 1), for example, was not reprinted after its original appearance in July 1935 until I published it half a century later in *Prophetic Allegory*.[5] Of course there are a number of books on comics varying in character from nostalgic reminiscence,[6] to encyclopedic reference,[7] from surveys,[8] to axe-grinding studies,[9] but it is very rare to find systematic runs of daily strips.[10] It is like trying to study movies by looking at stills, or Italian Renaissance painting from details of ears. To assemble the sequence in *Prophetic Allegory* took long and hard digging through back files of newspapers, the only place where complete sets exist. Comparable situations exist in most areas of popular/commercial arts.

Difficulty of access alone cannot explain this pitiful lack of primary working data on popular/commercial arts. It is difficult to get data about many artists whose value has been recognized posthumously, in striking contrast to the legions assiduously amassing the most obscure details about the most obscure people in Fine Arts: as in the *Creative Canada* project, for example. Vast projects of archival work are underway in every area of Fine Arts, from cataloguing every single architectural drawing from the six-teenth century to memorabilia of Emma Lake, on the premise that sooner or later scholars will need such material to work from—as indeed they will. It is often difficult to dig out data on material culture. Yet here too we find endless pains expended to preserve ephemera, busy teams out interviewing denizens of the deep marshes, or recording rail fences on the high ridges. But the comparable data-collecting of popular/commercial arts, the basis for any serious analysis, is neglected. Why?

There are two basic reasons, I suppose. First, popular/commercial arts are not thought to be artifacts in the way that word is used in material culture studies. A plow or a pigpen has a Maker, whose Hand is discernible in the object, if not via actual marks of saw or adze. It is otherwise with panels from comic strips, stills from movies, photographs, beer cans, automobiles. But surely this means only that the "handicraft" in popular/commercial arts occurs at another level? Some Hand is responsible for the popular/commercial artifact ultimately—in the case of E.C. Segar, at his drawing board. He sent his India-ink drawings into the Syndicate, where they were translated into cardboard matts from which the Syndicate's subscribers printed them in their papers, the originals apparently being discarded.[11] But does disappearance of the original mean that the strip as reproduced is somehow not a product of a human mind and craft? It is, and remains so. The creative process is not invalidated because it occurs at another stage. No; if any such argument is maintained it is not because intelligent people find it convincing but because their judgement is being affected by prejudice deep-seated at an unconscious level—a subliminal assumption that popular/commercial arts *cannot* involve any serious intellectual endeavour, and that those who expend serious intellectual endeavours on them deserve no academic credentials. This feeling, this assumption, is pervasive in modern culture. Its origin, I believe, is to be found in an élitist defence mechanism protecting Modernism from serious analysis, which material culturalists, of all people, should be most aware of and the best able to understand.

Let's begin with the young Clement Greenberg's "Avant Garde and Kitsch," written for *Partisan Review* in September 1939. Greenberg later went on to great fame as an art critic, creating artists like David Smith *ex nihilo*. This article, plus a follow-up, achieved canonical status in the academic and critical artworld, and had been reprinted several times before it appeared in *Pollock and After*, a collection of essays edited by Francis Francina in 1983. Culture, says Greenberg, is Picasso; the artist's socialist (Communist) views and anti-bourgeois attitudes are culture's only hope in fact. Over against him stand arrayed the evil forces of kitsch—"decayed remnants of bourgeois culture, in tin pan alley songs, Eddie Guest poems, comics." No one example of kitsch is ever analysed.[12] Timothy J. Clark, in another essay reprinted in *Pollock and After*, picks up on this article and puts kitsch into more precise Marxist terminology: "the sign of the bourgeoisie contriving to lose its identity." But Clark too, never analyses anything specific but merely uses "kitsch" as a term of indiscriminate abuse, as "bourgeois" was for Marx.

"How is this virulence of kitsch, this irresistible attractiveness...to be explained?" Greenberg wrote rhetorically, and went on to give the standard avant-garde answer since the de Goncourts' introduction to *Germinie Lacerteux* in the 1860s: the taste of the public is incurably depraved, pandered to by capitalist culture-mongers; this taste prevents appreciation of what we great critics define as great art and destroys genuine folk culture.[13] But this is not an answer, it is more like ideological abuse. What is needed is analysis of specific examples, not generalized denunciations of a whole genre.

The moment serious analysis of popular/commercial arts is made—the moment we begin actually *looking* at them, how they are put together, how they develop—one fact becomes decisively apparent: in no way can it be demonstrated that these are the detritus, the worthless remains of older high arts, "a culture of instant assimilation," as Clark calls them. Quite the opposite. Compare the appearance of new forms in popular/commercial arts with new forms in avant-garde arts since 1850, and there is no doubt: quite contrary to the Modern myth of being a vanguard, it is in popular/commercial arts that the new forms appear first. In one case after another, forms invented first in popular/commercial arts are then taken over by the avant-garde, put on a pedestal as it were, and made Fine Art. Examples of every kind abound.[14] But this is peripheral to the argument here. The place to begin is with a serious attempt to define "kitsch" by specific reference to examples and that, of course, means inquiring what given works were made to *do* in and for society.

Kitsch, I propose, is anything made just as art—i.e., not primarily made to serve any of the traditional functions of arts in and for society, but primarily for artistic expression—in a style that is no longer fashionable among the avant-garde. Made primarily, that is, not as a substitute image of anything, nor primarily to illustrate in the sense of telling a story, nor to beautify in the traditional sense of ordering human experience so as to increase individual awareness, nor to persuade towards or express convictions about some set of beliefs or values, but just to be a Work of Art. Not to *do* anything, just to *be* Art, an art without social function and in some style unfashionable at the moment. Kitsch is embodied in those little objets d'art that you buy at cheap stores and see on windowsills or fleamarket tables and that perpetuate styles of nineteenth-century realism and eighteenth-century Rococo. Kitsch is a reproduction of the Blue Boy from Woolworth's or of Meissen china from cheap jewellers. Kitsch could also, however, be a cheap print of a Cubist painting by Braque or Van Gogh's "Sunflowers" that adorn motel walls, or even Picasso's blue period works that hotel decorators buy by the job lot. Certainly the originals of these works weren't made as kitsch, to be mass-produced and sold commercially, but then neither was Gainsborough's Blue Boy or Meissen china. Any work made just as a work of art will eventually become unfashionable in style and so become kitsch; but a work made to fulfil a specific social function which still fulfils it can never be kitsch until its social function is lost. That includes most popular/commercial works today.

For in contrast to works made just to hang in galleries and be admired aesthetically or as evidences of human creativity, most popular/commercial arts have an obvious social function. At the very least they entertain; but it usually turns out upon analysis that their social functions are quite plain—substitute images, used to illustrate or beautify, to persuade or to compel. But let us take the specific example I promised.

At the time Greenberg was formulating his first thoughts on avant-garde art, *Thimble Theatre*, was one of the country's most popular comic strips. Greenberg would unhesitatingly have called it kitsch. But it was no such thing. After assembling the strip as it appeared day by day and reading it as it was originally read, one surprising fact emerges. These are not just "funnies," or simple entertainment. They are also commentaries upon utopian schemes. After Segar's death, when the strip was given by the Syndicate to other artists to draw, its character changed; but in the 1930s one long sequence strip after another played on the utopian theme and, once we read them, we begin to see at once the deeper reasons why comics like this—there were many others at the time—would be so distasteful to the contemporary avant-garde. These strips were not just about utopias; they were anti-utopian, satires upon utopian thinking opposed directly to the kind of Marxist utopianism popular in left-wing and avant-garde circles at the time.

Segar's art grows out of deep folk traditions of many sorts. For example the second character in *Thimble Theatre*, J. Wellington Wimpy, who first appeared in 1931 (Popeye appeared in 1929) could be thought of as the counterpart to Popeye in a body-soul dualism of the sort which Orwell found, in "The Art of Donald McGill," endemic in Western literature. Popeye and Wimpy are versions of Don Quixote and Sancho Panza, Mr. Pickwick and Sam Weller, or

Tamino and Papageno. They are natural foils. In an excess of idealism Popeye may exclude Wimpy from his new and perfect country; but they will not stay apart for long (Figure 2). But Wimpy is also a representative in his time of that figure whom literary critics call the American Adam in Eden, who in a new continent with new laws seeks Paradise restored in the form of freedom from the curse of work.[15] Wimpy is a late version of what was once, in the time of William Sidney Mount and George Caleb Bingham, a central theme in American painting ("Cider Making on Long Island," "Rafting on the Missouri"), all depicting free figures whom bountiful Nature feeds almost without work—what Marxist analysts would call "bourgeois ideal art," celebrating the bourgeois *rentier utopia*. Its long decline is a central theme in the history of subsequent American painting. Superficially the typical themes of painters like Winslow Homer and Frederick Remington in the next generation from Mount and Bingham are much the same—concerned with individuals in a direct relationship to Nature. But what they paint are individuals *alienated* from Nature in many ways, "lost in a world they never made." Archetypal is the black man in Homer's Gulf Stream, drifting helplessly in a wrecked boat with sharks circling all around, far away indeed from those jolly flatboatmen and jovial farmers drinking cider in a benign landscape or Remington's solitary Indians and cowboys set punily against vast expanses of hostile, implacable plain and sky. American regional painting of the 1930s (Bohrod, Shahn, Hopper, Grant Wood's *American Gothic*) presents lonely, somber, frozen scenes, lamenting the lost American dream. Parallel popular/commercial arts seemed to reinforce the message—all is lost. Chaplin, Laurel and Hardy, L'il Abner, Mutt and Jeff, all in their way mocked the very idea of a utopia; the American Adam in Eden becomes a caging moocher, like Wimpy. All in their way proclaimed the absurdity of *rentier* capitalism's promises.

Yet opposed to this is the left-wing message: the economic system is at fault. Change the economic system and paradise may yet be realizable, the perfect society achievable! This is the message of the leftist avant-garde of the 1930s. Amongst these believers all the American Dream's repressed utopianism revives. And it necessarily collides directly with all those arts which deride its possibility. The regionalists' laments are easily enough silenced; Greenberg's generation of critics polished them off by the end of the 1930s. But the popular/commercial arts are not so easily silenced. Their base was broader, their roots in contemporary social life deeper.

Unlike those painters who were heirs to the utopian aspirations of the early Republic, popular/commercial artists never at any time

Figure 2: The worm in Paradise: J. Wellington Wimpy constructs an artifact. First two panels of 27 May 1935 strip, and last three of 28 May 1935 strip.

Reproduced courtesy of Alan Gowans, *Prophetic Allegory: Popeye and the American Dream,* Watkins Glen, American Life Foundation 1983.

held any illusions about utopian possibilities. Their art was rooted in the common sense of common people. Their constant message was: utopias of *all* sorts are risible. Promoters of utopias are not heroes essaying some lofty quest, tragically to fail; they are deluded people, like drunks challenging everybody at the bar, lunatics pretending to be Napoleon. Furthermore, not only do they proclaim the impossibility of realizing any sort of utopia, they specifically cite the dangers of trying to do so. That is surely their most dangerous fault in avant-garde eyes; good reason to attack them as bourgeois *detritus*, to bury them with abuse, to call them kitsch (Figure 3).

Yet this "kitsch" was as politically engaged as any high art of the time. In the years when *Thimble Theatre* was running its anti-utopian satires, millions of Russians were being starved and murdered and tortured in slave labour camps. Slavery, deportation, and superstitions reappeared in virulent form. References to this situation and an explanation for it—a society based upon physical repression must end in secret police cellars (as Orwell was writing in this same decade)—permeate the strip presented here.[16] Popeye's search for *The Pool of Youth* results in the discovery of primeval forces of terror, primitive horrors whose monstrosity only Wimpy (the representative intellectual of the strip) is unable to see. The ideal society, which Popeye promoted in the long *Popeye's Ark* series, likewise brought as much misery and frustration as the old one had. So it was not just the old, exploded, bourgeois utopia that popular/commercial arts like these was mocking, it was the new socialist utopia as well.

No utopia can stand laughter. Hence the unreasoning hostility of the avant-garde to *all* popular/commercial arts, its insistence on lumping them all together as kitsch, its refusal to analyse any of them. Hence the avant-garde ban on laughter, in such marked contrast to the high arts of the past. The Globe theatre might ring with laughter at comic parts even within the great tragedies; broad farce tickled the groundlings watching *The Magic Flute* in the Frei-haustheater auf der Wieden. No such thing in Museums of Modern Art, only occasional mockery of those poor aspirants to the Artworld Establishment who fail to catch the latest turn of critical opinion. They cannot afford to allow laughter, it is too dangerous. For what produces laughter is perception of the incongruous. Given any encouragement, the contradiction between the high professions of the Artworld to purity of intent, and the present state of the New York art-market-critics-connoisseurs-dealers-curators-investors complex would be enough to provoke uncontrollable mirth. But the matter goes far deeper than that. There is a basic incongruity

Figure 3: Among the many perils and absurdities of utopian adventures satirized by popular/commercial arts in the 1930s was a relapse into naked force (in the Pool of Youth, Toar), and in Spinachova, the resumption of old powers under new names—Milton's "New Presbyter is but old Priest Writ Large." Marxism was just state capitalism, according to Proudhon. Dictatorships can turn into republics and vice-versa, according to E.C. Segar. (3 December 1935). Recognize Mussolini's balcony?

between Modernism's claim to be based upon scientific materialism, and the present state of Science—and popular/commercial arts reveal that fact.

Late nineteenth- and early twentieth-century Science seemed to have shown that reality was determined by how the mind perceives it. It followed, vulgarly, that such bourgeois virtues as courage, integrity, appreciation of beauty, sense of duty, were figments of the mind; that only material rewards are possible for material actions. So orthodox Modern arts were to be judged by expressions of process and should not appeal to any outward standards. Popular/commercial arts did not follow this development. They remained based upon older criteria. Hence the judgement: bourgeois detritus, decrepit survivals of exploded bourgeois art. But the basic assumptions of Science have been rapidly changing over the last twenty-five years or so and now it is the avant-garde that seems out of date.

Dramatic evidences of changed mindset are to be found in almost any publication dedicated to scientific philosophies nowadays. For example it now appears that the reason the brain has evolved certain nerve endings capable of responding to given drugs is that these receptors were intended to respond to certain chemically similar substances which are manufactured by the brain itself as a reward for satisfactory responses to calls of duty, accomplishments of things difficult or dangerous or heroic. Thus the brain itself certifies that those older concepts are real, have an objective existence, are necessary for full humanity. Their expression is not "bourgeois," but simply human. Courage, integrity, beauty and the rest are not concerns of Modern arts. A painting like Picasso's *Guernica*, painted in 1937 and still often called the greatest Modern work of art, has nothing to do with heroism, despite its ostensible subject. It has to do with the mechanics of picture-making, into which demonstration some can read a message if they choose;[17] it thus corresponds to reality as formulated by late nineteenth- and early twentieth-century Science. By contrast, the work of Picasso's contemporary, E.C. Segar, abounds in panels depicting old-fashioned heroism: Popeye confronting some monster with such words as (I translate from Popeyese), "Before we go on with the battle, let me tell you something—you can't win because you're a crook and I am fighting for what's right" (Figure 4). The brute responds, "The biggest man will win and I'm him"—a sentiment the avant-garde would applaud, shuddering delicately at Popeye's faux pas, his lapse into nineteenth-century bourgeois sentimentality. Lower and middle-class culture preserved the old values that early Modern science professed to have debunked—precariously, vulgarly, but tenaciously. And now it seems these old values are realities after all.

Figure 4: The noble sentiments of a past age—and, perhaps, of a coming present one again. A panel of 13 May 1936.

Reproduced courtesy of Alan Gowans, *Prophetic Allegory: Popeye and the American Dream*, Watkins Glen, American Life Foundation 1983.

Thus the truth of Greenberg's 1939 claim that it's a choice between Picasso or kitsch on which to build a culture—indeed so, but the solid foundation is not Modernism, but popular/commercial arts. For in a coming age whose science acknowledges the reality of the old virtues there will be no art corresponding to or speaking for those virtues except popular/commercial. It's kitsch (using Greenberg's epithet for all popular/commercial arts) or nothing.

In "Escape from Modernism" Frederick Turner wrote that

> In the heyday of high modernism the world of the future seemed impersonal, cool, centralized, inorganic, tidy, sharp-edged; a world-state with equal prosperity for all, tall rectilinear buildings, cool atonal music, abstract art, imagist free verse, novels purified of the fetishism and hierarchy of plot and character; a world-state without represssion, alienation, and ego, free from the shibboleths of honor, beauty, sexual morality, patriotism, idealism, religion, and duty.

This future now appears dated, even dreary....A much more decentralized world seems likely: personal, warm, custom-made, organic, untidy, decorated. Our music will be full of melody again....Our visual arts will be mainly representational, with abstraction reserved for decoration. Our architecture will recapitulate the panhuman village clutter, and all functions—domestic, religious, commercial, industrial, educational, political—will be jumbled together. Our poetry will be, as all poetry was until seventy years ago, richly metrical and rhetorical, full of stories, ideas, moral energy, scientific speculation, theology, drama, history. Many of these changes have already begun, though a rearguard of modernist reactionaries still holds much political and economic power, and it will take decades to deprogram middlebrow taste from its masochistic preferences (1984:52).[18]

All of which is at present, as he says elsewhere, in the nature of prophecy more than observation. But it will surely come to pass. This new art will not grow out of Post-Modernism, at least not, as we said, unless Post-Modernism shakes off its present subservience to the tyranny of *Zeitgeist*. It will grow out of the despised popular/commercial arts, which alone constitute the necessary reservoir of vocabulary and skills to produce it. No longer seen—by some of us at least—as derivative remains of bourgeois utopianism, popular/commercial arts now appear to present a dynamic, rich foundation for a vital material culture in touch with past and future alike.

Notes

1. It is not always realized that what goes under the title "Popeye" these days is very different from the original creation. In the 1930s it was, and in some respects still is, normal practice for the artist who creates a strip to sell it to a Syndicate, which thereupon owns it and can elect to continue the strip with someone else drawing it if the originator becomes incapacitated or dies, or indeed even in case of a quarrel—as was the case when Walt Disney's original strip, *Oswald the Rabbit*, was taken from him in the 1920s (he had to invent another, which he called *Mickey Mouse*). The classic *Popeye* dates essentially from 1929 when Popeye the Sailor made his appearance, to early 1938 when Segar's work had to be ghosted because of his approaching death.

2. What biographical information there is about Segar is collected in *Prophetic Allegory*, chapter 5, 33–44. I learned something more about him in connection with the opening of a small show which I organized on Segar's work, called *The Case for Culture Heroes*, exhibited in the National Museum of American History at the Smithsonian in 1983 (now in the custody of the Maltwood Museum, University of Victoria, B.C.). Attending the opening were Segar's daughter Mrs. Marie Claussen, and son Tom. I questioned them extensively about their father's intellectual

life, what books he was fondest of, his schooling, the usual. To my surprise they couldn't think of any intellectual life. Their father's formal education was very sketchy (which I knew), but whatever time he spent away from his drawing-board — and the life of the creator of a syndicated strip is very exacting, far more so than the average painter's — was spent duck-hunting (the Sunday strip had numerous references to this sport and there is one also in *Popeye's Ark (Prophetic Allegory*, 280). The utopian imagery in Segar's mind had apparently sunk into his unconscious from an early schooling in American history as promulgated from the Civil War to the 1930s, which he spontaneously extrapolated from (see the argument in *Prophetic Allegory*, 142). The only recreation other than duck-hunting which the children remembered was that at Christmas-time Segar on occasion got out a revolver and shot the glass ornaments off the Christmas tree!

3. These four functions are described succinctly in *Prophetic Allegory* 18–23 and at book length in *Learning to See: Historical Perspectives on Modern Popular/Commercial Arts*, Bowling Green, Ohio, Popular Press, 1983.

4. One could go on indefinitely; that's a reason for writing *Learning to See!* A particularly good example is funerary arts as focal points for community and family awareness. See *L.T.S.* 90–99, and, for an extended treatment of one theme Rubin (1979).

5. More precisely, it was first republished in *RACAR (Revue de l'Art Canadien/Canadian Art Review 1(1) (1974), 3–19, a sort of preview of part of Prophetic Allegory*, which was in fact being written then, though it took ten years to appear. I also used it as an illustration in "Popeye and the American Dream," a short article in J. Salzman (ed.), 1979 — despite which, it does not yet seem to have made it to The Hundred Best-Known Works of Western Art.

6. Typical examples: Bill Blackbeard and Martin Williams (1977); George Perry and Alan Aldridge (1967).

7. E.g., Maurice Horn (ed.) (1976).

8. E.g., David M. White and Robert H. Abel (1963); it has a bibliography listing previous surveys.

9. Typical examples: Les Daniels (1971); Reinhold C. Reitberger and Wolfgang J. Fuchs (1971; 1974).

10. One can find, of course, runs of daily strips published as *fliegendeblätter* such as *the real free press Amsterdam* of the 1970s and a number of others, fly-by-night outfits many of them; I have seen sequences of *Thimble Theatre* from the early 1930s which consisted of the end of one episode and the beginning of another, as if there were no awareness of complete stories being involved. There are comic books such as Limited Collectors Editions (of *Dick Tracy*, e.g., also *Little Orphan Annie*) and the Nostalgia Press (Woody Gelman, ed.) has done a number. Dailies were collected in old comic books as well, the first

being the Mutt and Jeff comic book of 1911. I am referring to systematic publication where you could go to find a complete run of a strip for specific years. A good overview of the kind of sources available is provided by M. Thomas Inge (1975).

11. As far as I have been able to ascertain, not a single original from Segar's hand exists. King Features seems to have kept none, the Segar family has none. I have never seen one anywhere else.

12. A curious attitude that remains common to this day. How often have I been asked, "Do you like comics?" as if all comic strips were exactly the same! To which the only possible reply is, "Do you like Italian painting?" "Do you like German music?"

13. "The Goncourts charge the public with corrupt and perverted taste; with preferring false values, pseudo-refinement, pruriency, reading as a comfortable and soporific pastime, books which end happily and make no serious demand on the reader. Instead, they continue, they offer the public a novel which is true, which found its subject in the street [it is about the erotic life of an elderly maid] …."

Erich Auerbach (1953) from chapter 19. The whole analysis rewards study in this connection.

14. Some convincing examples are given, especially of photography's influence on painting, in Gowans, 1971:65–82.

15. See, e.g., David W. Noble (1968) and R.W.B. Lewis (1955).

16. References to Orwell on the rising tide of primitive barbarism, & c., are to be found in the section on Toar's appearance in the *Pool of Youth, Prophetic Allegory*, 71–79.

17. "Everything that has been considered inherent in the art of painting, even by the most advanced schools: light, color precision or plasticity of drawing … .are here conspicuously lacking. The most that can be said to remain is a clean surface upon which we follow the alternate syncopations of blacks with grays and whites, in a mysterious drama of vital disorder, with marked tendencies towards triangulation…. Clearly, then, the reality conveyed by the Guernica is not a physical but a mental reality alike in this to language or writing…a dream world, with images flowing together, not related particulary to Guernica, basque country, or anything else … ."

Juan Larrea, *Guernica*, New York, 1947, 13, 28, quoted in my book *The Restless Art* (1966: 376), in context of a discussion of *Guernica's* social function compared to political cartooning.

18. *Harper's Magazine*, 152/11 (1984) 52. I have drawn liberally on Frederick Turner's thought in this article (47–55) in the concluding paragraphs of this essay.

On the "Art" In Artifacts   7

Jules David Prown

Ever since I began working self-consciously with "material culture," I have, as an art historian, been troubled by the relationship between what is considered art and what is not. The word "art" is neatly embedded in the word "*art*ifacts," and works of art are indeed a sub-set of the larger category "artifacts" which includes *all* man-made things. But in the practice of material culture, the category of material we call art does not fit into the larger universe of objects we call artifacts nearly as comfortably as it would appear to do etymologically. The very first time that I gave a course in "material culture" I discovered that the introduction of aesthetic issues tended to stop object-based material culture analysis dead in its tracks. First, the persistent imposition of twentieth-century values—moral as well as aesthetic—that inevitably accompanies the discussion of art as art, that defines what *we* mean by art, compromises the objectivity needed for a clear-eyed reading of the object and the formulation of hypotheses for further investigation. Second, and more importantly, art raises special questions of authorial intent ("what did the artist mean to say"), and occasionally questions of possible psychological deviance from social norms by the artist as communicator. These complications of intentionality and abnormality seem peculiar to art and threaten to compromise the validity of art as cultural evidence. If art is different from other artifacts, then art poses special problems for the analyst of material culture.

In order to gauge the extent to which the special character of art affects its validity as cultural evidence, we need to understand clearly *how* artifacts express culture and then to address the question of whether art differs in cultural expression, leading us into the study of ethnoaesthetics. In the course of asking how artifacts express culture, I arrived at what were, for me, some new understandings of the mechanics of artifactual cultural expression.

A few years ago I argued that the potency of artifacts as cultural evidence is not as bearers of information (Prown 1982). Words and numbers convey factual data with much greater precision. Rather, artifacts are indicators of belief, of value, and my argument is that they primarily express belief and value metaphorically. Man is a metaphor-making animal—a framer of tropes, images and similes, of signs and symbols. The human mind functions analogically, both consciously and unconsciously. In material culture it is useful to look for the metaphorical structures embedded in artifacts.

What follows is an abbreviated example of object analysis leading to the uncovering of metaphors. The first stage of analysis in the procedure that I advocate is purely descriptive, recording data about the physical and formal properties of the object. The object under consideration (Figure 1), is 6 3/8 inches high, 4 3/4 inches wide at the widest part of the body, and 7 7/8 inches wide overall from spout tip to handle. It is wider than it is high, and could be inscribed within a rectangle. The primary material is pewter, with the handle and lower ring of the finial made of wood. There is a small hole in the top of the lid (Figure 2), and inside the vessel there is a circular arrangement of small holes where the spout joins the body.

Viewed two-dimensionally, the vessel is divided by a horizontal line three-fifths of the way up. This is the rim where the lid joins the body. The lid and the body are also each sub-divided by horizontal mouldings, the lower one exactly midway between the base and the top of the handle, and at a height exactly equal to the height of the lid. Viewed from the side the object presents a series of S-curves, including the handle, the spout, the outlines of the body, the lid and the finial. The spout and the handle rise above the rim. The vessel stands on a 3/8 inch raised base.

Seen from the top, the object presents a series of concentric circles surrounding the finial. The spout, finial, hole, hinge, and handle are aligned to form an axis through the vessel at its largest dimension.

The object consists three-dimensionally of five separate parts— lid, body, handle, spout, and finial. The lower section of the body is a flattened ball; the upper part a reel. The lid is bell-shaped and

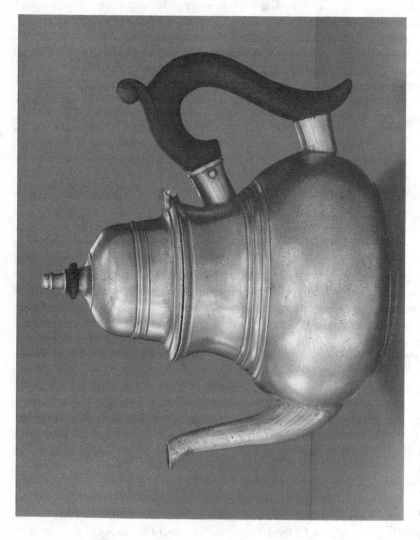

Figure 1: Thomas Danforth, 18th century pewter teapot. Yale University.

Figure 2: Thomas Danforth, 18th century pewter teapot. Yale University.

surmounted by a finial that echoes in simplified form the shape of
the vessel—a flattened ball surmounted by a reel, with a hemisphere
above.

After the object is described, the analyst proceeds to make
deductions on the basis of physical and intellectual interaction with
the object. This involves a certain amount of feigned innocence in
order that preconceptions do not close the mind to the gradual
emergence of metaphors. In other words, conclusions should be
reached gradually rather than jumped to or assumed immediately.
It can be inferred that this hollow-bodied object is a vessel or
container, that the larger opening at the top when the lid is opened
is used to put some substance into the vessel, and that the spout is
used to redirect that substance into a smaller container. The small
holes in the body at the base of the spout suggest that the contained
substance is strained in the act of pouring to retain in the vessel
particles larger than the holes. Since liquid would overflow when the
vessel were full if the spout were below the rim, the fact that the
spout rises above the rim suggests that the substance contained is
liquid. The use of wood in the handle and in the finial which is
grasped to open the lid suggests that the liquid may be hot, since
wood is a less effective conductor of heat than metal. The fact that
an attached rim raises the bottom of the pot off the surface on which
it stands reinforces this deduction. Direct sensory engagement—
manipulating the object—suggests the use of the handle and the
finial. Opening the lid indicates that the finial makes contact with
the handle, and the absence of wear suggests that the handle, and
perhaps the finial disk as well, is a replacement. The bell shape of
the lid suggests sound, and actual sound results from opening and
closing the lid.

The next step, emotional response, is almost invariably the one
in which an object is "broken open," and the unpacking process
begins. In "Mind in Matter" (Prown, 1982) I included emotional
response as the third step in the deductive process, since, like the
preceding intellectual and sensory deductive steps, it involved interaction with the object. But emotional response is really a different
stage because, although it is triggered by interaction, it does not
involve further exploration of the object. Rather it involves reaching
into the analyst's conscious and sub-conscious mind to retrieve
experiences that for some as yet unconceptualized reason resonate
with the object. The analyst tries to account for feelings, even vague
or imprecise feelings. The object triggers responses and recollec-
tions, and the identification of the links between the object and the

memories of experience for which it stands as a sign, is the key to unlocking the cultural belief embedded in it.

James Fernandez (1971) has written of the importance of metaphor to anthropologists in decoding culture, an important process he referred to punningly as an-trope-ology. Although he was discussing verbal metaphors, several of his discriminations are also applicable to understanding how artifacts function as metaphorical expressions of culture. First of all, he distinguishes between two kinds of metaphor: structural metaphors which conform to the *shape* of experience, which resemble actual objects in the physical world, and textual metaphors which are similar to the *feelings* of experience. Structural metaphors are based on physical experience of the phenomenal world, textual metaphors are based on the emotive experience of living in that world. When my students are asked to express their feelings about this object following extended analysis, responses have taken the form of such words as "solid," "substantial," "cheerful," "comfortable," "grandmotherly," and "reliable." If you ask what in the object triggered such words as "solid, substantial and reliable," the respondents will point out that the object is wider than it is high, and the flattened ball of the lower part of the vessel gives it a squarish and bottom-weighted appearance, suggesting stability. The responses are based on experience of the phenomenal world. The words "cheerful, comfortable and grandmotherly" reflect more subjective life experiences that also can be located with some precision by asking questions based on the previously deduced evidence. Under what circumstances do we drink warm liquids? When we are cold, warm liquid warms us inside. We drink hot liquids when we are ill—soup or tea—again because it makes us feel better, perhaps by promoting perspiration and helping to break a fever. When we are ill and incapacitated, warm liquids are often brought to us, and the care of another person is comforting.

Hot liquids are also drunk on social occasions. Coffee and tea drinking are marked by a sense of well-being that derives from the drink itself; by the physical act of giving or pouring and receiving; and frequently by conversation. Drinking hot liquids and talking seem to go together. Thus the object, which we can now identify as a teapot on the basis of external information without distorting our reading of the object up to this point, invokes multiple *textual* metaphors—cheerful, comfortable, reliable, grandmotherly, etc.— based on the feelings of experience.

The teapot also embodies structural metaphors based on the shape of experience. For example, the lid and finial can be read as a bell metaphor. And the bell shape of the lid suggests calling for service—whether a dinner bell or ringing from a sick bed—calling for and receiving help or comfort or sustenance. Another structural metaphor, equally obvious, is less easily retrieved however, because it is usually repressed. But if you ask the respondent, what is the "*ur*-experience," the earliest human experience of ingesting warm liquids, the immediate response is that it is as a baby feeding from a mother's breast. Now structural analogies become immediately evident between the shape of the lower section of the body of the vessel and the female breast. And when the object is viewed from above (Figure 2), with the finial at the centre like a nipple, the object is even more breast-like. The teapot is revealed, unexpectedly, as a structural metaphor for the female breast.

Fernandez defines a metaphor as a sign, a combination of image and idea located between perception and conception, between a signal and a symbol. A *signal* is a perception that orients some kind of interaction. For example, a picture of a teapot could function literally as a signal hanging outside of a tearoom beckoning the tourist, or at a tea party the teapot itself serves as a signal for pouring and serving. At the other end of the scale, a *symbol* is a conception whose meaning is fully realized. For example, a common denominator linking the various circumstances cited in which warm liquids are ingested is that all involve an act of giving and receiving, which is, in its largest social sense, the act of charity. The Roman story of Cimon and Pero (Figure 3), of the daughter who visits her elderly father starving in prison, and nourishes him by feeding him from her own breast, is generally known as the legend of Roman Charity. Thus, fully conceptualized in meaning, the teapot could become a symbol of charity, a symbol of the act of giving. One could, for example, envision an image of a teapot with an accompanying moralizing text on a page in an emblem book, as an emblem or symbol.

Located between signal and symbol, this teapot as a *sign*, a metaphor both structural and textual, embodies deeply felt but unconceptualized meanings relating to such things as maternal love and care, oral gratification, satisfaction of hunger and thirst, comforting internal warmth when cold or ill, and conviviality. And it is thus as a sign or metaphor that the teapot works as evidence of cultural belief.

If artifacts articulate cultural expression metaphorically, what *kinds* of insights can they afford us? What, for example, does the teapot tell us about belief? The object has given us a clue that the drinking of tea, and perhaps the entire ceremony of tea drinking,

Figure 3: *Roman Charity: Cimon and Pero*. Dirck van Baburen. Courtesy of York City Art Gallery, England.

may be related metaphorically to the fundamental human act of giving and receiving, and has the potential of being a symbol of generosity or charity, of *caritas*. The humanness as well as the humaneness of the act is suggested in this teapot by the fact that the liquid is encased in an organic, breast-like form. But as we well know, a teapot can be precisely the opposite in form (Figure 4); it can deny the humanly anatomical or personal aspect of giving or charity, and by using purely inorganic, intellectual, geometric forms deny personal involvement and emphasize the cerebral character of the act. In so doing it conveys something about the different character of a different culture.

Nevertheless, the fundamental structural linkage of warm liquids, breast feeding and charity—the human metaphor—is a constant potential; the extent to which it is generated, tolerated or rejected by a culture is an index of belief. Objects are evidence, and material culture enables us to interpret the culture that produced them in subjective, affective ways that are unachievable through written records alone.

So the teapot, then, might function as an indicator of beliefs about giving and receiving, generosity, charity, and definitions of the self in relation to others. Can one go on to describe with greater precision the terrain of cultural belief expressed by artifacts? That is a large, important, and largely unanswered question. The most persistent metaphors that have emerged to date in student papers in my graduate seminar relate to fundamental human experiences: mortality and death; love, sexuality and gender roles; privacy (seeing and being seen) and communication; power or control and acceptance; fear and danger; as well as giving and receiving. I suspect, however, that the terrain can be described with greater precision. What I have to say now is tentative; it brings us back to the problem of art with which we started.

Metaphors, Fernandez says, locate beliefs in what he calls the "quality space" of a culture.[1] Among several formulations he noted as to how metaphors locate belief is one which accords closely with the polarities of belief I have encountered in my analysis of American artifacts, using W.T. Jones' seven "axes of bias" (1961). These are lines of predisposition, along the calibration of which beliefs are located.[2]

Although these axes of belief can be noted in artifacts like teapots, I find that works of art—paintings, for example—often embody even clearer and more powerful expressions of belief locatable along these axes. The essential difference is, of course, that works of art are usually *conscious*, intentional expression of belief.

Figure 4: Loring Bailey (1740–1814), American Teapot, 1790–1800. Silver, 7 in. high, 5 3/4 in. long. M.967.40. Hood Museum of Art, Dartmouth College, Hanover, N.H.

This brings us to the problem of applying material culture analysis to works of art, especially the issue of "authorial intent" that I raised at the beginning. The intentional expression of belief embodied in works of art is quite different from the unconscious expression embedded in teapots and other artifacts.[3] Although many artifacts in categories other than art clearly have an artistic component (clothing, decorative arts, and architecture are obvious examples), these objects also have some clear utilitarian orientation—indeed *use* is primary. Art as a category is distinctive by virtue of having self-conscious or imposed *aesthetic* quality as its primary characteristic. If a work of art is metaphorical, and it often is, it is, as a rule, intentionally so. Works of art are fictions. Indeed, as cultural evidence, art more resembles literature than it does other tangible artifacts. Works of art are painted or carved, as novels and poetry are written, to communicate something. They are usually, like literature, conscious expressions of belief, and to that end are built of a vocabulary of line and colour, light and texture, enriched by tropes and metaphors. As cultural evidence, works of art therefore have many of the same liabilities as verbal fictions with their attendant problems of intentionality. If we accept the visual messages of art as sent, we can, as with literary fictions, be deceived to the extent that the sender intended to manipulate the audience or, even worse, to the extent that the sender who formulated the message laboured under cultural misperceptions or self-delusions. Material culturalists are interested in objects *as* expressions of belief. Art is quite clearly material that *is* expressive of belief. It would be absurd to exclude art from material culture. Yet how do we penetrate the self-conscious or self-deluded cultural disguise of art to reach deeper structures of meaning? The key lies in the capacity of art for unconscious as well as conscious metaphorical expression. That is the route through which it is possible to locate the unintended metaphors of cultural expression in works of art, just as it was possible to do with the teapot.

Notes

1. I am not comfortable with the spatial or topographical model of imaging cultural belief, but neither is Fernandez.

2. They are Static/Dynamic, Order/Disorder, Discreteness/Continuity, Process/Spontaneity, Sharp/Soft, Outer/Inner, and Other World/This World.

3. In "Mind in Matter" I arbitrarily divided the entire spectrum of artifacts—the material of material culture—into categories. These were arranged in a sequence that proceeds from most aesthetic to most

utilitarian, with considerable overlap: (1) art (paintings, drawings, prints, sculpture, photography); (2) diversions (books, toys, games, meals, theatrical performances); (3) adornment (jewelry, clothing, hair styles, cosmetics, tattooing, other alterations of the body); (4) modifications of the landscape (architecture, town planning, agriculture, mining); (5) applied arts (furniture, furnishings, receptacles); and (6) devices (machines, vehicles, scientific instruments, musical instruments, implements).

Form and User   **8**

Style, Mode, Fashion, and the Artifact

Dell Upton

Is the artifact important to material culture studies? Is there any way to treat objects more directly than we do? Do we understand the relationship between artifact and user as well as we do the relationship between object and maker? Can we define a "consumer's" view of the physical world? These questions raise issues that have occupied art historians and material culturists since the nineteenth century and in asking them we reopen old questions for re-examination. The authority of the old formalist art historians in the Swiss-German tradition, pioneers such as Heinrich Wölfflin, Alois Riegl, and Paul Frankl, was first undermined by art historians over half a century ago, and most contemporary students of material culture ignore these early theoreticians. The problem with traditional formalistic treatments is evident: too often forms seem to exist in a world of their own, apart from human agency, and thus from human history and meaning. Beginning with the iconographers, later art historians, as well as historians and material culturists have turned their attention from form toward meaning, from object toward maker, by asking about intention and thematic content. The history of artifacts became first an intellectual, and later a social and economic inquiry. In the process critical insight was lost.

For all their limitations, formalist scholars recognized that their stock in trade was the object, even though their ultimate aim was to turn their work back to the human subject. Although our understanding of material culture has advanced considerably in substance and sophistication in the past two decades we have, by and large, sidestepped artifacts. By this I mean that we are more comfortable with describing intangible social phenomena surrounding the possession and use of objects than with direct exploration of the object-person relationship.

Historically oriented scholars, for example, have rigorously examined the social and economic dimensions of artifacts, some seeking to make correlations between status, economic ability, and possession, others to question the spatial dimensions of social relations (e.g., Michel 1981). Because the objects are charged with conveying abstractions, the artifacts act simply as examples or counters in these studies. The objects are little more than names. To put it another way, these studies are easier to do with probate inventories than with the things themselves. Even studies based closely on archaeological or architectural fieldwork serve mostly to verify documentary descriptions or to substitute for missing documents. Studies of objects by geographers and folklorists use artifacts in a similar manner, to trace well-documented migrations of people through space and time or to define regional characteristics (Kniffen 1965; Glassie 1969; Lewis 1975). Again, nothing intrinsic in the artifacts is essential to the study.

Anthropologists have been more successful in using the physical characteristics of artifacts as keys to understanding. For example, James Deetz (1967) and Henry Glassie (1975b) have tried to establish a direct correlation between artifactual form and mental structure. Three-dimensional objects are indispensable to their work; no name or verbal description could substitute for the artifact, as they often might in the historical studies. Glassie's, in particular, is an ambitious study of the process of spatial design that is a necessary starting point for any subsequent inquiry. It establishes that mental structures shape the individual artifact, and it describes a process through which this might happen. In addition, Glassie attempts to account socially and culturally for the patterns that emerge from many such individual creative acts.

To emphasize the maker and the content is to make an important assumption, namely that objects are intended to communicate some concept of the maker's, an assumption accepted by American scholars for over thirty years (Robinson 1960:576-77). As early as the 1930s, European folklorists had gone even further, suggesting that if artifacts communicate, they should be thought of as "signs" that may share structural properties as well as communicative

functions with linguistic signs (Glassie 1973). Linguistically derived
semiotic models have been particularly popular among scholars of
material and immaterial culture since the late 1960s. Deetz uses
one derived from structural linguistics. In the first half of *Folk
Housing in Middle Virginia* Glassie applies another, borrowed from
generative grammar, to rural houses. But his model has not
achieved as wide a currency as the less rigorous applications of the
linguistic analogy to material culture so common in anthropological
and folkloristic studies during the last decade. The linguistic or
"communications" approach to artifacts has contributed significantly to our understanding of things not only in demonstrating ways to
avoid the metaphysical implications of formalistic theories, but in
teaching us to see the object as a mediator between creator and
perceiver. However, if we presume communication, we must ask
what is being communicated (Sperber 1977).

The descriptions of what objects communicate have been of two
sorts. The first stresses the autonomy of art. In his essay "The
Essence of the Visual Arts," semiotician Jan Mukarovsky concludes
that "the artistic sign" as opposed to the linguistic sign, refers only
to itself, communicating at most an attitude rather than a thing, by
which I assume he means a concept or idea (Mukarovsky 1966:236-
37). This claim resembles the orthodox art historian's assertion of
the "irreducibility or autonomy of art" (Podro 1982:xx). Both acknowledge the "inextricability" of the object from the context in
which it was made.

The object's message is also described by historians and material
culturists. In recent years, these scholars have begun to look more
closely at the phenomenon of consumption, asking about the im-
pulse to consume and the meaning of material goods for their users.
This is appropriate. Few people make things, but everyone uses
artifacts. Typically, however, those who study consumers adopt
semiotic assumptions (but less often methods) in rather heavy-
handed ways, searching for simple correlations between possession
and status that tell us little beyond what we would expect. The
traditional semiotic emphasis on the creator or maker assumes the
primacy of the sender of the presumed message. Consequently even
consumer studies stress the transmission of the consumer's self-
conception to others through objects: it is a maker study in another
form.

The importance of this work is undeniable, but I argue that there
is more to the story. We need to look beyond economic incentive and
social communication. To understand the meaning of artifacts in
the broadest sense, we need to focus on the imaginative act by which

people fuse their surroundings into a meaningful whole. It is an act more prosaic, but more ambitious, than that of making the most perfect basket or the cleverest tale, because its scope is so great. Yet because every person performs it constantly, it receives less attention and no romantic celebration.

If we ask about the formation of understanding, rather than its communication to others, and if we are to do this in a way that proceeds from the object, we must analyse the physical cues through which the consumer (or user, or observer) organizes and understands the physical world. One approach might be to return to the study of formal qualities that many scholars of material culture have rejected along with formalism. At the same time, we might want to reclaim and redefine some of the formalists' terminology.[1]

Style, for example, is widely accepted by makers and users of objects to be a "real" quality of things. The concept of style has the advantage of appearing commonsensical and artifact-based rather than mentalistic. It might allow us to describe intuitive relationships between people and objects in ways differing from the propositional forms that linguistic analogies promote.[2]

If we accept the idea of style, it is still necessary to define it. Part of the reason that style has been rejected is that several conflicting concepts have been wrapped up in the word. One is an art historical concept, discussed at length by Meyer Schapiro in his famous article in *Anthropology Today*. For Schapiro, style is "the constant form — and sometimes the constant elements, qualities and expression — in the art of an individual or group" (Schapiro 1953:287). As such it has an organizing function, as a "recurrent way of structuring and presenting" (Mills 1957:72).

Another concept of style is an evolutionary definition argued by some recent archaeologists. Style is a left-over, the accidental element of form that seems to have a separate existence but does not contribute to the explicit purpose of an artifact (Sackett 1977; Dunnell 1978; Meltzer 1981). As a contingent attribute, style is useful as an independent index of chronology. Paradoxically, the incidental quality of style subjects it to evolutionary changes that resemble the ahistorical formal developments suggested by the early art historians.

A third concept of style is found in popular culture. Here it is a changing assortment of specific visual motifs and decorative gew-gaws. It is above all concrete. In contrast to the art historical definition, and even to the archaeological one, this style can be photographed, described, classified, and catalogued in handbooks (Whiffen 1969; McAlester and McAlester 1984). Many scholars

dismiss these popular books as misreadings of the concept of style
(Longstreth 1984), but they represent an accurate and widely accepted understanding of one aspect of visual form.

This is a mixed bag of definitions. The first emphasizes artistic
intention and *Weltanschauung*, the second contingency, and the
third the concrete image. To recast them from the point of view of
the "consumer," we must assume that visual form organizes the
environment and embodies meanings invested in it by the observer.
We might describe this as a three-level organization.

Style in this model has an establishing function, acting "as a
signpost or banner advertising the arena for which an object is
intended" (Sackett 1977:370). As Meyer Schapiro wrote, style is "a
manifestation of the culture as a whole, the visible sign of its unity"
(Schapiro 1953:287).

Despite the implication of a unifying mental temperament underlying style, much of its visual unity comes more from generally
accepted conventions arising from functional necessities than from
undefined cultural harmony. In architecture, for example, conventional sizes of building materials, standard ratios of part size to
building size, moulding planes of fixed profiles, allow the maker to
work with limited training and a small chest of tools to create a varied
but coherent group of buildings. As semioticians have shown,
convention is an important element in understanding what we see,
even if we play down the communicative function that they assign
to it. Contrasts between materials and finishes as well as contextual
contrasts between light and dark, decorated and plain, serve to
establish identity and difference, which is the fundamental task of
visual forms.[3] For the maker, then, convention eliminates the need
to rethink every technical problem. For the user, it helps to sort out
one's surroundings. For the historian, it shapes the characteristic
look, or style, of a group of artifacts.

Style is pervasive. It provides a context, or system of common
understanding, for the members of a society. To refer once more to
linguistics, style resembles what sociolinguists call a code: a con-
cise, bonding body of implicitly understood assumptions that need
not be rehearsed. Allusions suffice (Upton 1979). Style is in this
sense consensual.

In contrast to *style*, I propose the term *mode* for the popular
sense of style, represented by the small-s styles catalogued in style
manuals. Artifactual modes serve not to unify but to distinguish.
They refer to the divisions within society, emphasizing and perpetuating old differences, recalling them to attention by clothing
them in striking new garb. Modes work to create new differences as

well, casting an identifying cloak over individuals not apparently related, or set apart, before.

Although the modes of élite and avant-garde groups are most likely to attract historians, modes can be used by groups of any social status wishing to set themselves apart (Hebdige 1979). Eighteenth-century forms in furniture, oriental designs in rugs, and antique Chinese porcelain are modes among certain élite twentieth-century Americans of conservative taste. The distinctive costume, buildings, or furniture of doctrinally plain groups like the Shakers and the Amish Mennonites also depend on visual modes. In both cases the modish forms identify people in a group with one another and at the same time demonstrate to themselves and to outsiders their differences from the larger society. Modes are limited, as well as limiting: by definition, they are small-scale phenomena standing highlighted against the background of style. That is, they are used selectively, rather than permeating or defining a particular physical environment.

The descriptions of style and mode I have offered so far are indistinguishable from semiotic interpretations in treating style and mode as signs of status and belonging. But they do more than simply mark. The semiotic approach is limited because material objects are more ordering than meaning-bearing. That is, they are symbolic, rather than significant.

Students of symbolism distinguish carefully between the sign and the symbol, a distinction not always made colloquially. A sign, a conventional marker that stands for some more cumbersome or abstract concept, is a more limited and a more easily defined entity than a symbol.

Consider a building with columns. Some observers might react to its reference to Greek antiquity or to the quality of its proportions or construction, but for most people, the initial reaction would be to its familiarity or rarity in their experience. That is, they respond to the setting in which the building is found. The observer requires extrinsic, contextual information to interpret the scene. A semiotic analysis would suggest that this information is used to extract explicit, grammatically encoded messages from the scene, but there need be no message to interpret.[4] Significant order is inserted by the viewer and takes a different, less propositional form than that implied by semiotics.

Recent studies of symbolism demonstrate that it is more useful to speak of a symbolic process than to attempt to identify and interpret individual symbols. Symbolism is rooted in the epistemological necessity for order. Our actions are based on the

assumption that our environment is not random, but structured
and predictable. At the same time, the structure of the world is a
human invention. We learn it from other people, who teach us to see
certain relationships in our social and physical surroundings. Consequently, the symbolic process is a reciprocal one: we look for the
relationships we expect and we find them because we put them
there. In this sense symbolization is the act of creating and recreat-
ing the world; we continually invest our environment with an order
that we find in it over and over again. Correspondences and resonan-
ces appear in unlikely places, and the imagined structure begins to
take on a life of its own.[5] When that happens, the symbolic order is
effective (Dolgin, Kemnitzer and Schneider 1977:3-44; Sperber
1977).

The establishment of correspondences alone is inadequate.
Some interpretation of their significance is required, and that interpretation can vary from observer to observer (Sperber 1977). But
effective social life requires that individual interpretations be knit
together by a common ideology. An ideological interpretation suc-
ceeds when its assumptions or propositions are made to seem
self-evident—when they are transformed into common sense. Then
they appear to be neutral depictions of the natural (Gramsci
1971:157). The interpretation achieves legitimacy, what Antonio
Gramsci called "hegemony," and inspirits the conduct of those who
are convinced by it. That is, it permeates one's relationship to one's
surroundings, explaining them, ordering them, guiding and justify-
ing action. Ideology is symbolization socialized, or adapted to a
particular social setting.

Artifacts are uniquely powerful tools of this process precisely
because they do not convey explicit messages. Rather, their visual
forms suggest identities and contrasts that make it possible for us
to perceive an implicit order based on commonsense understandings of contingency and causation. The concreteness of the
material world is more real and persuasive than verbal propositions
because of the apparent otherness of objects (Upton 1985b). From
this standpoint the semiotic and status communicative interpretations are trivial. A rich physical environment presents many
simultaneous orders to the symbolic imagination.

Let me offer a brief example drawn from eighteenth-century
Virginia and its established Church (Upton 1986). It necessarily
builds out from a semiotic interpretation, but is intended to
demonstrate that an adequate explanation of the relationship of
these artifacts to their users requires something more: an understanding of the ideologically charged symbolic process.

The Anglican Church reinforced the power of the state by promoting morality and respect for authority among the parishioners. There were several signs in the local parish churches that served this end. The Ten Commandments, "those grand rules of the Christian religion," were displayed prominently over the communion table. Above them hung the Royal Arms. Contemporary commentators noted that the conjunction of sacred and profane authority was intentional.

At the same time, the church had an explicit other-worldly end. Theologically, after all, the state was an instrument of divine purpose, even if the institution of the Church was an instrument of the state. The importance of the Church's message was reinforced by traditional physical language, notably the use of canopies and pediments, over the Ten Commandments, the pulpit, and the doorways. In the most expensive buildings, the entire auditorium was often vaulted. All three devices—canopy, pediment, and vault—were derived from the dome of heaven, a traditional language of honour with a history stretching back thousands of years (Smith 1950; Smith 1956). Colonial Virginians need not have been familiar with this history; by the eighteenth century the reference was obscured, but Virginians knew from experience that these architectural devices were intrinsically honorific.

The Anglican Church was organized territorially, and Anglican parishes in Virginia usually coincided with county lines. Thus, the traditional English use of the church as a device for display by the local élite was transferred to Virginia, even though it was altered in some details. The parish was controlled by the vestry, a self-perpetuating body of local gentry. They controlled the construction of the church building and the purchase of its furnishings. They frequently made gifts of goods or services to the parish.

The churches that the vestries built employed the standard structural and decorative elements—the style—of Virginia architecture. Their proportional systems, structural systems, and much of their decoration proclaimed them to be indigenous parts of the Virginia landscape. They established a visual relationship with the houses of planters and slaves of all varieties. But at key points they stood out. Their size was conspicuous. Churches, the largest buildings in the colony, equalled or surpassed the size of gentry houses, but dwarfed everyone else's. Similarly, their quality was closer to that of a mansion than a farmhouse. Churches had plastered walls and glazed windows; many planters' houses had neither of these. Other aspects of the church and its fittings established even more explicit identity with the world of the gentry. Some elements—

pilasters and capitals and entablatures, gilding and japanning, tables of certain shapes, silver vessels — were like the possessions of planters; no one else owned them. Similarly, the honorific elements were also confined to élite domains, such as the courthouse and the plantation house. Finally, many artifacts given to the church by the gentry were marked with the names and coats of arms of their donors.

There is no doubt that the modes of the wealthy served as signs of social standing. Modish artifacts that accorded with élite tastes and that were not available to everyone demonstrated native gentry familiarity with the aesthetic preferences of an international élite with whom they wished to be identified, and differentiated them from the ordinary planter. They had a bluntly communicative intent, and a semiotic interpretation is unavoidable. However, the visual elements needed to be fused into a symbolic order that transcended individual manipulation, otherwise they were transparently fraudulent. They demanded the otherness of artifacts. The metaphor of the house of God animated the Virginia church, lifting it from a collection of miscellaneous rich people's things to living truth. The ideology of host-guest and divine-human obligations, of grace and hospitality, provided the context within which the parishioner could understand the interpenetration of common religious language and élite visual modes. Through them, abstract theological propositions were concretized in the daily world at the same time that existing social order appeared timeless.

Having explored style and mode, we need to reconsider one more common term, fashion. Fashion is usually equated with mode, or treated as a kind of *deus ex machina*, a providential force that can be used to explain otherwise inexplicable preferences. But fashion is as definable as style or mode and is distinct from both. It is a relatively recent phenomenon that emerged from the greatly expanded availability of consumer goods in Euro-American society after the mid-eighteenth century. Emulative behaviour certainly existed in a limited form before that time (Williams 1982:19-31), but it was transmitted through small groups; it was restricted to élite, usually courtly, society; and it revolved around scarce, rather than plentiful, goods (McKendrick, Brewer, and Plumb 1982; also Bushman 1984:363). After the mid-eighteenth century, it was no longer a distinctive achievement merely to own desirable things, or those in a particular taste. Large-scale manufacturing made goods that had previously been restricted to the well-to-do available to middling purchasers. This was accompanied by the invention of marketing strategies that goaded individual consumers not simply to maintain acceptable standards within their own social groups but to keep pace with the rapidly and capriciously changing forms created by designers and manufacturers. Fashionable late-eighteenth-century consumers learned to adapt rapidly. Status was no longer a stable condition, but had to be maintained constantly by a quick grasp and speedy adoption of the newest material goods (McKendrick, Brewer, and Plumb 1982).

The commercial exploitation of fashion thus differs from the marketing of élite modes in several respects. Élite modes depend for their appeal in large part on their inaccessibility. Fashion plays on this premise, drawing on a tension between sentimental allegiance to archaic social hierarchies and the values of competitive consumption. New-style entrepreneurs of the eighteenth century charged artificially high prices for their new goods and released them initially to a small, prestigious audience, thereby whipping up demand for them when they were made available for general sale (McKendrick, Brewer, and Plumb 1982). Old-style modes revolved around the tastes of the ruling class—around patronage. In the new order, the élite were as much the tools of fashion as its guides; they were often manipulated by merchants and manufacturers to enhance the saleability of new goods. The patron-producer relationship was replaced by the merchant-customer relationship, although the commercial transaction was still described in the language of patronage. The change was not simple or sudden, and once fashion was established it outgrew the manipulation of individual men like the potter Josiah Wedgwood, who had pioneered its selling techniques (McKendrick, Brewer, and Plumb 1982:99-145). The important point is that producers now emphasized the quick acquisition of generally available goods and ideas over restricted access to scarce commodities.

Because the definition of visual forms as stylish, modish, or fashionable is based on the user's viewpoint rather than on the maker's intent or the original source of the forms, no form belongs intrinsically to any of the three levels. Old modes can feed new fashions, in the sense that they are incorporated into fashionable objects for the purpose of drawing on their hierarchical content for fashionable ends. At the same time, forms created for a fashionable market can be used for modish ends, for instance when their currency is past and knowledge of them must be developed as a taste in the appreciator. Fashionable forms can also become modes when they take on special meanings for a particular group apart from that recognized in the wider society. Again, the development of a personal ability to discriminate among similar objects is necessary in the absence of authoritative public pronouncements. Finally, both modish and fashionable forms can attain recurrent, but not continuous, currency, as frequently happens with works of art (Haskell 1976). The phenomenon of the rise and decline of reputations reinforces the description of style, mode, and fashion as collective transactions, and suggests once more that the maker is perhaps the least important figure in the maker-object-user triad, and can readily be replaced by the entrepreneur. Both can be equally effective in helping to establish the conventions or ideological lenses through which the artifacts are interpreted (Robinson 1960).

This analysis implies that the creator, user, and requisite abilities are different at each of the three levels. The ability to use styles is conveyed through craft training and the appreciative ability embedded in commonsensical categories of control and quality. The language of style once called on artisans to do "workmanlike," "decent," and "proper" work. The maker of élite modish items is the artist, their consumer the cultivated patron. In both artist and patron the ability to use modes is conveyed through what the eighteenth century called taste. Although for ideological purposes taste was described as innate in the patron and governed by immutable aesthetic rules in the artist, a learned ability to manipulate and to recognize the manipulation of modes in knowing ways served as a kind of test of belonging.

In the realm of fashion, it is the entrepreneur who establishes the context in which objects are seen. The language through which goods are described—taste, distinction, quality—is retained from traditional uses, but the standards of judgment are based not on the perceiver's learning, but on personal testimony of the entrepreneur. Advertising serves this function for ordinary goods, while professional and artistic credentials certify more costly goods. Taste rests in right choice rather than in knowing command.

Architecture is an intriguing test of the fashionable process, and of the necessary interpenetration of ideology and object; ideological claims alone cannot animate an unconvincing material world.

Although it might seem impossible for architectural clients to respond to rapidly changing fashions, this is not true. Robert Adam, a pioneer of the consumerization of architecture and interior decoration, was able to find clients, such as Robert Child at Osterley Park, who could be persuaded to rework at least part of their houses at very short intervals to keep up with the demands of fashion. Yet while ordinary fashionable behaviour is theoretically possible in architecture, it is not practicable for most clients.

Nevertheless, architectural entrepreneurs staked their fortunes on fashion after the early nineteenth century. In common with other professions, architects made claims to objective scientific knowledge (Upton 1984). At other times, they stated their claims in the traditional language of taste. And they cast the mysterious cloak of art over their work (Saint 1983:1-18, 161-66). Yet architects were neither scientists nor artists. Both labels were metaphors that hurt as much as they helped. As architects formulated it, the science of architecture was not abstruse, but consisted of a codification of common knowledge that could be understood by anyone. On the one hand, the technical part of architecture—the engineering—was quickly and willingly handed over to a separate profession. On the other hand, to apply the ideology of art to architecture was to throw every architect onto his own resources, in competition with every other architect. Each had to produce a uniquely personal product. This was fine for a few—the Richard Morris Hunts and the Henry Hobson Richardsons—but to do so carried them out of the world of fashionable mass consumption into that of producing distinctive and inaccessible (or modish) works for the élite. Although popular architects sounded the chord of art, they relied on the mechanism of fashion to generate business. They argued that architectural fashion progressed so rapidly that no client could keep up with it. The architect, who built houses year in and year out for all sorts of people, proposed to be a surrogate consumer for the client, taking it on himself to keep abreast of fashion, so that the client could jump into the tide with confidence.

If we look back to our earlier analysis of the role of objects, however, we will understand why architecture has never been successfully subjugated to fashion. Architects used traditional forms, but they did not transform them. Consequently, the ideology of architectural design was not supported by the material world. The buildings popular architects offered the middle-class consumer were thinly disguised traditional buildings. The animating fusion of ideology and material world never occurred. Ordinary builders found it easy to pick and choose from the architects' offerings without succumbing to the consumers' ethic of fashion. Architecture remained, and still remains, a technical profession serving large corporations and a modish pastime of the urban élite.

At the beginning of this paper I claimed that material culture studies had somehow relegated its most distinctive aspect—the object—to a secondary role. Too often, we simply confirm propositions made by historians and anthropologists. We use objects purely instrumentally, and we envision that the instrumental is their historical function as well. At the risk of sounding too formalist, I suggest that we need to come to terms more directly with the thing itself. Yet Glassie and others have made it clear that we can never go back to antiquarian or formalist views of objects, to the object exclusive of its human setting. This is why I am looking for answers in the conjunction of symbolism, ideology, and the psychology of perception of the physical world. This proposition leaves us with strong and entirely appropriate ties to social history and cultural anthropology, but it also suggests to me where our own contribution might be: in providing insights about human understanding of the material world.

Notes

1. The suggestion is appropriate for two reasons. First, older traditions of material culture study, including art history, have produced a body of sophisticated scholarship that we need to be able to use. Second, those who apply linguistic approaches in material culture have never been able to escape the theoretical metalanguage. One consequence is that most theoretical studies of material culture have been unable to analyse artifacts authoritatively. In addition, their findings are inaccessible to traditionalist historians of art, architectural, and decorative arts because of the specialized language. Material culture study does represent genuine progress both in its conceptual scope and in its ability to analyse many more kinds of artifacts, but the effort is futile if it is directed only to ourselves. The need to synthesize our predecessors' work with our own, and the desire to make our insights useful outside our own circle, suggest to me that we should co-opt commonly accepted concepts to our purposes. In doing so, we would draw on longstanding funds of meaning while reinterpreting the traditional concepts in critical ways.

2. This is not a call for a return to old-fashioned formalism. The iconographer, semiotician, and other critics of formalism have shown us that it is not possible to think of artifacts or style in pure ways separate from their thinkers, and that there is a propositional or communicative content to artifacts. Instead, the approach I am suggesting supplements, rather than replaces, the insights offered by the linguistic analogy.

3. In an important essay on the interpretation of artifacts, Jules Prown argues that the creator of a historic object and its modern interpreter share certain givens of perception: "rough is rough, wet is wet, hot is hot, and red is red to all human perceivers. Corollary assumptions are that physical man himself provides a constant measure in regard to scale (big, small) and that there are constants in man's experience of the physical world (the pull of gravity, the cycle of day and night). In confronting authentic objects of another period or place ... we do in fact

perceive something of what its producers and users perceived" (Prown 1980:208). In my argument, we need only presume the ability to distinguish among sensations. Whether our responses resemble those of the past only historical study can determine. It is not necessary to assume any continuity.

4. In addition, it seems likely that the observer interprets the scene through the experience of physical contingency—through having seen forms associated or used in particular contexts before—rather than grammatically. I am thinking of something analogous to the billiard-ball example offered in David Hume's argument about causality in *Dialogues Concerning Natural Religion* (Hume 1779; Copleston 1964: 68-72, 78-96). Similar arguments to mine were made by nineteenth-century theorists in explaining the "associational" qualities of visual forms (Hersey 1972). They thought that the viewer's response to the physical world was emotional and concurrent rather than rational and sequential.

5. A corollary of this statement is that, for analytical purposes, the maker is the expendable element in the maker-object-user triad. In his essay "The Essence of the Visual Arts," Jan Mukarovsky comes close to making this assertion. Mukarovsky considers whether a natural stone in which a viewer perceives intention might not be considered an art work. As a semiotician who maintains the existence of a "message" in the object, he must finally reject the notion, but the indispensability of an audience or user is clearly established by his discussion (Mukarovsky 1966:230-32, 236).

Ideology

"In a Very Tasty Style"

9

"Folk" Portraiture and the Purchase of Status

John Michael Vlach

When confronted with the work of sixteenth-century limner Nicholas Hilliard, a daughter of George III is said to have exclaimed: "Christ, what a fright!" (Strong 1969:57). Judgments of "folk" painting have rarely been so frank. Yet many of the so-called folk portraits done by amateur and self-trained professional painters in the United States during the first half of the nineteenth century probably merit similar assessments. Poor Mrs. Hepzibah Carpenter (Figure 1), for example, has a bizarre neck and a head tilted at an angle calculated to appeal mainly to a chiropractor; her image is but one of thousands of flawed pictures generally presented as characteristic of American folk art.

While such works were actually attempts to employ the idioms of studio practice and thus should be regarded as examples of popular, if not fine, art, they have, for over half a century, been claimed as expressions of the American folk tradition (Vlach 1988). This error in attribution has been accompanied by a congratulatory and up-beat rhetoric. These paintings are often said to be bold, fresh, imaginative, and direct and even equal to the greatest achievements of fine art (Lipman 1980:11). Yet this is not at all how these pictures were perceived when they first appeared in nineteenth-century homes. Observers contemporary with these paintings often made derogatory comments similar to that uttered by King George's daughter. These comments have been largely overlooked and ignored by the current aficionados of American "folk" portraits.

Figure 1: Portrait of Mrs. Hepzibah Carpenter by an unknown artist, ca. 1835. Courtesy of the Abby Aldrich Rockefeller Folk Art Center, Williamsburg, Virginia.

This painting, possibly done by the sitter's sister, reveals the desire to work within academic conventions in spite of a less than perfect command of those requirements. During the middle decades of the nineteenth century, subjects were often set in relaxed poses with the body inclined to one side and the head slightly tilted. The artist hoped then to present, particularly for women, a romantic image marked by gentle, curving lines. In this case, however, the head tilts but the body does not follow, producing a disastrous, even comic, result.

Preferring to see these paintings solely in positive aesthetic terms, they have struggled to ennoble these works as outstanding artistic achievements. In the process, the paintings and their painters have become entangled in a web of rosy assumptions that support a spurious vision of an antique folk era when, it is supposed, common man created folk art happily, effortlessly, and instinctively (Ames 1977:21). While the formulation of this propaganda is an interesting topic worthy of thoughtful comment, it is the intent of this essay to reconnect so-called folk paintings to their actual social and historical contexts and thus hopefully demystify the notion of a simple, charmed life so frequently claimed to be a feature of folk culture.

In 1807 Washington Irving commented in the first issue of *Salmagundi*: "Everyone is anxious to see his phiz[iogamy] on canvas, however stupid and ugly it may be." There existed at this time a national passion for portraiture that was to burn for more than six decades. Aaron Burr called it a "rage for portraits" (Flexner 1954:200). The demand was so great that apparently any picture would do. Russian diplomat and water colourist Paul Svinin noted this tendency as he travelled through America in 1811. He commented: "For that reason portrait painters are constantly in demand and are well paid. The most wretched paint-slinger receives no less than twenty dollars for a bust portrait and some men get as much as a hundred" (Yarmolinsky 1930:33). The trend continued unabated into the age of Jackson. Reviewing the condition of American art in 1829 the self-anointed critic John Neal wrote: "Our head-makers are without number and some without price." And he added with characteristic irony "They are more than we know what to do with." While Neal was generally optimistic about the potential for American painting, he basically felt that there was nowhere to go but up, so deficient was the public taste and the general performance of the majority of American painters. Of the numerous pictures that hung in American homes, Neal wrote that they were "things for everybody, familiar household furniture." He continued:

> Already they are quite as *necessary* as the chief of what goes to the embellishment of a house, and far more beautiful than most of the other furniture. If you cannot believe this, you have but to look at the multitude of portraits, wretched as they generally are, that may be found in every village of our country. You can hardly open the door of a best-room anywhere, without surprising, or being surprised by, the picture of somebody, plastered to the wall and staring at you with both eyes and a bunch of flowers (McCoubrey 1965:125). (See Figure 2.)

Figure 2: *Eliza Welch Stone* by Thomas Skynner; National Gallery of Art, Washington; Gift of Edgar William and Bernice Chrysler Garbisch, 1953.5.56.

Eyes and flowers dominate this portrait in the manner described by John Neal. The painter, one Thomas Skynner, knew something about the rules of perspective since he placed one eye higher than the other as if he (and the viewer) were looking up at the subject. However, he made both the far and the near eye the same size and thus negated the illusion of the third dimension. The picture mixes frontal and three-quarter from the side points of view drawing extra attention to the strangely positioned eyes which stare back without any hope of blinking.

Neal's critique, launched as it was from the lofty perch of a self-declared expert, might be expected to be snobbishly hostile. However, alarms of dismay were also heard from other sectors of society and they too point negatively to the public's preoccupation with self-likeness. For example, an 1822 editorial appearing in the *Western Sun and General Advertiser* of Vincennes, Indiana, complained of the wasteful extravagance of the local citizenry: "Instead of paying 12 or $15.00 to a portrait painter, why was not that sum of money appropriated to support a clergy man whose character, whose interest, and whose hopes were identified with our own?" (Peat 1954:21). It was not uncommon for inordinate sums of money to be spent on paintings. In fact, the economic success of one Cincinnati artist was so great that in 1841 it was reported that he offered loans at ten percent interest and held mortgages and real estate for security (Peat 1954:21).

That some artists made huge profits was no guarantee that the quality of their paintings was improving. According to Henry T. Tuckerman as late as 1867 the average artist was badly affected by "imperfect training, the pressure of necessity, the hurry and hustle of life, the absence of a just and firm critical influence, and a carelessness." The common people, alleged Tuckerman, were easily fooled by artists who "dash off likenesses cheap and fast" (Figure 3), artists who painted pictures filled with "violations of drawing, and absurdities of color, apparent to the least practiced eye" (Tuckerman 1867:23).

Not much had changed since Neal's first appraisal of the American art scene. At mid-century the popular taste for wide-eyed, flat, brightly coloured, shadowless portraits seemed firmly entrenched. At the same time, criticisms became even more caustic. Comments by Mark Twain provide not only the most thorough survey of domestic decoration during the period, but also have the most critical bite. In *Life on the Mississippi*, Twain describes in detail the southern domestic routine between 1850 and 1855. Here he sketches the common furnishings for the average "two-story 'frame' house":

> Over the middle of the mantle, engraving—*Washington Crossing the Delaware*; on the wall by the door, copy of it done in thunder-and-lightning crewels by one of the young ladies—work of art which would have made Washington hesitate about crossing, if he could have foreseen what advantage was going to be taken of it...
>
> In big gilt frame, slander of the family in oil: Papa holding a book ("Constitution of the United States"); guitar leaning up against mamma; the young ladies, as children,...both simpering up at

Figure 3: *The Letter*, Anonymous, American School, XIX century; National Gallery of Art, Washington; Gift of Edgar William and Bernice Chrysler Garbisch, 1953.5.79.

The great numbers of paintings of this type distressed Henry Tuckerman and other commentators. In this picture there is an attempt at likeness that results primarily in distortion of the features of the face. It is hard to believe that the subject was pleased to see his forehead so high or his nose so long. The writing equipment on the table is more convincingly painted and perhaps that compensated for the artist's failures in the depiction of human anatomy.

mamma, who simpers back. Those persons all fresh, raw, and red—apparently skinned (Twain 1883:276–277).

When Twain wrote as a journalist rather than as a novelist, his observations concerning "folk" painting leave no doubt regarding his disgust. In 1864 he declared "California and Nevada Territory are flooded with distressed looking abortions done in oil...and in every substance that is malleable and chiselable or that can be marked on, or scratched on, or painted on, or which by its nature can be compelled to lend itself to a relentless and unholy persecution and distortion of the features." The world, Twain felt, would be a better place without the makers of "sleepy-looking pictures" that were "blank, monotonous, over-fed, wretched counterfeits." He added that "There was no more life or expression in them than you may find in the soggy, upturned face of a pickled infant, dangling by the neck in a glass jar among the trophies of a doctor's back office, anyday" (Branch 1969:61–62).

That such works might even be termed art was considered by one commentator akin to a criminal act. In 1861 Oliver Wendell Holmes went so far as to refer to the numerous itinerant painters of New England as "wandering Thugs of Art." They were in his view, scoundrels who duped their customers into "murderous doings with the brush" as they:

> ...passed from one country tavern to another, eating and painting their way—feeding a week upon the landlord, another week upon the landlady, and two or three days apiece upon the children, as the walls of those hospitable edifices frequently testify even to the present day (Holmes 1861:14).

While one might expect self-proclaimed arbiters of taste to offer indictments against middle class paintings and their painters, the artists themselves were also self-incriminating. Chester Harding, a social portraitist who attained great celebrity as a painter of American statesmen and members of the European nobility, first worked—as all artists must—as a novice amateur. Starting out on the Kentucky frontier, he received enthusiastic patronage but he quickly realized that his canvases did not deserve the praise they were given. In his memoirs, entitled *My Egotistigraphy*, Harding remembered of his early days in Paris, Kentucky: "I painted nearly one hundred portraits, at twenty-five dollars a head. The first twenty-five I took rather disturbed the equanimity of my conscience. It did not seem to me that the portrait was intrinsically worth that money; now, I know it was not" (1866:43). (See Figure 4.)

A similar admission of inadequacy is found in the letters of Tom Moore, an itinerant painter from Virginia. He wrote in 1838: "I feel

Figure 4: *The John Speed Smith Family*, 1819 by Chester Harding; Collection of the J.B. Speed Art Museum, Louisville, Kentucky.

This painting is one of the few works that survive from Harding's early days in Kentucky. As a group portrait, however, it represents a move toward a level of sophistication that he certainly did not manifest in his first commissions. One can see in this canvas that the group is rendered as three distinct images. The notion of clustering the three subjects into a single entity had not yet occurred to Harding.

the want of instruction—and I have the idea of taking an excursion through the land for the purpose of endeavoring to raise sufficient funds to secure me a good master either in Philadelphia or New York" (O'Neil 1960:43). Moore's colleague, John Toole, had a similar plan but he was able only to obtain prints by Thomas Sully which he copied to improve his compositional technique. These exercises, as well as a partnership that he formed with a daguerreotypist who doubtless taught Toole a good deal about anatomy, led eventually to his greater competence in rendering accurate, convincing like-nesses.

The most revealing account of a nineteenth-century "folk" painter is found in the diary of James Guild which intermittently covers his career from 1818 to 1824. During this period he engaged in a range of trades—peddler, tinker, wrestler, profile cutter, pen-manship teacher, and portrait painter. His narrative is important because it reveals not only his views, but the attitudes of some of his clients. From his surviving account it is apparent that Guild was not universally received with open arms. On one occasion when he was bargaining with a New York farm wife to paint pictures of her children, the woman's husband, a Mr. Marvin, objected strenuously. When he saw the samples Guild had provided, Marvin grabbed him by the collar and dragged him into the yard, threatening all the while to horsewhip the presumptuous artist. But Guild got the better of the confrontation and threw Marvin head first into a goose pen where he struck his face on a board. Guild afterwards bragged "I guess he carrys the mark until this day" (1937:268).

Even though Guild admitted that he "lacked very much for instruction," and saw that he should "go to N.Y. and receive instruc-tion from the first artists," he was not deterred from presenting himself to the public as a portrait painter. He wrote of his first attempt at painting:

> I put up at a tavern and told a Young Lady if she would wash my shirt, I would draw her likeness. Now then I was to exert my skill in painting. I operated once on her but it looked so like a [w]re[t]ch I throwed it away and tried again. The poor Girl sat nipped up so prim and look[ed] so smileing it makes me smile when I think of while I was daubing on paint on a piece of paper—it could not be called painting—for it looked more like a strangle[d] cat than it did like her. However I told her it looked like her and she believed it (1937:268).

The intent here to deceive could not be any clearer and yet no offence was taken as the sitter was willingly duped. This sort of encounter apparently occurred repeatedly in the nineteenth century. It was an age of pretence during which a sham artist was not likely to be unmasked even if his ineptitude was plainly obvious. Paintings that were "wretched," "slanderous," "murderous," or "looked like strangled cats," were all judged acceptable. That these paintings were cherished despite all their flaws is made clear by one overwhelming reality: scores of thousands of these paintings were commissioned. Their existence constitutes a mute testimony to the fact that many people believed that they needed those pictures even if they contained flaws of execution.

Compelling social forces were at work in America during the nineteenth century which caused the degree of resemblance usually required in a portrait to be somewhat suspended. Because the American public wanted works of art more than they wanted artistry, they would accept a painting even when it was poorly done. Having *a* painting was more important than having a *good* painting. Indeed a wretched picture might be quite satisfactory so long as it cost a considerable amount of money.

For their owners, a desire to possess these less than fine paintings was tied to the pervasive materialism of early nineteenth century America. Many social commentators from the period noted that money and property ranked highest among the concerns of American citizens. Ralph Waldo Emerson, for example, stated: "You will hear that the first duty is to get land and money, place and name" (Ellis 1979:219). Michel Chevalier, a French traveller, wrote in 1839: "At the bottom of all that an American does is money, beneath every word, money... His motto is 'Victory or Death!' But to him, victory is to make money, to get the dollars, to make a fortune out of nothing" (Pessen 1969:29). This analysis restates the earlier observation of John Vanderlyn who noted of his Hudson Valley neighbours in 1825: "Property is after all the most important thing, in this country particularly. Fame is little thought of, money is all and ever the thing" (letter to John Vanderlyn, Jr.). In such a social context, paintings were highly charged objects. They could be used as proof that one controlled the discretionary income required for the purchase of luxury items. They could be used to demonstrate wealth and thus serve as a means for claiming higher social rank and its accompanying greater prestige. It was no wonder then, that the anonymous tavern girl who sat for Guild smiled so. She was getting a painted likeness, a proof of success just for washing a shirt. A painting had the ritual power of transformation; it seemingly boosted one up a rung on the social ladder. While the tavern girl would never advance her station simply by owning Guild's awkward picture of her, she could at least feel richer. Consequently, she was happily deceived and she accepted her unflattering portrait as if it were a masterpiece. The social gain she anticipated caused her to overlook her alleged resemblance to an asphyxiated feline.

A few years later a similar ritual of arrival was enacted in Orange County, New York. The first quarter of the nineteenth century was a productive period for a local farmer named Alexander Thompson. In 1819 he won the county prize for the most improved farm; in 1822 he redesigned his house adding "fancy rooms" for which he purchased all new furnishings in the latest style; in 1823 he and his wife had their tenth and last child and he accepted local elective office. The next year he and his wife had their portraits painted. Thompson had secured all the elements of the Emersonian formula for success — land and money, place and name — and he underscored his achievement with images of self, portraits to be hung in the new parlour. However, he chose Ammi Phillips as the artist and the paintings he got for his money were considered "cheap and slight" (Figure 5). Still the brush work was careful and the paintings were judged suitable enough for their purpose. In fact, Thompson recommended Phillips to all his kinfolk in the county and the itinerant artist painted his way from door to door, capturing the likenesses of the entire Thompson clan. If we follow Thompson's career for a few more decades, we find that he acts with less expedience in the matter of portrait painting. In 1848 when he retired from an eleven-year term as Town Supervisor, his portrait was again painted but this time by John Vanderlyn, a studio-trained artist of international repute (Figure 6). Thus as Thompson climbed the social ladder of success, he also moved up through the hierarchy of art (Larson 1980:40–41). His taste for "folk" portraiture had been replaced by a preference for canvases that would be clearly recognized as works of fine art.

Opportunistic social climbing was one of the symptomatic behaviours of the Jacksonian age. This condition is effectively captured in an apocryphal tale reported by Godfry T. Vigne in 1833. The captain of a steamboat, during a meal aboard his vessel, asked in a loud voice of a distinguished guest seated next to him, "General, a little more fish?" and immediately twenty-five of the thirty men seated at the table answered "Yes!" (Pessen 1969:31–32). The country was full of pretenders to greatness and one of the most common strategies used was to imitate the behaviour of a local grandee. We have already seen that Alexander Thompson's less prominent kin followed his lead when they commissioned portraits by Ammi Phillips. Chester Harding reported a similar copy-cat syndrome in Kentucky. When he began to paint portraits, he first

Figure 5: Portrait of Alexander Thompson II by Ammi Phillips, 1824. Courtesy of Cheekwood Botanical Gardens and Fine Arts Center; 86.16.20. Gift of Mr. and Mrs. Walter G. Knestrich.

Figure 6: Portrait of Alexander Thompson II by John Vanderlyn, 1848. Courtesy of Neil and Lee Larson, Troy, New York. In comparing Figures 5 and 6, note that Phillips renders Thompson in relatively bright light which tends to emphasize the outline of his head and torso. Vanderlyn's version emphasizes shadows through an adept use of chiaroscuro, a technique that establishes a pronounced sense of three-dimensional reality. Phillips thus renders Thompson more over a surface, while Vanderlyn locates him in a space. That space appears to be more real because one senses that the light in it comes from a specific direction—above and from the left. In Phillip's painting the light is diffuse and less realistic. Further, by cloaking Thompson in shadows, Vanderlyn concentrates the viewer's attention more directly on the subject's face and thus heightens one's awareness of his personality. Phillips, in contrast, gives Thompson essentially the resigned countenance of a man waiting for the painter to be finished.

did a painting of a "very popular young man, and made a hit." He was then thrown in with the "tip-top of society" and he found himself beseiged with requests to paint more portraits (1866:43–44). Since these were likenesses that Harding would later judge to be inferior, it is fairly certain that his work was solicited mainly because of the prestige associated with the first sitter rather than the quality of the portraits. An 1840 newspaper article from the Richmond, Indiana *Palladium* counselled "ladies and gentlemen of taste and fashion" to patronize S.S. Walker, a portrait painter then visiting that town. The reporter took pains to note that an economic depression had created a scarcity of money, but he argued that the "finer feelings of nature" merited indulgence (Peat 1954:88–89). He essentially dared the well-to-do of Richmond to spend their limited funds on art to prove their social position. The act of commissioning a painting in such circumstances may be more significant than the actual painting itself.

The sort of paintings under consideration here were by the 1830s becoming less expensive and more readily available with an increase in the number of rural portrait makers, but the acceptance of these works is connected to complex matters which should not be overlooked. In the United States, the period roughly from 1830 to 1850 is characterized in most histories as a time of the prominence of the ordinary citizen, as an age of egalitarian feeling. Yet, ironically, what the supposedly egalitarian, democratic art of the populace demonstrates is competition for position and reinforcement of strict class boundaries. So powerful was the general desire for advancement via property that art became one of the prime means of brokering one's movement in society. Any artwork, even the very plain, possessed sufficient charm by association to flatter the ego of its owner. This is why unsophisticated and awkward portraits could be willingly accepted; they may not have looked like fine art, but they worked like it. They gave partial admittance into the style of culture practised by society's first people. "Folk" paintings were important as elements of family rituals; yet more important was their promise of advance in the wider realm of taste and fashion. Painters constantly advertised the matter of status. William Matthew Prior of Boston offered works "in a very tasty style"; R.B. Crafft promised his Indiana clients portraits "in a superior style"; Ezra Ames of Albany, New York, vowed likenesses "in the best manner" (Bishop 1977:40; Peat 1954:111; Bolton and Cortelyou 1955:21). This was a time when, as Charles Dickens noted, Americans had a predilection for high-toned language; when working girls earned *compensation* not wages, when household cats might be called *quadruped members of our establishment*, and women could happily give their sons names like *Altamount* (Pessen 1969:32).

The rhetoric of "folk" painting and the paintings themselves gave lip service to the ideal of advance, yet the consumers of those paintings were held in place, victims of a hoax that things were getting better. Between 1825 and 1850 the highest echelon of society tightened its control over the United States; by mid-century one percent of the population controlled close to 50 percent of the nation's wealth (Pessen 1973:383). This increase, up from 25 percent, was achieved mainly at the expense of the middle classes who were severely affected by a number of disastrous economic depressions in the 1830s. The statistics were exceedingly dreary for people of modest means; in 1850 when the mean value of real estate holdings was $1,001, 78 percent of the households counted in the census were below the mean (Soltow 1975:178). A study of property holding in five New England towns has shown that by 1860 30 to 50 percent of the men over thirty had failed to gain even minimal wealth levels (Doherty 1977:54–55). Thus, even as "folk" paintings became cheaper, fewer and fewer could afford them.

For most citizens the age of Jackson was an age of ruin, a period during which the bases for even middle-class status evaporated while political orators provided a constant flow of smooth and reassuring promises. So-called "folk" portraits were unwittingly drawn into this process of appeasement since they appeared, like any artwork, to signal a degree of success. Because they provided relatively imposing images during an era of crisis, they served as an extension of the spoken propaganda of general well-being. As they satisfied their owners' perceived needs for luxurious property, they deflected potential criticism away from the élite group who were determined to keep the common people under command. Consequently we should read in these pictures not the celebration of the common man so frequently heralded, but his containment and his control.

Edward Pessen has written that: "An expanding capitalistic society everywhere dips into the less privileged strata to provide some of the manpower it requires for entrepreneurial leadership" (1969:57). Thus while a few may advance, most will stay put where they are or actually fall to a lower status. Ownership of "folk" portraits served a relatively small group as a faint sign of success. Those who afforded them may have seemed to rise through the ranks, yet most remained anchored in a subordinate position. The owners interpreted their portraits as congratulatory images that saluted their industrious habits, their aggressive thrift, and their new aesthetic discernment. But because their pictures were actually failed works of art, these paintings only reinforced the hegemony of the old-money élite. So long as ordinary people consumed "folk" paintings, they were contained by—and mocked for—their "bad" taste. The age of Jackson was neither an age of egalitarianism nor the common man. While a two-dimensional rendering of an ancestor may have promoted family solidarity in the home where it was displayed, as an agent of social stratification, it was devastating.

Although James Thomas Flexner has written that the thousands of "folk" portraits commissioned during the nineteenth century include "some of the ugliest social portraits the western world has ever known," they are far from uninteresting (1954:209). As suggested above, they provide a valuable key to unlock the workings of a complex social history for a period during which economic conditions ran counter to prevailing social rhetoric. During the age of the common man, the so-called common man was losing ground. The paintings said to represent this group (actually they depict members of the upper middle-class) signalled a seemingly improved status at the very moment the owners' status was falling. Rather than confront representations of financial and social failure, these people sought luxury items like paintings. Convinced that their paintings possessed prestige, they accepted them even when they were flawed by anatomical distortion, faulty perspective, or botched technique. These men and women of aspiration were, after all, more concerned with buying status than with buying art.

The Fashion System in American Furniture

10

Michael J. Ettema

One of the common complaints of material culture scholars is that researchers in other fields do not make serious attempts to incorporate material culture into their work. But the problem works two ways. The others may not be serious about our work because we have neglected to demonstrate that what we do is, indeed, serious.

Material culture is not really a field or a discipline. Rather, it is a set of conceptual tools. The best work in material culture has taught us how we can learn about human thoughts, motivations, feelings, and attitudes through the study of objects. What it does not teach us is how to interpret that information. Material culture provides an ever growing body of valuable data on human behaviour, but the more longstanding disciplines such as anthropology, sociology, and history continue to provide the theoretical and interpretive frameworks in which that data takes on meaning and usefulness. In other words, material culture study has no issues of its own other than those of methodology.

I am particularly interested here in one of the major problems that keep historians and artifact specialists apart. We can think of this problem as one of categories: the categories we use to identify, classify, think about artifacts. Historians have great difficulty understanding artifacts because the categories normally used to define them are based on the concrete physical attributes of the objects themselves or on the conditions of their manufacture. Historians, however, find great comfort in abstract categories such as political movements or social philosophies. Unlike anthropologists, historians have no training in the intricacies of uniting objects and ideas. But more to the point (and also unlike anthropologists), historians have seldom built their historical questions around artifact types. Ideas and actions—not things—are what define the groups of people that historians study. This is not to say that material culture specialists do not have or do not use ideas, nor to say that historical inquiry is not based in the world of the concrete. The point is that, for the sake of intellectual progress, we need to overcome the limitations of traditional categories in both history and material culture. The study of artifacts presents historians with an opportunity to expand their data base and with a nonverbal, non-linear way to organize human experience. To material culture study, traditional historical inquiry extends the opportunity to think about the ways in which artifacts have meaning outside the context of design and manufacture. The potential for gain is on both sides and the old suspicions, one for the other, are unnecessary.

Let me be a bit more specific about the problem and possibilities. The categories traditionally used in material culture study are derived from formalist studies of artifacts. They usually are based on analysis of the formal qualities or structure of artifacts and the physical circumstances of their manufacture. Therefore we have categories such as "handicraft" and "industrial" or "vernacular" and "high-style." Formalist categories also include "period styles," regional designations, and material types as well as taxonomies of form or configuration (such as Georgian, half-Georgian, I-house).

In any event, the assumption behind this type of categorization is that the formal qualities are what constitute meaning in artifacts; it is what makes objects historically and culturally important. The extreme version of this view is that form is culture itself. It follows from this formalist assumption that cultural change will be signalled by formal change. For example, Deetz, Glassie, and many others have observed that the adoption of Georgian symmetry in architecture and other artifacts signalled the rise of a worldview of individualism. Mapping such change is the basis of most material culture study, and certainly much thoughtful analysis has been done within formal categories; that is not at issue. What is at issue is what else can be done. What do these formalist assumptions *not* account for?

Formal analysis tends to obscure a central problem: while form usually signals meaning (which is only to say that objects are given specific appearances for some cultural reason, that goods have meaning), meaning is not inherent in form. In other words, the categories by which people comprehend objects may change even though the forms do not. And conversely, the forms may change even though the categories do not. This is because formal categories are not the only categories people have used to identify objects. An easy example is an eighteenth century turned, rush-seated, "fiddle-back" chair. When new, it was apprehended as a chair of lower-middle price range, appropriate to a wide variety of social circumstances and used in different rooms of the house. By the mid-nineteenth century, such chairs occupied the lower end of the economic spectrum and were only used in non-status activities. By the late nineteenth century, the form was considered a symbol of the virtuous simplicity of our forbears as well as an excellent example of the "country Queen Anne" style, and, for the first time, found a treasured place in fashionable parlours. So, even though the form did not change, the terms by which the chairs were understood changed dramatically. In the eighteenth and early nineteenth centuries, the categories were those of economic level and social affiliation—the change in meaning was only a change within the categories. But by the late nineteenth century, the economic and social terms were supplemented by categories of style and cultural iconography: a change across categories.

Objects may therefore be organized into many different categories, certain of which are not inherent in their manufacture or appearance. Many such categories are defined by associations that accrue through use. Formal categories are therefore useful only for certain types of historical issues. Generally speaking, they are most helpful in understanding issues arising from production such as the culture of craftspeople, social relationships of production, or the relationships of producers to local communities. Issues tied to use frequently require some other type of categorization which students of material culture have not yet adequately developed.

And this, I believe, is one of the reasons material culture has been so hesitantly adopted by historians of the written record. Often our formal categories are not unuseful to them. For example, the historian who is studying crowd actions during the American Revolution finds that objects (especially as commodities) are at the centre of the story. The seizure and destruction (or more equitable distribution) of goods and commodities by an angry mob were aimed at disciplining greedy merchants or selfish consumers. In puzzling out the meaning and role of artifacts in this instance, the careful measurements of houses, chairs, and dinner plates are meaningless; detailed analyses of roof construction and silversmithing techniques are pointless; stylistic categorizations for chair splats are absurd. What the historian here needs to know are the categories that allowed people during the Revolution to understand the place of objects in the moral economy. Did tea and tea wares have certain associations of class or politics which made them culturally charged or symbolic commodities? In this case organizing goods into the historian's abstract categories would be productive.

The trick to constructing categories, however, lies not in the triumph of historical over material inquiry, nor vice versa, but in attempting to recreate the categories used by the people we are studying. The key to understanding the role of goods in other cultures is to understand the terms by which they thought about goods and how they manipulated those terms. They are bound to be different than the terms we use today. Material culture analysis and historical inquiry will move closer together if both are respectful of the various ways that people have organized their worlds.

By way of example, I want to sketch the broad outlines of an historical argument about the relationship between objects and cultural authority. The historical problem I've been working on is the relationships between fashion and materialism. The area of fashion I chose was home furnishings, particularly furniture. I quickly found that studies of fashion usually talked about furniture in aesthetic terms, particularly as the progression of styles; in almost every case fashion was tied to art. A little primary research, however, revealed that before the 1880s things that were considered fashionable were not always, indeed not usually, discussed in terms of art. Instead the public understood home furnishing in terms of their functions: physical functions, but especially their ritual or symbolic functions. It was from the 1880s on that writers increasingly discussed furnishings in terms of their aesthetic qualities, especially style. This was happening at a time when the middle classes dramatically increased consumption of home furnishings and when participation in fashionable consumption was penetrating deeply down the economic scale. What was the relationship between these phenomena? I want to argue that the change in categories was an integral part in a shift in the cultural authority to channel and promote consumption. More specifically, business people seized cultural authority for consumption of home furnishings.

In the period from the 1840s through the 1870s fashion was defined, in official Victorian culture, primarily according to functional categories, especially categories of ceremonial function. Being up to date stylistically was usually a positive value and not ignored, but fashion was mostly understood as having furnishings that were designed to be used in genteel social situations. These situations were defined by codes of etiquette. For example, Ken Ames has shown in his famous article on hall furnishings that hall stands and chairs were adjuncts to the elaborate rituals of calling (Ames 1978). Similarly, the formal entertaining carried on in the reception room or drawing room supposedly required furniture such as parlour or reception suites, pier mirrors, etageres, pedestals, easels, cabinets and centre tables which were specifically designated as formal furnishings intended for presentation and display to visitors. Less formal situations also had their appropriate furniture types; rocking chairs, reclining chairs, easy chairs, and lounges were usually reserved for more private times when the rules of etiquette could be somewhat relaxed, or at least when public appearances were not at risk. Thus furniture was to be formally varied, but it was primarily categorized by social situations of use.

Why these categories? To answer that we must look at the cultural context of use, the official ideas of what the home was for and how it should be used. Domestic ideology in this period has been summed up under the phrase, "the cult of domesticity." To simplify greatly, this ideology held that the purpose of the home was to serve as antidote to the moral and spiritual depredations of the world of society and commerce. It would do this in three ways: by structuring and therefore controlling social interaction with outsiders, by providing a place of retreat, and by providing nurture and regeneration through the agency of the loving family circle. The latter purpose was to be accomplished mainly through the habits and activities of the family such as dining together, sharing books and entertainments, and particularly through all the attention that the mother paid to every detail of homemaking.

Nurture and regeneration had relatively few material manifestations. The material environment of the house was primarily shaped by the first two purposes: retreat and controlled social interaction. The control of social interaction was to be accomplished by carefully segregating activities by room and then by establishing a strict code of behaviour for each room and activity. In general, rooms and activities were differentiated by degrees of formality: the hall was most formal, followed by reception room, drawing room, dining room, library, sitting room, bedroom, kitchen, and finally, servants' rooms. Each level of formality had its appropriate ceremonies, postures, gestures, and topics of conversation and even number of participants. Genteel visitors supposedly knew the code and conformed to the behaviour indicated by the particular room in which they found themselves. Privacy was controlled in the same way: the less formal the room the more private it was. In most houses this also coincided with the layout of the rooms; the further one penetrated back or above in the house, the more one's activities were to be shielded from public view. Only close friends and family were to be invited into the sitting room or bedrooms.

This desire for control and privacy was the reason that furniture of this period was thought of in terms of its ceremonial function. The purpose of furniture was to serve as a guide to the appropriate behaviour in each room. It did this primarily through its physical function. Rocking chairs were for relaxation, relaxation was an informal occasion, and therefore an invitation to be seated in a rocker indicated an informal social circumstance. Conversely, reception and drawing room chairs were small in scale with straight backs and taut upholstery, made more for perching than relaxing. But sitting upright and at attention was a formal posture appropriate for such a formal space. Thus, formal qualities of furniture did not dictate the categories, but rather were signs of the social usages which defined the categories by which they were understood. The objects took on significance within the ideology of domesticity.

But this ideology can also be located in a larger cultural context—mainstream Victorian culture in the third quarter of the nineteenth century. In this culture, shared largely by educated, middle- and upper-class whites of Anglo-Saxon ancestry, adherence to the tenets of domesticity was considered essential to social order. The home, they believed, was the centre of value and truth. It was where the individual character was formed and nurtured. Sound character depended on both the moral rectitude and worldly success of the individual citizen. And, in the republican scheme of things, on the virtuous individual depended the well-being and progress of the whole society. Therefore domesticity became charged with a moral urgency that now seems shocking and absurd. And by extension, conforming to the codes of domestic etiquette was also a moral imperative. Learning the correct way to furnish a home and the correct usage of the furnishings would both cultivate and symbolize a sound character. Fashionable consumption, then, had a basis in moral principle.

In this situation where fashion had become a moral duty and social obligation, it was important to get fashion down right. But who made the codes of etiquette? Individuals could not do it for they cannot make codes. Since consumption was infused with such cultural importance, etiquette and domestic advice usually appeared in the context of general cultural and social commentary. Domestic advice books often took the form of guides to general principles of sound living; they were heavily moralizing and usually explicitly religious. Typically they combined dictates on decoration, manners, cooking, hygiene, childrearing, and marriage all in one volume. Popular periodicals such as Godey's and Peterson's did essentially the same thing through the vehicles of fashion tips, fiction, poetry and book reviews. So the fashion authorities—the authorities for correct consumption at mid-century—were Protestant ministers, upper middle-class housewives, and the self-appointed guardians of genteel culture who dominated the popular press. They were cultural authorities because they articulated the ideology of domesticity and its rules of etiquette and fashion. In their ability to articulate the codes of genteel behaviour, they established the categories by which objects were understood, and therefore they had enormous influence over the reasons that the goods were purchased.

In the late 1870s this cultural system began to show signs of breaking up; by the 1920s, the system was largely transformed. On the level of home furnishings, we can see that the categories began to change. Middle- and upper-grade furniture was still identified by function, but ceremonial functions were de-emphasized and physical functions were identified with less specificity. In particular, the fine gradations of formality were minimized. For example, the categories of hall chairs, reception chairs, drawing room chairs, and parlour chairs were replaced simply with easy chairs and occasional chairs by the 1920s. While the categories of low-end goods remained largely unaltered, middle- and upper-grade furniture for the front rooms tended to become less function specific, less identified with social ceremony.

But as the use of ceremonial categories waned, aesthetic identifications waxed. The first type of furniture identified primarily by its aesthetic qualities was called "art furniture" and was based on the English aesthetic reform styles. Through the decade of the 1880s this furniture identified by style was thought of as an alternative to the more conventional goods identified by function. In the 1890s, however, the identification of furniture by art styles became the norm for middle- and upper-grade goods. Thus the idea of period styles became the primary organizing principle for furniture design. Since the functions of furniture were less specific—a given item could be used in many different rooms or situations—the most important feature of a furniture item was its style.

If the set of categories used to identify furniture was changing at the turn of the century, we might also find that ideas about the purpose of the home were changing at the same time. In the culture of domesticity, the home became even more intensely private than had been the ideal at mid-century. Rather than understanding the rooms of the house as a set of filters which progressively screened occupants from public view, domestic ideologues increasingly pushed the bounds of privacy out toward the front of the house. The front rooms were now supposedly more for the comfort and pleasure of the family, than for the entertainment and benefit of guests. This is why there was less need to differentiate among formal furnishings; the reception room, drawing room and formal parlour had all been replaced by the living room.

As the need to carefully structure social interaction was minimized in the middle-class home, nurture and regeneration, the other side of domesticity, were maximized. The home was to be devoted to every aspect of personal development and success. But in these years surrounding the turn of the century, the meaning of nurture and development also changed. Rather than learning the rules and attributes of a genteel lifestyle, character formation increasingly came to mean the development of inherent personal virtue. This is what Warren Susman has called the shift from character to personality (Susman 1984). Being a virtuous and successful individual was not just a matter of learning how to behave, it also depended on bringing out that combination of desirable personal qualities that supposedly made the individual unique. This newly perceived need was summed up in the term "self-expression."

An important part of self-expression was aesthetic expression or, as was often said, the "cultivation of taste." It was in service to this new need for expression that the style categories of furniture became useful. It was thought that each style was the product of a specific culture or historical epoch and was that culture's peculiar way of seeing aesthetic truth. In other words each style was aesthetically worthy, but each revealed a different set of cultural characteristics. For example the "Adam style" (based on eighteenth century, English neo-classical design) was considered rational, formal, genteel, sophisticated, learned, and republican, while the "Louis XIV style" was romantic, impetuous, luxurious, smacking of monarchy, yet was also sophisticated, formal, and genteel. Each style, then, supposedly expressed the culture that produced it. Individual taste was cultivated by learning to distinguish the various styles and selecting those which best matched one's personality. According to the domestic advisors, individual expression consisted largely of adopting a personal combination of the approved style categories.

So, we can see that the shift from functional to aesthetic categories in home furnishings was part of a shift in domestic ideology. This shift, I believe, had profound consequences for the history of materialism. In the earlier version of domesticity, desirable personal attributes lay in behaviour towards others, in conformity to the rules of etiquette. The objects were only tools used to guide and facilitate this socially-oriented behaviour. In the revised ideology, however, the use of goods was not meaningful, so much as their appearance. Domestic furniture had moved from signal to symbol. Formal qualities were no longer simply guides to character, they contained character. Value existed less in the behaviour of people than in the style of their objects.

This act of reification is aestheticism: the willingness to categorize the world and the self using the terms of aesthetics and fashion. When such value is placed on aesthetic categories (when fashion is defined in this way) fashion authorities are those who can explain the aesthetic philosophies on which they are based. Cultural authorities are those who can explain the meaning of style. Since the meanings of the styles were derived from highly specialized learning in history and aesthetics, these authorities had to be specialized experts. Merely being educated and genteel was no longer enough. By the twentieth century, domestic advice tended increasingly to come from professional artists, designers, scholars, and critics.

The social and moral commentators—Protestant clergyman and women authors—were replaced towards the end of the century by furniture manufacturers and retailers, interior decorators, art critics, connoisseurs, and museum curators. Although these people were generally from the same social group as their predecessors—white, upper- middle-class, Protestant males of the northeastern United States—they differed in one very important respect. Authority had always accrued to the people who defined the categories by which objects were understood; this fact gave them the greatest individual control over what made objects desirable. But now the authorities for consumption also had a direct interest in the production and sale of those very goods. By virtue of this growing ability to manipulate the categories of culture, authority was increasingly passed on to capitalist business organizations.

Now, it is easily argued that not everyone became an aestheticist caught up in the fashion system. And that is certainly true; this is a study of official culture, and the people most affected by it tended to be of a privileged social and economic situation. But the purpose here is not to explain the history of a specific group of people, but rather to explain the workings of a specific cultural system in which individuals participated to a greater or lesser degree, based on their particular histories and circumstances. Although this cultural system of gentility and aestheticism had existed in some form in the West at least since the late middle ages, it burgeoned in both scope and intensity in the late nineteenth century. In the twentieth century it is still one of the primary underpinnings of our popular culture of materialism. In the course of that expansion, some of the components or terms of that culture changed in a way which has helped to strengthen the larger culture, the culture of capitalism.

If it is true, as students of material culture claim, that making and using objects are fundamentally social experiences, then the names people give to objects and the categories in which they identify their artifacts are guides to the way people order their thinking about their place in the world and interpret their social experience. Being respectful and sensitive to the categories of culture that people have used in the past can only help historians strengthen and deepen their interpretations of the past, and help material culture specialists continue to uncover the complexity and diversity of material life.

Artifacts and Cultural Meaning

11

The Ritual of Collecting American Folk Art

Eugene W. Metcalf

We live in a world we make for ourselves. It is built not simply of bricks and mortar, but of meanings which frame our understanding and expectations to support the significance of what we experience. Primary materials in the construction of society, meanings are stored in symbols and passed from one generation to the next, perpetuating culture by giving form and order to the world as we collectively experience it.

Every society is organized around regularized activities which attempt to determine and express what is important to that group. These activities are called rituals. Rituals dramatize social meaning, thereby channeling the flux of our experience into established, and knowable, conventions. Although many rituals are purely verbal, some of the most effective ones employ objects to help manipulate, establish, and record important meanings.

In any society, at a given time, certain rituals assume special importance. Related to the development and articulation of what are perceived to be significant meanings which need to be conventionalized or expressed, such rituals, and the symbols they use, are central to the development and maintenance of key patterns of culture. Understanding the importance of such activities helps unlock the significance of other related behaviours. Artifacts used in such rituals are particularly useful subjects for material culture study (Ames 1980:619–641).

In American society, for the last half century, one such ritual has been the collecting of American folk art. The power of the ritual of folk art collecting comes from its ability to synthesize and make available to modern American society a broad variety of important beliefs and activities, which help define the nature and promise of America.

As it is commonly understood by most Americans, American folk art is the representative art of the American nation. Said to be produced by artisans untrained in the skills of academic art, it is thought to embody the vision and accomplishment of the common American. Folk art is believed to be an everyday art form, made by ordinary people from the materials of everyday life. It exists as shop signs, weather vanes, paint-decorated furniture, and crude paint-ings. Although often described as naive or primitive, these objects are said to evidence the positive attitudes and values of an in-dividualistic, unpretentious, and democratic nation.

Despite its social value as a symbol of American democracy, folk art is nonetheless evaluated by collectors primarily as an aesthetic entity. Objects called folk art are categorized as painting and sculp-ture and judged in terms of formal qualities like design and colour. Known for their spontaneous expression, vigour and simplicity of line, rather than their original social uses, these objects are removed from the particular cultural and historical contexts in which they were made and placed in art museums and galleries. Thus the fraktur of Pennsylvania Germans is viewed as bold painting, not as social or secular announcement; cigar store figures are considered vivid and powerful sculpture, devoid of commercial or social sig-nificance. Although this aestheticizing isolates objects called folk art from their original social meanings and thus limits our knowledge of these artifacts, it also raises an interesting issue which might help us to begin to understand these objects in a new, and expanded, way. As Henry Glassie has observed, perhaps folk art is only made by *other* people (Glassie 1986:269).

Belonging to all cultures, art is a common human gesture—yet it assumes a local character, representing the particular forms and meanings of the society in which it is produced. What was art in Puritan Massachusetts or in the antebellum South, what it is in Italian neighbourhoods or on Amish farms is not the same (Geertz 1983:97).

But not so for folk art. Folk art does not exist at all as such in the culture or consciousness of the people who make it. Instead, folk art is produced by the perception of an outsider. Objects are called "quilts" or "taufschein" or "weather vanes" or even termed "art," but are never "*folk* art." The adjective "folk" seems always to refer to someone else's artifact. It designates a difference between the observer's art and that being described. Folk art is thus a translation of the complex artifactual and social reality of one group into generalized terms that another group can use and comprehend. Consequently, objects called folk art belong, in an important way, to the observer's perception. Defined by the knowledge and subject to the needs of the observer, they are constructions of his or her culture, emblems of the observer's values and world view. Subjected to an outsider definition, folk art objects may be able to tell us only a little about the people who originally made and used them, but they reveal much about the society and people that designate them as folk. This becomes especially evident when one examines the nature of folk artistic production.

Regardless of its aesthetic dimension, art is primarily a social phenomenon; it represents not only social values, but also the social organization, or art world, which supports the art. As forms of social organization, these art worlds include the people and the co-operative system involved in creating, defining, promoting, and sustaining a particular artistic interest (Becker 1982). In terms of folk art, this group includes collectors, dealers, gallery owners, museum workers, those who read the *Clarion* folk art magazine, and others who contribute to the interest in folk art.

This sociological view of folk art may seem at odds with the one that is generally used to understand this art form. The approach employed by students of folk art (and by students of art in general) places primary emphasis on the art object and its original creator, not on the co-operative system of artistic manufacture and promotion. As a result the people who make folk art are (when they can be identified) regarded as the sole creators of the things they assemble. They are given an elevated social position and honoured as "artists": the possessors of unique talents and inspired imagination. Likewise, the things these people produce are also said to be special. Imbued with what are believed to be innately aesthetic qualities and regarded as icons of American experience, these objects are valued as artifacts whose importance transcends their original social utility.

Yet this view of the uniqueness of folk art is no more accurate than the conception of the folk "artist" as the sole creator. For once we recognize and accept the importance of the folk art world in sustaining—and even creating—art, we can see that rather than being an innately aesthetic or unique object, a work of folk art is simply *any* artifact that has been designated as such by members of the folk art world. Of course, the notion that an interested society can enforce its own artistic values on virtually any kind of object is not peculiar to folk art. But it allows the folk art enthusiast a particularly creative and powerful role (Robbins 1976:14).

Appropriating in part the function of the artist, folk art collectors and critics have created an entire artistic corpus. They search for and select existing artifacts, redefine them as folk art, and give them new meanings and relationships within a new social context. Through this process utilitarian objects often become objects of beauty and art. Redefined, revalued, and thus in a sense recreated, these objects become more a product of the social network that remade them than they are of the person who originally fashioned them. Consequently, for the purposes of the examination of American folk art, the circumstances in which an artifact existed before it entered the folk art world may be less important than what happens once it enters. It is in this sense that the "makers" of folk art objects are not so much those craftsmen untrained in the techniques of high art, but those collectors and dealers who find crude objects and infuse them with folk art meaning. Likewise, the society that produces folk art is not the so-called primitive or simple society which may have nurtured the original fabricator of the folk art object, but the modern American society in which folk art collecting functions as an important ritual. It is a ritual that interprets historical experience to give significance to contemporary life by dramatizing and transfiguring the meaning of a central American activity—the acquisition and ownership of goods.

It is difficult to study American folk art for very long and not come to the conclusion that it is, at the most basic level, an economic commodity. For although we may feel uncomfortable admitting it, our behaviour as Americans indicates that the ownership of goods is a major goal in American life. Once this truth is acknowledged, we realize that the commercial matrix in which Americans live is not incidental. It is not, as some have argued, a kind of artifactual overlay superimposed on the real structure of life; it *is* the structure, the fundamental network holding society together. As a product of co–operative labour, and a commodity in an artistic marketplace, folk art represents some of the important and prestigious goods of an economic system. These goods acquire meaning as a form of investment and exchange, and their aesthetic value is connected to their market value. Yet, as the work of Mary Douglas and Baron Isherwood suggests, the consumption of such commodities represents much more than mere greedy consumerism or simple conspicuous consumption. Rather, consumption is "an integral part of the social system" and "itself part of the social need to relate to other people." It is a system of communication by which people come together to establish, accept or reject, the meanings and values of their society. They do this through the judgments they exercise in the marketplace. By choosing what to consume or not, by deciding what they are willing to pay for a particular object, consumers join together to rank the values that commodities represent and to help establish their worth (Douglas and Isherwood 1979:14). Thus, consumption can be seen as an important arena in which culture is negotiated, fixed, and codified. In the ever present human attempt to select and determine the common meanings of culture, consumption is a ritual process which publicly establishes the visible, and commonly agreed on, categories of culture (Douglas and Isherwood 1979:65).

In recent decades the prices paid for American folk art have escalated remarkably. New auction records are set each season as the price of folk objects rises in parallel to (though of course not equalling) such privileged art forms as impressionist or old master paintings. But what values are being established through folk art, and what is being communicated? To consider these questions we must glance at the historical significance of the ritual of folk art collecting.

So great is our need to understand and contain our experience that any breakdown in our explanatory apparatus results in considerable anxiety. One such epistemological and cultural dislocation occurred in the early years of the twentieth century, when American folk art was first defined and popularized. It is through understanding the relationship of folk art to this dislocation that we can begin to comprehend why folk art has such important ritual meaning in America.

The discovery and popularization of American folk art happened in the first decades of the twentieth century at a time of rapid, and disquieting, social change. Most important was the growth of the city, completing the transition from a rural nation to an urban one. Over half the population lived in large cities and, in the minds of many Americans, rural life appeared dull and sterile. Nevertheless, as much as Americans seemed to welcome the glamour and vitality of the city, they also feared other aspects of encroaching urbanization. To a nation raised on Jeffersonian ideals, the city still represented images of sin and decay. It was a place of debauchery and crowding, a haven for crime, and home for unassimilated foreigners. The conflicting hopes and fears about the city were not new to America, but in these years they were deeply felt, and they represented a pervasive ambivalence.

Hand in hand with demographic changes went new mechanization and industrialization. Revolutionary technological innovations such as the moving assembly line and the widespread use of the electrical motor created new or radically altered industries like those producing automobiles, light metals, chemicals and synthetics. Yet as fervently as Americans welcomed the unprecedented increase of new consumer goods, they were also uneasy with the technology that manufactured them. Fear of dehumanization and standardization was part of the general reaction to the machines. The fear was often voiced that man himself was becoming little more than a machine—a "robot" to use a word that appeared at this time.

Demographic and technological changes exacerbated the changing roles of women, alterations in religious practices, changing family structure, and new patterns of immigration. Despite prosperity, a culture was being created that felt deeply threatened. Battered by the forces of change, and unable to make sense of contemporary events through the use of old systems of belief and feeling, Americans struggled to develop new conventions to accommodate modern experience, and new symbols to mark and contain not only new categories of meaning but bygone ones too. Hence American folk art.

In the face of the complicated dilemmas of modern life, folk art was enshrined by collectors as a representation of the simple and elemental truths of American life as Americans wanted to believe (and remember) them. Understood in terms of preindustrial and pastoral meaning, folk art was said to celebrate individuality, democracy, the virtues and values of handcraftsmanship, and agrarian society—ideals which were now fundamentally challenged by the reality of modern American experience. As a ritual activity collecting folk art allowed, and still gives, Americans the reassurance and hope that by coming together to exchange and venerate the symbols of traditional American values, those values are still somehow available. They can be protected and enshrined. Yet as ritual, the ultimate significance of the consumption of folk art goes beyond even this historical meaning. It acquires an almost religious significance.

As Clifford Geertz has pointed out, religion is that aspect of cultural activity which operates to synthesize a people's sense of the meaning and value of life with their view of the way things actually are (Geertz 1973b:87–125). It connects their moral and aesthetic sense, their attitude toward themselves and their lives, with what they experience and know of the world firsthand.

The consumption of folk art can function as a religious ritual because it operates to connect important social and historical meanings (embedded in terms such as "individualism" and "democracy") to mundane things or activities (weather vanes or handcraftsmanship) sustaining each element and integrating the American experience as it is lived and as it is imagined. More important, however (and this is the case for all religious symbols), the meaning which is fused into folk art objects is generally *transcendent*. Representing concepts of ultimate truth, these interpretations affirm the American vision of God's holy plan.

It has long been recognized that in America there are common elements of religious orientation which operate outside of established church structures and which have played an important role in the development of American ideology and institutions, an orientation Robert Bellah calls civil religion. Springing originally from the seventeenth–century Puritan vision of America as a place where God's kingdom can be realized, and codified as a national ideology at the time of the American Revolution, American civil religion provides a transcendent dimension to the understanding of American history, and a spiritual justification for American action. In this quasi-religious view, the American Revolution can be interpreted as a kind of exodus from Egypt; the Declaration of Independence and Constitution as the holy scriptures of liberty; and American nationalism as a divinely sanctioned obligation. Interpreting history and national destiny as religious imperative has historically resulted in the justification of many questionable ethnocentric American activities. Yet they have been influential in establishing a national identity and sense of purpose (Bellah 1967). This identity and transcendent purpose is embodied and contained in civic symbols like the flag, George Washington, and even the Arlington National Cemetery, and is likewise expressed in a particularly meaningful way through objects of American folk art.

Not only do folk art objects often assume and use traditional civic images, they turn them into art. Folk-made representations of the flag and George Washington come to carry aesthetic as well as political significance. Now objects of beauty, the appreciation of such things evidences good taste and social sophistication, as well as patriotism. Yet it is not only folk art objects in the form of civic symbols that embody the values of American civil religion, it is *all* folk art objects. First popularized during a period when the historical identity of America was called into question, folk art reifies the qualities that made America God's chosen land. Through collecting and venerating folk art, Americans can hope, if only subconsciously, to reclaim and reaffirm God's mission for themselves and their country. This is why objects called folk art, and the behaviours associated with them, can never be understood in purely rational terms. With its religiously motivated component, folk art moves beyond the realities of everyday life to a transcendent view. As in all forms of religious belief, it is ultimately responsible not to the dictates of everyday experience, but to an *a priori* acceptance of the transcendent religious authority which expands that experience; folk art transforms the mundane to the miraculous. In other words, to *know* American folk art, and to participate fully in the collecting of it, one must first *believe*.

So in the end, folk art objects are best understood not as objects at all, but as part of a constantly developing process of cultural meaning. As an evidence of material culture, works of folk art—like all artifacts—should be seen not simply as things, but also as notations which give form to changing social and historical meanings. As Douglas and Isherwood have observed: "The stream of consumable goods leaves a sediment that builds up the structure of culture like a coral island" (1979:75).

Yet finally in order to completely understand American folk art, it must be comprehended not only in terms of its relationship to the folk art world, but also in relationship to the world of high art. For although American folk art is considered to be an art form fundamentally different from high art, the differences are in reality insignificant. Instead of threatening or changing the world of high art, the introduction of folk art supported it.

The first discoverers and promoters of American folk art were American modern artists. These artists were interested in naive American paintings and sculpture not because they represented new and unknown techniques and genres, but because they seemed similar in feeling and form to the modern art the artists were themselves making. As Daniel Robbins has pointed out, folk art became popular at a time when high art began to be dominated by a striving for vigour, simplicity, and a return to origins: "Works were sanctified that seemed to hark back to periods when vision was fresh or to stages in life when conventions had not yet corroded personal spontaneity." Yet, as Robbins has also shown, naive artifacts were valued by artists not only for aesthetic reasons, but also because they seemed to give modern art the historical and cultural roots of an indigenous American tradition. This was a reply to critics who complained that American modern art was only another version of decadent European civilization (Robbins 1976:19). Consequently, although these artifacts were believed to be productions of unsophisticated craftsmen untrained in academic artistic traditions, they were discovered by members of an emerging élite art world and defined according to the sophisticated artistic canons which governed that group. Interest in such objects did not result in the development of new artistic conventions and co-operative networks, but rather in the support of existing, or already emerging, ones. Although a new art world was indeed developing when American folk art was first popularized, it was not one centred on folk art, but on modern art into whose social system folk art, and most of the activities related to folk art, could be assimilated.

Thus American folk art must be understood as an essentially high art form. That it is still popularly identified as different from high art is testimony to the power of the cultural needs it satisfies. For whether folk art does or does not exist as the art of the common man, we still need to believe that it does. It is this belief that continues to function as a mainstay of American social ideology.

Invisibility, Embodiment and American Furniture **12**

Stanley Johannesen

This essay is concerned with a moment in the history of taste, of acquisition, of social power, and of a distinctive form of spiritual life which is considerably diminished in the modern world. My thesis is that Western furniture from the late Middle Ages until the late eighteenth century was a feature of a humane and civilizing process having to do with the rationalizing of the perception of personhood. The modern person was progressively understood in the West as a body in a comfortably furnished interior. Between the enchanted invisibility of things in traditional society, and the capitalist invisibility of things in the fully rationalized present, there was a classical age of naive embodiment that embraced both human bodies and other things in the furnished interior. American furniture occupies an illustrative if problematic place in such an account.

The object illustrated here—a Newport secretary-bookcase of the Townsend-Goddard workshops (Figure 1)—is familiar enough. Far from representing a class of things in need of being brought to light, it represents a class of things that has for at least the past century been the object of intensely competitive acquisitory zeal by wealthy Americans. Such things have become icons of a taste both patrician and patriotic, and at the same time sources of a still-living tradition of popular decor promoted through most of the twentieth century as "colonial." Like all extremely scarce luxury goods for which a standard of connoisseurship is established, original examples of American antique furniture embody social power: both the power

Figure 1: Secretary-bookcase. Attributed to John Goddard, Newport, Rhode Island, 1761. Courtesy of the Rhode Island Historical Society.

that accrues to one who possesses rare "originals" as evidence of discrimination and surplus income, and the power that accrues to one whose taste and pattern of consumption are emulated on a lesser scale by others.

So much is easily understood as characterizing the meaning of these objects in what we might call their second age—that social and temporal medium in which they are "antiques," in which they have ceased to age or become obsolescent in the ordinary sense but have rather become encysted in social codes, social force-fields, and cycles of taste and evaluation separated from their original or first age by a chasm of disuse, neglect, and destruction. Indeed, the miraculous survival of some of these things across that chasm is a considerable part of the meaning of these things in their second age, when they are often accompanied by stories of discovery, rescue, restoration, as in a drama of moral rehabilitation.

The pursuit of distinction, as Pierre Bourdieu reminds us, may take virtually anything as its field of operation: any class of objects or forms, and any conceivable system of aesthetic inclusion or exclusion (Bourdieu 1984). From the vantage point of this thorough-going skepticism, one need only apply two stringent principles: that one cannot tell what a thing means merely by looking at it; and that professions of taste, along with claims of distinction on the basis of taste, are infallibly operations that make virtue of necessity. These principles of interpretation applied to the second life of the objects before us mean that the content of connoisseurship in these things does not arise naturally or simply out of the forms of the things themselves, but is rather a position constructed and taken up as an exclusive piece of social territory. Once the urgencies of social power are felt, the appropriate field of new cultural capital will not fail to present itself, and the objects of these tastes will be discovered to have properties of beauty and value of an absolute character.

What does this recognition of social power in the second age of these objects have to do with the interpretation of these objects in their first age? First of all, one must recognize that there is an element of continuity in the meaning of social power between that age and this, between the societies of late colonial America and our own society. If any analysis of luxury goods in our society should properly begin with an understanding of distinction as social power, apart from the techniques of connoisseurship that are generated within the practice of this social power, then such an approach is also appropriate in late colonial America. This is a crucial point about these particular sorts of objects: unlike many other things that enter into fields of distinction in modern society, objects that came into existence first in exotic social contexts with an "affecting presence" (Armstrong 1971) wholly irrecoverable under modern conditions of social life, American Chippendale furniture came into existence in a society that is one of the immediate predecessors of our own. The social system that produced the eighteenth-century gentry republic was in important respects very different from the social system of modern America. However, a useful starting point for putting those differences in a proper scale is to note what is familiar and already "modern" in the system that produced this furniture. To put the relevant issues in sharp contrast, let us digress for a moment to take in an episode in a distant corner of the transatlantic world.

The books of Pierre-Jakez Hélias (Hélias 1978) reflect a rare personal experience of social and spiritual migration from tradition- al society to modern society in a single lifetime. Hélias was born and raised in one of the last outposts of peasant culture in Western Europe, the village communes of Breton-speaking Armorican Brit- tany in the northwestern part of France in the early twentieth century.

Among other things, Hélias' reflections on this experience show how traditional societies sustain themselves, in the absence of central administrative direction and functional specializations, by a web of shared memory, daily reinforced by an extraordinary specification of detail. Everything and every practice, from the head-dresses of the women to the heft of particular tools, serves both to enlarge the content of mental culture within the group to satiation and to separate tiny, otherwise indistinguishable, social units from each other by an intricate code of differences.

One of the experiences Hélias remembers is being put to bed in a carved wooden bedstead with doors. He recalls the distinctive warmth and safety of these beds, and how the perforations in the carving of panels and doors provided peepholes, often in the shape of crosses and other mystically charged emblems, through which a child could spy on adults and hear their talk. Hélias then describes his own reaction as an adult to seeing these same bedsteads, or perhaps just their doors, carted off to fashionable Paris antique shops and then to suburban parlours to be recycled as stereo cabinets and liquor cabinets (Hélias 1978:333). What had been part of a web of collective memory, a thing whose form, placement and details of execution were fully charged with the lines of social, religious and even political force that made up the totality of that culture, had become mere cultural capital, something easily interchangeable with, say, African granary doors, or Chinese lacquer panels.

To see why this commonplace transformation of artifacts presents problems central to the understanding of culture in the modern West, we may usefully study the situation of objects of perception when the collective element is introduced. Consider an analogy with objects of play in a spectator sport. Under conditions of collective inter-subjectivity objects disappear, in the way that a football, visible as a thing made of such and such materials, of such and such dimensions, when it is inert in our hands or on a shelf, becomes invisible, as a thing, when it is in play in the context of the rules of a football game.[1] To extend the simile, we might say that the Breton bedstead in its original setting is invisible too, and in precisely the sense in which the football is invisible in a football game: that is, in the context for which the object in question was conceived and fashioned. The way in which the doors of a Breton bedstead become invisible when they are the doors of a suburban liquor cabinet is like the way a football would become invisible if it were mounted on a stand in a trophy room because it bore the signatures of members of a famous team in the early years of the game. In the first simile the object is a transmission point of social practices, invisible as an object but essential in exactly that form to the practices themselves. If we could imagine the practices without that form we would be imagining something that did not in fact ever happen, for the practices and the forms evolved in the same social and temporal reality. This is equally true of the football in a football game, and objects of communal practice and memory in traditional societies.[2]

This necessity is clearly not present in the second simile, in which an object is like a football on a display stand. The object in this case is a transmission point in a set of social practices, but since the practices turn on the demonstration of distinction, and the field of cultural capital in which distinction is earned is determined by the principle of constant expansion of fields of cultural capital as old fields are exhausted, the form of the object has not the slightest relation to its chief function.

Hélias himself, it should be said, was not particularly shocked by the new uses to which these things from another age were put. What did surprise him was the suggestion that he might wish to enter one of these bedsteads from his childhood and spend a night in it (Hélias 1978:334). One could never return to the time of a lost world, and to try it would be a species of sacrilege, an offence against sacred memories.

There is a moment in every social transaction involving a thing, that the thing ceases for all epistemological purposes to exist, and all that remains is the transaction — membership, superiority, nostalgia, anticipation, and so forth, phenomenally experienced.

For pieces of American furniture, we can see that although it is tempting to read meaning directly from some aspect of their appearance, such a reading will be worthless if we have no proper framework of comparison. There is nothing about the scale of these pieces, their quality of finish, their details of ornamentation, their tendency to particular degrees of centripetal or centrifugal extension, their general opulence or virtuosity, that cannot be projected into a plausible social psychology, and perhaps correctly. Yet what if the meaning of these particular objects, to take the extreme possibility, has always been, in both their first and second ages, simply that they were luxury goods in transactions that involved little more than invidious distinction, social power through display, and the exercise of taste as itself a good, a prerequisite of wealth and position? We might still imagine a child, or any person of sensitive imagination, storing his or her memory with the details or the general aspect of such things, and feeling affection, fear, morbid identification, mere obsessive fascination, or any other feeling in the repertory of people's relations with things. Yet we would not feel that the forms, the placement, the details of these things were fixed in a web of communal memory in such fashion that any break in these features would threaten the entire fabric of community. The reason we know that this is so is not because any of the features of these objects, isolated as symbols, or conceived in sentimental and affective terms, could not, in some conceivable community, under the pressure of extraordinary transactions, bear the burden of intense social import. Rather, we know things about late colonial American society that make such a reading of these things highly suspect.

The consumers of these luxury objects were not a community dependent for survival on ritual practices and world-making at the intensely local and detailed level of European peasant villagers. Colonial élites were integrated into social and economic connections both inter-regional and transatlantic. These factors were true in every colonial centre, whatever variations there were in regional institutional and economic base or in the character of popular piety and local demography. Élites everywhere surrounded themselves with the sumptuary trappings of players in a game of social power.[3] The appearance of concerted movements for sumptuary virtue in the struggles with Britain, from the imperial crises of the 1760s right through to the 1812–1815 period, should be seen as the flourishing of the shapes of provincial things under moral banners such as "simple," "homely," "unrefined," "manly," or simply "American." It is under these rubrics that actual things tend to disappear in the republic of virtue, made invisible by these collective perceptions — just as people may be said to disappear from view when ideological purity comes to be associated with virtue in the modern revolutionary state.

There is of course something about these objects that lent them readily to the purposes of new and modern systems of discourse, and it is not in their material or aesthetic features as such, but in the inner histories of design and taste to which they already belonged. The names of the forms that attach to pieces of furniture, the names in the decorative vocabularies that apply to furniture, the names of fashionable designers associated with "styles," the experience of being in fashion or out of fashion, were all features of a wider discourse on cultural goods, and features of a progressive rationalization of lifeworlds, already long familiar by the end of the eighteenth century. This rationalized discourse served to alienate things, and the particular material features of things, from the enchantment that surrounded things in a more emblem-conscious age, and also progressively to alienate things from intimate involvement in social ritual. Instead, things are understood to occupy specific temporal and spatial junctures according to the logic of the spread of styles and of tastes: from high to low, from early to late, from major population centres to lesser, from skilled craftsmen to indifferent copyists, from the metropolis to the provinces, from town to country. These are also the categories of connoisseurship in the second age of things, but they were in the first age already primary categories of entry into the discourse of cultural capital.

In one decade "provincial" or "simple" might mean something inferior, or perhaps the best one could do, or as reflecting the virtues of frugality or of acquiescence in the unformed tastes of one's neighbours. In another decade these terms denoted the high ethical and aesthetic tastes of a Spartan age, the conscious rejection of effete luxury in favour of an environment conducive to the classical virtues. In both of these situations, however, there was at least tacit recognition of a rationalized narrative of things as belonging to a series: a series whose particular devices and shapes were conventional. In other words, variation in things from one place and time to another were not attributed to variation in the particular genius of places and times (unless these were very long distances and widely separated periods, as in Montesquieu's famous speculations on the effects of climate on political culture), but rather to the uneven reach of universal standards of taste, and hence of criteria for social power. Every Breton child could identify his or her village by the mere cut of the women's caps. By contrast, there is little reference in the travel literature of late colonial America to suggest that people noticed variations in the style of Boston, New York, Newport, Philadelphia, or Southern furniture, except to note degrees of luxury, costliness, fashionableness, sophistication, and impressiveness.

I have so far taken the well-known piece of American furniture with which we began, as a text, or occasion, for emphasizing two issues: the distance between modern things and things in traditional society; and the kinship between modern things in their first age of meaning and those same things in their second age of meaning. In the remainder of this essay I want to balance this account with a different sort of perspective and a different sort of question: can we construct a rather more genetic and less starkly contrasting inter-pretation of this furniture, one that takes into account broad continuities of meaning in the cultural experience of Western Europe?

I should like to describe three loosely circumscribed historical contexts, one fitting inside the other, from an outer circumstance toward more inner, or local, ones. The first one is Northwestern Europe in the late Middle Ages and early modern periods. The second is the Anglo-American tradition (mainly as opposed to the French tradition), as it became visible in developed fashion in the eighteenth century. Finally, I shall suggest a defining element in the American idiom in furniture, in the context of each of the foregoing, and in the context of the history of American design generally.

Let us begin with Penelope Eames' definitive catalogue and survey of medieval furniture (Eames 1977). The evidence consists of the handful of fully authenticated pieces that survive, together with pictorial and literary evidence. Many things, such as strongboxes and lockers, survived because they were out of the way, and belonged to institutions such as churches and colleges that were likely to go on using them for their original purpose, or to forget about them when they were no longer used. Many furniture forms, particularly seating furniture, did not survive in any numbers. In part this was because they wore out, but also because in many instances these were roughly joined structures meant to be com-pletely concealed by fine cloths, furs, specimens of needlework and so forth, which were more likely to constitute personal and household wealth than were examples of joinery. Furthermore, a medieval household likely to be substantial enough to require a good bit of furniture was also one on the move, spending many parts of the year relocating from one drafty hall to another, taking down hangings, placing them in chests, and hanging them again somewhere else. Solid furniture was either knocked together for temporary need, or so massive as to be impossible or unprofitable to steal during the periods when buildings were empty and unguarded.

We must imagine, in other words, a world in which interiors underwent radical transformation rather quickly: seasonal investitures and divestitures not unlike the transformations of the church altar in the liturgical cycle. The use of vestments in interiors was part of a characteristic way of occupying and representing social life at the same time. Social life was at once carried out—in and through the work of designing, making, hanging, and moving all these things—and illustrated—in the decorative opportunity created by cloth coverings (perhaps a practical and material reason for the importance of heraldry and the elaborate figural and colour symbolisms of medieval costume and decoration). A person of high status or great wealth would be recognized as such in his meanest castle as well as in his greatest. Social space was filled with representations and symbols of the orders and degrees of the society, while domestic space was filled with persons both engaged in the considerable labour of such a household, wearing on themselves and on the furniture the flags and pennons of the status of their master.

More interesting from our present point of view, however, is the specific grammar of use relating to furniture, particularly seating furniture, which corresponded with a general feeling for social space: position in space did not pertain to, or belong to, particular persons, but rather to their relative statuses. High, chief, or central places belonged on any particular occasion to the highest ranking person present. It did not matter that a chair or a place at table was the property of a particular person or his or her customary place: that person would slide along to the next less favoured place in the presence of a person of higher degree, and everyone above or below would slide accordingly to an appropriate position.

Let us try to connect these impressions—a sense of interiors as densely packed social medium, and a sense of personal location as something supremely relative, changing with every change in the surrounding social medium—with the sense of furniture as "created" by temporary and constantly adjusted arrangements of portable stuffs and coverings. And we see that there is a curious reciprocation within social space between persons and things. The king is no less a king for having the high place in the meanest lodging. The lowliest of knights may sit in that same place on another occasion without an offence to majesty. The stool on which they sit, on these two occasions, is, however, in one instance merely a stool, and in the other a throne—at least functionally. The loose and shifting integrity of "a piece of furniture" (implied in the nature of the material arrangements of mobile and portable households) gives rise to these opportunities. A stool or box properly covered is like a man properly attired. The richness of the stuff and the heraldic sign, with a strong collective sense of precedence and degree, indicate honour, and perhaps, in a sense it is difficult for us to phenomenally appreciate, *is* honour in that moment. Honour is movable. A man may be degraded by the withdrawal of his relative standing, even by so much as the entry into a room of a person of higher precedence; likewise the things that shared this same social space occupied a similarly insecure and transient identity. Both the social system and the system of socially significant things were extraordinarily stable over long periods of time, but the identities of elements in these systems were relatively unstable.

The principle that seems to be important in all this, as the fertile bed from which quite heterogenous practices would grow, is that while architecture marks the site of social power—the terrain on which the game of social power is to be played—there is another class of things that supply a kind of grammar of power. Furniture does this, I would argue, not only in the way that any socially generated form of invidious display does—anything costly or rare or demanding of investment of time and money—but also by participating in the spatial positioning of bodies, by altering the shape and height and attitude of bodies, by extending, preventing, elevating, diminishing, the reach or the perceived scale of bodies, and by occupying the same space with bodies. Already in medieval practice we see the tendency toward a convergence of the treatment of furniture and bodies, and already in this case toward a certain common phenomenon of "disappearance": the disappearance of things in themselves in favour of points of reference in a highly structured social space.

It was still an open question in medieval culture how far persons were to be permitted to stand out from the viscous medium of that social system to be persons, that is, purely and simply. When European culture swung toward an increasing recognition of the separate person as the focus of human dignity, that movement was accompanied by a systematic crowding of interior space with a flood of specialized, and highly and permanently individuated objects, many with obscure functions, to a degree that is surely unique among civilizations and is not easily accounted for.

In an intriguing passage Elaine Scarry notices this excess of adjuncts to the various functions and articulations of the human body in furniture and even in the specializations of industries and whole cities in the West, in the context of torture and its systematic "unmaking" of precisely these features of the world (Scarry 1985:39). Her essay describes how the classical forms of torture focused on the dislocating of the joints in precisely the places that in the Western *habitus* are those places of the body that are supported by furniture, those places at which the human body is imagined to articulate naturally and as though these were not cultural contrivances and achievements. Racking and dislocation are typically called by torturers by the names of household objects, as "the chair," "the bed," and so forth. In torturing, furniture is perverted from its fundamental idea of extending and furthering the healthy activity and articulation of the body in favour of practices in which dehumanizing is the essential aim. Here we have a small clue that points to an interesting moment: a point of arrival of furniture in Western humanistic culture that is not entirely captured by the sociology of invidious consumption and cultural capital, but requires a certain theory of the body.

The evolution of furniture forms is to a certain degree a play of wit around the potential of the human body. One of these potentials is certainly for the realization of novel forms of comfort. The invention of modes of taking one's ease subtly changes the body itself so that from henceforth these ideas of comfort seem natural requirements of the body. Another of these potentials is for the exercise of mechanical contrivance, as a bodily acting-out of a cultural demand for classifying and ordering: the chest of drawers, and all the other forms that follow, great and small, that introduce an entirely novel repertory of thought and action in putting things away and retrieving them again: the stooping, pulling, shutting; the employment of elbow, backside, knee, belly, forehead, foot; the bracing, balancing, tugging, slamming: all unknown to the medieval householder in this variety, in this potential for expression and dramatic self-presentation, for the indication of mood, for the filling of time, for the development of that elusive sense of muscular and skeletal embodiment which is one of the latest of the senses to be acknowledged in our formal epistemologies.

If we look at the Rhode Island secretary-bookcase with these considerations in mind, it is not difficult to see a certain manifest declaration, or exuberance, of witty and playful challenge to the human body. This façade is a *working* façade. It does not conceal the invitation to pull and shut, reach, stoop, stretch and kick, but instead subordinates other possible aesthetic and practical ideas to it.

Of all questions of interpretation of human culture, those that touch on the body and its social significance are perhaps richest in deliberate ambiguity, in downright evasion. We have by now certainly come to understand this about the representation of the body in art, which, as in a dream, bears many interpretations. Is an image one that reflects what the beholder imagines himself to be? Is it what he wishes to be? Is it what he fears he may be? Is it a projection out of some unacknowledged social condition or experience? What, for that matter, does the beholder make of the spatial medium that contains both image and beholder? And all these ambiguities must surely be as richly textured when we move away from the relatively controlled issues of pictorial space, into the cultural medium of the "interior," into space where the relation between persons and things is not taken to be the relationship of beholder to image but rather the relationship of things, including human bodies, living together.

The complexity of the issues involved in ways of seeing and their relation to Western art have been brilliantly suggested in Svetlana Alpers' study of Dutch art in the seventeenth century (Alpers 1983). The Dutch "art of describing" differed significantly, she argues, from Italian Renaissance theory and practice. The Dutch eye trained itself to see the world in terms of the optical experience of light and shadow, to take in the world as it presented itself from things out there, through an atmospheric medium, to a receptive plane at the eye, or a lens, or a canvas; whereas the Italian eye was the instrument of an intellectual force imposing on the world the laws of perspective, creating the world in terms of an intellectual scheme. Suppose we take this argument, as Alpers herself does, to be suggestive of important social and cultural factors at work in Northwestern Europe in the seventeenth century. The direction that Dutch and English experimental science took in this period in the direction of empirical study and description, and a social organization of knowledge around systematic comparison and checking of observation, bears a striking resemblance to the experimental and empirical program implicit in Dutch art. So much might also be said about the relationship between geographical exploration in these societies and the intellectual fascination with maps—maps frequently appear in Dutch painting, as Alpers points out—which are, notionally, the flat impress of the actual appearance of the world.

Consider then the content of so many Dutch pictures of the seventeenth century. What social practices correspond to these images of absorption in reading, writing, gazing, flirting, day-dreaming, sleeping, idle conversation: all images of people with secrets, people whose motives are in the nature of their activity opaque to the beholder? An answer is particularly important, because, as Alpers convincingly demonstrates, Dutch painting represents an intensely worked out method for the establishment of an idea of truth. Let us say that the subject matter of these paintings is the same rigorous agnosticism that informs the method of the paintings: the painter sees only the surface of things. The painter can only describe. The appropriate challenge for an art based on such a perceptual scheme would be therefore the representation of bodies – what is visible – during just those social events that are most intricately interior and inaccessible to vision.

Let us carry this just one step further and say that the subject matter of Dutch painting of the genres we are referring to is embodiment in what we may take to be its natural environment. The site, in other words, of the human activities which are the main subject matter of these pictures is the modern interior. The extraordinary technical achievement of this art in the representation of furniture in interior space both underscores the embodiment of these dreamers and readers and gazers as subject-matter (we no more know what they are thinking than we know what the chairs and chests are thinking), and establishes a normative condition for the *habitus* of the modern person. This person thinks, dreams, reads, does nothing that is perceivable at all, in a social and personal space that is shared with and counter-balanced by furniture, whether or not other people are there. It is not as though people in human society did not share cultural practices in which furniture figured crucially before this, but in Dutch painting we see intense and prolonged investigation of the crowded interior as the image of social reality itself.

The cautionary lesson in this episode of the European spirit is that anywhere we encounter things of human manufacture made to occupy this naturalized interior landscape, however conventional they may be, or from some points of view reducible either to the evolution of artisan technique or mannerism, or to the history of taste and consumption, we are dealing nonetheless also with mirrors of embodiment, both in relation to muscular corresponsiveness and the repertory of bodily actions, and to radical embodiment itself as a spiritual and political ideal. Certain things fill customary positions in social space. It is not clear what they intend, nor what they do or are good for, but it is a kind of decency and completion that they be there. That the "thing" may be a chest of drawers as well as another person is a form of modern civility.

Modern, urbane, cosmopolitan life began in the great cities of Northwestern Europe in the seventeenth and eighteenth centuries, in London and Paris and their provincial satellites all over the Western world. These cities and their respective hinterlands may also be understood to be loosely interconnected and reciprocating yet intelligibly different clusters of attitudes: moral, aesthetic, and political. In each of these clusters of cultural development and influence there is a characteristic conception of the human body in social space, and a characteristic perceptual bias in relation to the body. We cannot even allude here to all the ways this is manifest, in different traditions of urban planning and architecture, different traditions of theatre and of sport, different styles of politics. Let us notice only the detail that has to do with the shapes of domestic furnishings, and their homologies in certain characteristic moral attitudes.

Sophisticated French furniture, and furniture elsewhere developed in imitation of it, is constructed according to a specific scheme. Carcass work, or the business of making a framework to hold the piece of furniture together is, in this scheme, a preparatory process, and sometimes shockingly rough and ready. To the basic squared or rectangular units bits and pieces of scrap are fastened, then shaped to a surface for the elaborate veneering characteristic of the style. The highest level of craftsmanship is represented by the *ébéniste*, so called from the use of ebony as one of the exotic woods employed in the surface finish of furniture. The forms of French eighteenth-century furniture in all the conventional design periods exploit this manner of procedure to the fullest, a procedure which allows the finished article great freedom of movement, colour, and illusionistic play.

Now if we accept even a hypothetical relation between furniture in the modern interior and modern personality, we can see that there is at least a formal homology between the structural conventions of sophisticated French furniture and the moral conventions subsumed in the characteristically French social ideal represented in the terms *morale* and *moraliste*. In a tradition at least as old as Montaigne, the *moraliste* is understood in France to be a student not of morals, in the English sense, but of *moeurs*. The manners of a man or of a people, both in the ethnic sense and in the sense of polite usages, constitute the subject matter of human self-understanding. Self-knowledge is a disciplining of one's own manners so as to be open to the knowledge and civilizing gifts of others. A scoundrel is not deeper-dyed for having good manners, but is in some measure redeemed by them. People are understood in this tradition to have been improved by the usages of civilized life and not to have experienced degeneration in them. A tradition long associated with French metropolitan culture gives considerable weight to qualities of surface finish and to illusionistic graces.

The Anglo-American tradition, by contrast, has been shaped by a much more insistent pressure from its religious and cultural "left." From Puritanism, through the dissenting sectarians, right down to the Leavisite repugnance for Bloomsbury, there has been a downright suspicion of civilization, a feeling that something fundamental is lost in the veneer of polite usages, whether that something fundamental is a lively sense of sin, or a lively sense of sex.[4] A "moralist" in this English sense is precisely what his French counterpart is not: a person prepared to strip the mask from civilization and reveal the true condition of the soul. This is not the only tradition in English cultural life—although it is responsible for more of English poetry and art than is usually allowed—nor is the French cultural tradition devoid of powerful puritan impulses. It was nevertheless in the English-speaking world that a type of moral idea based on clear and transparent expression, in prose, in moral philosophy, in experimental science and in practical inventions, took root most abundantly and characteristically. And it was in America that this tradition in English cultural life institutionalized itself politically and socially as an offshoot of religious dissent, old and new, and as anti-Court political and cultural opposition.

The American interior belongs to this Anglo-American moral tradition. When we look at these dominating pieces of furniture, we can readily appreciate that behind the artisanal clichés, plainly adapted from the British tradition of cabinetmaking, lies a range of choices that pertain to the whole of the Anglo-American cultural world: a standard perhaps not of "truth," but certainly of sincerity, or what Habermas would call "truthfulness" (1984:23, 41).[5] This truthfulness, which we will not invest with an absolute moral value, but only observe to be a defining quality of Anglo-American ethnicity, is a matter of felt or perceived congruence between appearance and structure, a hatred of secrets, of hidden motives or unacknowledged structures. The frustration of the expectation of this form of truthfulness was a mainspring of the American Revolution and, perhaps finally, of the inability of the English to contest that Revolution wholeheartedly.

In a review of an exhibition of American furniture in London, on the occasion of the American bicentennial, Simon Jervis remarked that it was easy to see why American craftsmen made so much of such motifs as the Newport and Connecticut shell carvings: they are, he wrote, "among the easiest of motifs to set out and carve" (1976:186).[6] It seems to me that such a judgment leaves something unsaid: not only is the task of setting-out easy, the image is rationally and emotionally transparent. It holds no secrets. The method of setting it out and its meaning are fused. If we say that the craftsman had no choice, that he was a joiner with no fancy establishment, no carver or other specialist in his employ, that he worked in a provincial town with few motives for more demanding exertions, we have merely pushed the problem back to another level. Why in this tradition did provincial work move in this direction? What precisely has been simplified? Why is the setting-out simplified rather than the execution or the finish? Or, to put it succinctly, why should artisans "simplify" by abstraction, and not "simplify" by coarsening? And out of all the ways there are to imitate in a simplified way, why should it be certain elements in the adopted artisanal tradition that are sustained rigorously, when others are not?

American furniture, as Jervis points out, is far from simple. He prefers the phrase, "artisan mannerism," now applied in America to so-called country furniture, for virtually the whole of American taste in furniture, and thinks it can most profitably be compared with the regional variations of German furniture in the eighteenth century. Yet if American furniture is not simple, it does have qualities that were called by the term "simplicity" in the eighteenth century, and these are qualities missing in what Jervis himself calls the greater brilliance and virtuosity of decoration and execution in German practice.

Hogarth, for example (whose famous serpentine "line of beauty" is more exactly duplicated in American cabriole and ogee cabinet supports than in ordinary English practice), speaks of simplicity as one of the qualities of workmanship brought "to a very great degree of perfection, particularly in England; where plain good sense hath prefer'd these more necessary parts of beauty, which everybody can understand, to that richness of taste which is so much to be seen in other countries, and so often substituted in their room (1753:62–63)."

Might we project this ideology of simplicity forward into an hypothesis about the moral meaning of a form like the Rhode Island secretary-bookcase? Hogarth introduces some pertinent conceptions for our purpose. The following may stand as the text for which my argument is an elaboration:

> We must no longer confine ourselves to the particular notice of...surfaces only, as we heretofore have done; we must now open our view to general, as well as particular bulk and solidity; and also look into what may have filled up, or given rise thereto, such as certain *given* quantities and dimensions of parts, for inclosing any substance, or for performing of *motion, purchase, stedfastness* and other matters of use to living beings, which, I apprehend, at length, will bring us to a tolerable conception of the word *proportion*.
>
> As to these *joint-sensations* of bulk and motion, do we not at first sight almost, even without making trial, seem to *feel* when a leaver of any kind is too weak, or not long enough to make such or such a purchase? or when a spring is not sufficient? and don't we find by experience what weight, or dimension should be given, or taken away, on this or that account? if so, as the general as well as particular bulks of form, are made up of materials moulded together under mechanical directions, for some known purpose or other; how naturally, from these considerations, shall we fall into a judgment of *fit proportion*; which is one part of beauty to the mind tho' not always so to the eye (Hogarth 1753:84–85).

Hogarth supplies us here with a powerful insight into the kind of artisan mannerism we see in the Rhode Island secretary-book-case: it is a motif-mongering that relies heavily on the appreciation of factors of stored kinetic energy. How bent ought a foot to look under that sort of weight? How graduated in size from top to bottom ought a set of drawers to be so as to make weight and risk seem proportionately distributed? What sort of stiffening folds and creases would make this volume look suitably contained? These things are expressive of a culture that prizes a certain form of intelligence, an intelligence not fed primarily by literary sources or the exercise of literacy, but rather by the cultivation of the appreciation of things made for use.

Daniel Calhoun argues for the primacy of this form of intelligence in certain phases of American cultural development and points out how in time this reliance on "eye" and on an untutored but confident spatial judgment led to characteristically beautiful but dangerous objects (1973:esp. 230–256, 291–304). This furniture gives a very similar impression. Its grammar of broad, smooth surfaces, its openness and transparency of means, make it appear to be engineered for some purpose, like a bridge, or a cart: "moulded together under mechanical directions, for some known purpose or other," as Hogarth put it.

Calhoun's theory is that the oscillation of male- and female-dominated childhoods in American society, and a general rigidity in the demarcation of gender-specific zones of intelligence, produced observable deficiencies in both the verbal and the spatial-analytic products of American culture. A more cautious view of the spatial-analytic elements in this furniture is that they represent a narrowing and a compression, even a specialization, of a form of embodiment that is Western and modern, and more proximately Anglo-American, and that was to be profoundly altered in the nineteenth century by altogether different ideas about the scale appropriate to interior furnishing, and by very different ideas about the body. In other words, this furniture should not only be understood in the context of the history of American industrial design or of the so-called folk arts, which are parasitic on industrial products; it belongs as well to the long history of the Western interior, as a social and political universe of bodies.

It is on that social and political universe, the universe of bodies-in-interiors as the horizon of personal dignity and of political and moral self-representation, that the rationalized world of styles, of invidious consumption, and of the ordering of forms of cultural capital, is a parasitic growth and a parody. American furniture in the eighteenth century went about as far as it could go in bringing the new world of reason and experiment within the bound universe of the Western interior. Yet it is also clear in this furniture that its naive spatial-analytic "argument" introduces affecting elements of a less humane, more scientifico-mechanical nature. Its moment is a moment of transition from classical embodiment to new forms of invisibility.

Notes

1. I have borrowed this analogy from an argument in Lionel Rothkrug's Grey Lectures, delivered at the University of North Carolina in 1986. I am grateful to Professor Rothkrug for permitting me to read the manuscript, and for many stimulating conversations about charismatic objects and social practices.

2. This notion of "invisibility" is akin to "forgetting" in the following passage from Bourdieu (1984), p. 3, which he means us to take ironically: "Acquisition of legitimate culture by insensible familiarization within the family circle tends to favour an enchanted experience of culture which implies forgetting the acquisition." Armstrong (1971), p. 8, makes this point, but revealingly without irony, because he is talking about naive cultural conditions: "The terrifying sound of the bull-roarer is made with the clear intention of affecting. It is the transmutation of a material; it is not the sound of the paddle roaring

through the air which one hears, but the veritable voice of a totally different essence which has come to be."

3. In discussions of earlier versions of this paper I have received valuable help and criticism both from social historians of early America and from students of material culture and folklife. One general criticism that should be addressed is that the approach in this paper does not do justice to the complexity of subject matter in these fields, either in terms of the regional and historical variations in objects made in America, or in terms of the many sophisticated interpretive models American students of these subjects have formed around different classes of objects and different population groups and social interests. At one level the criticism seems to imply that because a field is intricately sub-divided it is somehow illegitimate to generalize about it at another level, or in relation to concerns outside these fields. Besides responding to this by saying that I am pursuing a different agendum from social history and material culture studies as these are frequently pursued, I should also like to suggest, by way of response, a counter-criticism: not of particular studies, but of the weight of them taken together. In spite of the very impressive achievements of the literature in these fields in calling attention to differences, gradations, separations embedded in the material record, there is an unacknowledged but decisive ideology implicit in the sheer impressiveness of the demonstration of these differences, gradations, separations. Every social group, every agent or school of cultural production, every class of object, is (in principle) textualized, or anthropologized, both within the closed universe of the "American," and within the (in principle) endlessly open and sub-divisible universe of a discourse of difference. These objects finally become sealed off from one another and from objects outside the canonical closure. They are mysterious to all but the specialists of particular differences, and also at the same time the component pieces of a vast mystery called America. The discourse of difference and the pre-emptively imperial idea of "American" are the twin mysteries that together tend to remove objects in the American past from a discourse that places them in other comparative situations, or that allows them to be seen as tools of social formations that are not so much mysterious as mystified.

4. At least since Charles Dickens, the word "veneer" has come to mean insincerity in the English speaking world.

5. Here Habermas (1984) not only equates truthfulness with sincerity of expression, but most suggestively aligns these modes of validation with what he calls the "therapeutic" form of argument, as opposed chiefly to aesthetic and moral-practical forms of argument. If by therapeutic we mean a test of argument as truthful as that which feels most authentically like ourselves, then that is what I mean below by the standard of truthfulness that characterizes American action and American cultural products.

6. Jervis (1976) is an interesting essay from several points of view: a shrewd discussion of the differences between American and English furniture, and of the importance of American materials as a body of provincial work, among others, at a particular distance from metropolitan taste. See also the important essay by Garrett (1970).

Concluding Statements

Material Culture or Material Life

13

Discipline or Field? Theory or Method?*

Thomas J. Schlereth

Three issues deserve attention for the future of material culture research. Questions of nomenclature: What shall we call what we do? Questions of methodology: Do the research strategies that we have developed constitute a field or discipline? Questions of theory: What hypotheses do we wish to answer?

NOMENCLATURE

The eclectic enterprise of those who see artifacts as significant cultural data has been called by diverse labels: from "pots-and-pans history" to "physical folklife," from "hardware history" to "artifact studies," from "concrete clio" to "above-ground archaeology" (Wood 1967; Dorson 1972; Lankton 1981; Fleming 1969; Rider 1984; Cotter 1972).

"Material culture," "material history," and "material life" now contend for acceptance as the most appropriate rubrics to describe North American object research. "Material culture" has been used in English-speaking research circles for over a century; the latter two are relatively new to our scholarly parlance, coming into vogue only in the past decade or so.

Nineteenth-century anthropologists first defined material culture. For example, as early as 1875, A. Lane-Fox Pitt-Rivers, in a paper, "On the Evolution of Culture," urged fellow researchers in the emerging social sciences to consider material culture as "the outward signs and symbols of particular ideas in the mind" (Pitt-Rivers 1906). Since then, the term has undergone redefinition and refor- mulation. Out of favour among anthropologists in certain decades of the twentieth century, it is presently enjoying an interesting resurgence among some of them (Dwyer 1975). More importantly, perhaps, it has gained currency among researchers in the arts and the humanities in the past twenty years. It is, of course, the official term used in the Memorial University conference and such scholars as Jules Prown, Henry Glassie, and James Deetz are among its advocates. For Deetz, material culture is "that segment of man's physical environment which is purposely shaped by him according to culturally dictated plans" (Deetz 1977a:10).

In Canada, however, another term, "material history," has both institutional and individual supporters. There is the *Material History Bulletin* (MHB) formerly published by the National Museum of Man in Ottawa and now jointly published as the *Material History Review* by the Canadian Museum of Civilization and the National Museum of Science and Technology. A new Diploma in Material History is offered by the University of New Brunswick in Saint John. The work of Ann Gorman Condon, Robert D. Turner, and Gregg Finley all address "material history" (Condon 1984; Turner 1984; Finley 1984).

There have been different definitions of material history during the brief time it has been used. A definition proposed by Barbara Riley and Robert Watt in the first issue of the *MHB* ("material history is the study of artifacts produced or used throughout history"; *MHB*, 3(1976) may be compared with one later advocated by Jean-Pierre Hardy and James Wardrop in a 1981 special issue of the same journal ("material history is the application of artifact-related evidence to the interpretation of the past"; *MHB*, 13(1981). In a recent essay, Finley attempts to amalgamate the two different em- phases in an extended definition:

> ...material history refers to both the artifacts under investigation and the disciplinary basis of the investigation. The word 'material' encompasses the broad range of historical objects which exist as concrete evidence of the human mind in operation at the time of construction and/or use, and as the three-dimensional, nonverbal record containing to a greater or lesser degree, the ideas, concepts, opinions, beliefs, intentions, and values held by people in the past. The word 'history' refers to the scholarly preoccupation with the human past and with historical change that is implicit in the practice of history (Finley 1985:34).

"Material history" appears to be completely of Canadian origin. The term was coined by Canadians (first usage is usually dated from the inauguration of the *Material History Bulletin* in 1972) and identifies many of the country's monographs, articles, serials, courses of study, and conferences (the Memorial University gathering excepted) dealing with artifact research.

To complicate things a bit more, a third term, "material life" (or its sometime synonym, "material civilization") has entered the terminology debate. Fernand Braudel's confessed attempt is to fabricate a label that would be an alternative to "technology" but "maintain a bridge to the material culture of anthropology and archaeology," and yet still convey an overview of "an economic culture of everyday life." Other explanations may be found among the French economic historians of the *Annales School* and their translators (Dupree 1981:685; Braudel 1973, 1977, 1981).

While French historians first used the phrase to describe an elementary economic culture more basic and pervasive even than the market economy that took root in it, the term's vogue on this continent thus far has been among American social historians of the colonial period. We have, for example, the recent work by Lorena S. Walsh, Susan Mackiewicz, and Cary Carson.

Carson, in a recent position paper, "Chesapeake Themes in the History of Early American Material Life," suggests some of the parameters and possibilities of the term. Postulating that "artifacts serve on one level as the devices men and women have always used to mediate their relationships with one another and with the physical world" and that "social history is preeminently a history of relationships," he argues that the study of material life would entail artifact research into social institutions and social relations both particularly "viewed as the consequence of complex choices among alternative standards and styles of living and the equipment needed to sustain them" (Carson 1984:6,9). In order to give specificity to his definition, Carson concludes his proposal with five thematic episodes from colonial Chesapeake history that would be included in a sample synthesis of its material life. These are such issues as settlements as economic units of production, investment in homesteading, assimilation and acculturation of European and African folk traditions, improved living standards, the consumer revolution, and the spread of genteel manners.

Does what we call what we do—whether it be material culture, material history, or material life—make any difference for the future of what we do? Perhaps not, yet encapsulated in our choice of labels are decisions about method and theory. In our future debate over the merits of these terms we need to recognize that each is problematic in certain ways, each has assets and liabilities, each betrays our scholarly predilections, institutional affiliations, and intellectual temperaments.

For example, arguments for adopting "material culture" as our covering term include: its common use in several disciplines, its embodiment of the culture concept, its extensive historical lineage, and its evocation of human behaviour and belief. Yet some critics could charge it with unmanageable comprehensiveness, a synchronic proclivity, and an internal contradiction. Nevertheless, this is the term I favour.

Advocates of "material history" champion it principally because "there is a distinct advantage to anchoring artifact studies to a clear disciplinary foundation, such as history" (Finley 1985:35). Objections to such usage, however, might include its limitation to a single disciplinary perspective, one exclusive of the object research of social scientists and the way it seems to restrict artifact inquiry solely to the activities of the past.

"Material life," of course, has some of the drawbacks of "material culture": indeterminateness, ambiguity, over-generality. It may also prove excessively beholden to economics and demography. Yet its merits include attention to ideology and the infra-economy of objects as well as to strata of human experience heretofore largely ignored by researchers in many fields: the habitual, routine, ordinary structures of everyday life.

METHODOLOGY

The problem of definition seems to hinge in part on the professional status of the work. Is it a discipline? A field? Or a method?

For each of these positions there have been various proponents. They range from those who propose, as has James Deetz, the establishment of university departments of Material Culture Studies to others who consider the undertaking as simply another technique in the general tool kit of cultural investigation (Deetz 1977b:12).

If recent surveys of practitioners (such as those who wrote in Simon Bronner's 1985 special issue of *Material Culture*) are to be believed, few envision material culture studies as a separate, established discipline in the traditional definition of a unique branch of knowledge with distinctive empirical data and special explanatory paradigms. While we have scholarly journals, academic conferences, and occasional talk of plans for a professional association, I do not think the present state of material culture research constitutes an academic discipline as usually defined.

As the late Richard Dorson used to remind us, for an activity to be considered as a scholarly discipline, it must be established in both a pragmatic and a philosophical way. Pragmatically, a discipline exists if it can reach an intellectual audience with scholarly works, earn a place in the accepted fields of learning of its day, preserve and enlarge its area of knowledge, attract converts and young disciples, and perpetuate itself. Philosophically, a discipline exists if it can lay claim to a distinctive methodology, empirical data, or explanatory theory important for humankind's knowledge of self and society (Dorson 1976:101). At this stage of its historical development, material culture performs several but not all of these requirements.

Jules Prown argues, however, we can claim material culture to be a type of discipline if we define "discipline" and "methodology" in specific ways. He suggests we constrict the definition of a discipline (such as Dorson's) to but one of its parts; that is, we define a discipline principally as a methodology, or to use his words, to think of it as "a mode of investigation" in order to differentiate it from a field of knowledge which he calls a "subject of investigation." In this, material culture differs from art history, for example, which is both a discipline (a mode of investigation) in its study of history through art, and a field (a subject of investigation) in its study of the history of art itself.

As a discipline, claims Prown, material culture must be content to be "a means rather than an end" in cultural study. It is disqualified from being a subject of investigation because the material evidence of its study (all manmade or modified things including art, diversions, adornments, modifications of the landscape, applied arts, and technological devices) is simply too vast and diverse to be manageable as a single field of analysis (Prown 1982:1).

Dell Upton, on the other hand, suggests it is appropriate to think of material culture as "a subject matter" comparable, in his judgment, to fields such as "traditional tales or the French Revolution." In proposing "a landscape approach" to the study of objects, he is not daunted by the immensity of material culture as a field. Rather this multiplicity could be an opportunity to take "all classes of artifacts into our purview." Upton urges us, therefore, to reclaim the initial catholicity of the first material culturists, those nineteenth-century antiquarians who were interested in numerous kinds of artifacts, from the smallest household utensils up to complete houses, and to set about developing material culture as a field of study that "would treat as many kinds and scales of objects as possible" (Upton 1985a:85).

Other scholars in various disciplines also seek to focus artifact research under the metaphor of "a field of study" or "a field of inquiry." Peter Rider would have it as "a field of history" (Rider 1984:92). The developers of the Diploma in Material History Pro- gramme at New Brunswick consider it a field of history with a particular institutional and vocational orientation. To wit: "the field of material history brings a necessary concern with how the objects of that study are preserved and interpreted to the general public. This necessitates for the prospective student of material history at the very least an introduction to the practical aspects of archival and museum work and of restoration techniques, all skills not tradition- ally a part of normal historical training" (Diploma in Material History 1983:3).

Those who tend to emphasize the content, the subject matter, or the field of material culture study are not, it should be noted, averse to developing its methodological possibilities. Upton, for instance, recognizes that "material culture studies might have the potential, as a method of analysis, like statistics or textual criticism, to expand the possibilities for inquiry in a number of established disciplines" (Upton 1985a:85).

Does it make any difference, particularly for the future of re- search, to think of material culture as a discipline or a field? Perhaps not, and yet it might orient our future efforts in certain directions, depending upon which perspective is emphasized. It could be ar- gued, for instance, that to opt for Prown's emphasis on discipline might mean increased concentration on material culture as novel methodology (rather than as special evidence), on only the "means" of material culture research, and on material culture as but a branch of cultural history or cultural anthropology. To press Upton's subject matter approach might mean more attention to material culture as novel evidence (rather than as unique method), to the "ends" of material culture study, and to its status as a research movement (possibly analogous to American or Canadian Studies) within a cross-disciplinary context.

My own preference in the discipline/field discussion is to see the enterprise, at least for the present, as a mode of inquiry primarily (but not exclusively) focused upon a type of evidence. Material culture thus becomes an investigation that uses artifacts (along with relevant documentary, statistical, and oral data) to explore cultural questions both in certain established disciplines (such as history or anthropology) and in certain research fields (such as the history of technology or the applied arts).

To use the term discipline (even in Prown's restricted fashion) conjures up too much confusion given the many meanings the term connotes in the varied institutional contexts (museum, academy, historical society, governmental agency) in which material culturists work. I am also not convinced that we are, other than in a limited bibliographical sense, yet a clearly articulated field of study. We have yet to reach a working consensus on how to fence the field. Should it encompass only traditional material culture as Warren Roberts would have it, or include the most modern objects of contemporary life as William Rathje would wish? Are its boundaries to be limited only to the extant, three-dimensional artifact or also to include public performance, behavioural gesture, and extemporaneous utterance? (Roberts 1985; Rathje 1981).

THEORY

No matter what we eventually become—a specialized methodology, a unique subject matter, or a departmental discipline—we will still need to concern ourselves with a third issue. What role will theory play in our efforts?

With a few exceptions, the theoretical premises of most material culture research has been largely derivative. We have been consumers, rather than producers, of research techniques and interpretive models.

This is slightly less true if we distinguish methodological theory from explanatory theory. In the past decade there have been several attempts to develop techniques of analysis that could be claimed as indigenous to material culture research. Here the goal (whether successful or not is another matter) has been to establish a plan of work that could be pointed to as something by, for, and of material culturists. E. McClung Fleming's four operations (Identification, Evaluation, Cultural Analysis, Interpretation), Jules Prown's three-stage model (Description, Deduction, Speculation), and, most recently, Robert Elliot's five-step scheme (Material, Construction, Function, Provenance, and Value) are examples of this quest (Fleming 1974; Prown 1982; Elliot 1986).

These models of artifact study were designed principally for the classroom and the seminar. They borrow much of their language and format from art history and archaeology. These how-to-do-it manuals can be criticized for being overly formalist in their prescriptions of the way a researcher's mind works, as well as excessively limited in their application; too often applicable to single artifacts (a press cupboard or a Bricklin automobile) rather than to large aggregates of material culture. Nevertheless these models are a start in the search for a more rigorous, more systematic, more verifiable theory that may eventually lay the ground for material culture studies in the future. Perhaps from these beginnings will develop a set of methodological procedures that will stimulate scholars in our own ranks and in other disciplines.

Yet in terms of what might be called explanatory theory in material culture, we cannot even claim a beginning. There are a few daring tour-de-force works that we all cite, but most of these draw their theoretical inspiration from other disciplines, particularly linguistics. They also remain largely untested by other scholars in other research contexts. When it comes to the production of new explanatory theories about human experience or persuasive grand syntheses that chart wide panoramas of human history, material culture students are debtors.

Some years ago I attempted an assessment of how widespread and diverse this borrowing has been in American material culture scholarship. I came up with nine conceptual positions (such as symbolist, functionalist, environmentalist, behaviourist, structuralist, and the like) on which we modelled most of our research (Schlereth 1982). Peter Rider applied the typology to Canadian material culture, particularly as published in the *Material History Bulletin*, and drew similar conclusions, although his analysis suggests that past Canadian work has been dependent on an even more limited theoretical spectrum (Rider 1984). To a degree, the program of the Memorial University conference reveals that this indebtedness continues, since there are interpretations of artifacts based on aesthetic, structuralist, and anthropological theories.

We need not be embarrassed by this current imbalance of payments in the scholarly world of explanatory theory. In fact, such a borrowing can be looked upon as an asset rather than a liability. As John Mannion and George Kubler recognize, it has assuredly nurtured our interdisciplinarity—a characteristic that may prove to be an emblem of our future identity, whether as a discipline, a field, or a coalition of varied individuals simply intrigued with the (possibly novel) explanatory power of physical objects as cultural meaning (Mannion 1979:21; Kubler 1969:9).

I hope interdisciplinarity in material culture research will expand in the future. If it does, it would have at least two implications in our search for useful theory. One would be the possibility of a still richer lode of explanatory concepts to adopt or adapt to our purposes. One area of current research that may prove profitable could be the behaviourial sciences, particularly social psychology, psychohistory, proxemics, and kinesics. A second possibility from interdisciplinary study would be to work with and possibly revive previously argued theories. James Deetz's *In Small Things Forgotten* and Merrit Roe Smith's *Harper's Ferry Armory and the New Technol-*

ogy are examples of macro- and micro-levels of interpretation. Modernization, urbanization, or embourgeoisement are three other concepts created out of documentary and statistical data, yet largely unexamined through artifactual evidence.

Of course, more ambitious scholars will want to do more than test (or contest) the theories of others. There is an understandable eagerness to prove what we can do on our own. In addition to taking methods and theories from others, we need to frame our own questions, to formulate our own hypotheses.

I am persuaded that material culture researchers might show a noticeable advance in our search for distinctive methods and theories, if we were to direct a large portion of our time and talent to probing the explanatory power of the artifact. As Upton has argued,

> ...whatever else they might be, artifacts are at the deepest level expressive forms. The manufacture of an artifact is an act of creation equal to, rather than reflective of, the manufacture of a social system or an intellectual concept. All are part of the symbolic process that continuously recreates the world by imposing meaning and order on it. As a primary phenomenon equal to social structure and intellectual reasoning, the artifact must be questioned on its own terms (Upton 1985a:87).

If we were to consider material culture as a "primary phenomenon" of human experience, what corollary hypotheses might follow from such a position? Perhaps several, at varying levels of theoretical discourse.

First, as a low level theory, we could systematically probe the assumption that all things are not created equal in evidential promise, that there is a scale of explanatory power within the categories of material culture. For instance, do arts reveal more than technics?

Second, we could press to their limits the claims that some of us have made (and not sufficiently proved) for an epistemological novelty within objects that differs from, complements, supplements, or contradicts what can be learned from other sources. Does, for example, an artifact have a unique veracity because it is a non-translated, sensory, three-dimensional, affective, historical event (Schlereth 1985a)?

Third, answers to questions like these could enable us to move onto larger issues such as the relations between behaviour and belief or the origins and operations of creativity. In venturing into such theory, we already have some provocative leads to follow.

In the first case, there is Braudel's parameter of the "limits of the possible" in material life, Carson's argument for a scale of "the state of furnishedness" in consumer behaviour, and Prown's concept of "intentionality in ethical and esthetic belief decisions." These may grow into models illustrative of broad cultural patterns (Braudel 1981; Carson 1984; Prown 1985). In the second instance, Glassie's formulation of "artifactual grammars," Cyril Stanley Smith's "esthetic origins of manufacture," and Hindle's "emulation and invention" inventory may provide new explanatory theories about the creative process, that most complex (and mysterious) of human acts (Glassie 1975b; Smith 1980; Hindle 1981).

To be sure, this proposal for an extended analysis of what Hindle, almost a decade ago, referred to as the unexamined "inner processes of material culture," is not a wish for additional taxonomy or typology. It is not a demand for expanded archives of artifactual evidence catalogued by those material culturists whom Carson has called "collector-compiler-describers." Nor is it a clarion for concentration on the object for the object's own sake, for seeing material culture as the beginning and end of our scholarly quest (Hindle 1978:14–16; Carson 1984:3).

Rather it is a proposal to subject the spatial and analytical understanding offered by artifacts to new questions about human behaviour. It is a claim to view material culture as a process whereby we attempt to see through objects (not just the objects themselves) to the cultural meaning to which they relate or which they might mediate. It is a suggestion to take our beginning forays into methodologies indigenous to material culture studies and apply them to exploring the subject matter of "thingness" in order to see just what discoveries such an inquiry might elucidate.

Finally, it is a request for material culture students to engage in the careful scrutiny of artifacts in appropriately large aggregates or samples, with verifiable research controls. There would be two ends in view: first, to uncover new information for hypotheses about culture, and, second, to explore various serendipitous, random insights that may be generated by systematic object research. Ultimately we seek ways of explaining the parts of human experience that heretofore have received little notice or understanding.

Notes

* This essay, published in modified form in *Cultural History and Material Culture: Everyday Life, Landscapes, Museums*, copyright c 1990 by Thomas J. Schlereth, is printed by permission of UMI Research Press, Ann Arbor, Michigan and the University of Virginia Press, Charlottesville, Virginia.

Researching Artifacts in Canada

14

Institutional Power and Levels of Dialogue*

Gerald L. Pocius

If the material culture on both sides of the border often seems remarkably similar, does scholarship enjoy the same similarity as well? Or is there a distinctively Canadian approach to studying and interpreting the artifact? If American theorists have had such a pervasive impact on the study of artifacts generally in the English-speaking world, then how does Canada differ, if at all, from these trends? To answer these questions, there are a number of issues that need to be examined concerning material culture studies as a distinct, if little unified, discipline. The documentation and analysis of the artifact takes place among three major groups in most countries: collectors, museologists, and academics. Each has its own focus, its own particular methods, and its own specific goals. Thomas Schlereth argues that an evolutionary sequence has characterized material culture research generally in the United States, with the earliest work marked by collection, the second stage by description, the third by interpretation (Schlereth 1982:6–72). Essentially, these categories parallel in general terms the interests of collectors, museum workers, and academics. When looking at the Canadian scene, these three kinds of researchers can be examined in order to see whether there are major differences among these groups themselves within Canada as well among their counterparts in the rest of the world.

Material culture research as a distinct intellectual pursuit is, for the most part, recently emerging in a number of academic disciplines, and, not surprisingly, like all areas of research, it is marked by competing factions with differing perceptions of the work to be done. A conference such as the Winterthur/Memorial University-sponsored "North American Material Culture Research" meeting, or the several anthologies of material culture essays (Bronner 1985b; Schlereth 1982; St. George 1988) may well give the impression that there is a group of researchers who, using one specific kind of data source—the object—are linked by commonalities. Yet, there are obviously different cultural categories of artifact researchers, and often their work is at odds with one another. Why is it, for example, as one museum curator now pursuing academic research asked, that at many museum conferences "academic historians and museum curators have respectively made presentations seemingly irrelevant to each other; the historians discussing political and social change, but not objects, and the curators talking objects, but without the framework of an historical thesis" (Tivy 1988:64)? Different approaches are often related directly to institutional settings: a museum demands a particular kind of exhibit, a history department requires publications that provide certain kinds of findings and that appear in specific types of journals. The question then seems to be less about the actual research and more about the scholarly audience and what kind of problems that audience considers interesting and important. In other words, one must look at the institutional framework. Such an analysis of the different approaches to artifact research should clarify the issue of how material culture studies in Canada resemble—and differ from—those in the United States. Well might one ask, is a unique approach being developed in this country?

In Canada, a number of different groups of artifact researchers can be identified, each sharing common attitudes about the scope and purpose of their work. Each knows about other groups, but often has little understanding of what these others are doing. Indeed, a group may well assume that the methods and/or theories of others are wrong, and may not be aware of their publications, believing that such theories have little application in their own work. In short, while using the artifact as a common data base, different researchers have all evolved separate paradigms as to what is considered significant.

While Schlereth claims his sketch portrays an evolutionary trend for material culture research in the United States, it is obvious that all three stages exist simultaneously in Canada today. Whether this is true of other countries is beyond the scope of my discussion, but clearly the research methodologies and goals during the "age of collection" and "age of description" are those of the connoisseur, while those of the "age of analysis" are those of the academic scholar. This dichotomy might also be thought of as the "public" material culture specialist as opposed to the "academic" artifact researcher. This is not to imply that either lacks theoretical skills or abilities; rather, the dichotomy has as much to do with the respective institutions as it does with specific interests. For institutions generate their own methods and objectives. Within both groups—the connoisseur and the academic—disciplinary orientations necessarily also influence those methods and issues; regardless of the common interest in the artifact, disciplinary paradigms regulate the dialogue.

REGIONAL AND GENRE RESEARCHERS

The private collector and the museum curator focus on a collection of material: one privately, the other publicly. According to the assumptions of these connoisseurs, certain artifacts are researched, either from particular places or by particular type—in other words by region or by genre.

First, the regionalist. Canada is called a community of communities, a country of regions, and it is fair to say that many of these regions are more interested in self-definition than anything that could be considered pan-Canadian. Publications and exhibits focus on the range and characteristics of objects or traditions found locally. The researcher becomes the expert on a particular locality, and rarely sees any need to relate his or her work to neighbouring traditions. The regionalist may be interested strictly in the artifacts within a certain political boundary or those things belonging to a particular ethnic or cultural group. The institutional structure of this research steers researchers away from what is considered typical of all Canada, from artifacts outside the particular province or ethnic group. In some cases, such a bias is logical; surely there is more in common, for example, between nineteenth-century Newfoundland, the Maritimes, and New England than there is between Newfoundland and Ontario or Québec. Yet the tendency is to become so intent on unearthing the details of every regional artifact, that research becomes paralysed with that strange disease called "unique-itis." And rarely is a cure sought, for if every aspect of a particular region is so unique, any communication of information can only be on the researcher's terms.

Then there is the genre specialist who develops expertise in one particular artifact category, whether a form (such as furniture), a material (such as metal or glass), or a type (such as folk art). Often a regionalist as well, the genre specialist is likewise interested first in the intricacies of identification of artifacts *per se*. Works of specific individuals, those exhibiting particular motifs or those of a particular time period become the primary concern, and are savoured, appreciated, even glorified. Publications or exhibits are intended to convey what are perceived to be simple unbiased historical facts. Communication with researchers in other places is minimal. The research from other areas is often unread, except perhaps if it has some comparative value.

Regionalists appreciate the object for its antiquarian emotional content, and the objects themselves through this antiquarianism become embodiments of the region. There is an unspoken belief that if too much interpreting goes on, if there is too much theorizing, then somehow the beauty and the essence of the object *per se* is lost, inflicting a kind of "aesthetic damage" (Prown 1982:13) whereby the object will no longer demonstrate how ingenious, resourceful, and downright brilliant the original settlers actually were. Instead the artifact might become the victim of such philistine intellectual tortures as semiotics, structuralism, or sociolinguistics.[1]

Yet there should be no necessary contradiction between regional focus and theoretical discussion. One of the deficiencies of previous artifact research has, however, been the lack of controlled regional data bases. Instead of deciding on a focused sample of objects that can methodically be investigated—such as those found in only one community—researchers look for the objects they want to find, although statistically they might not be the most representative. One particular artifact form considered the product of a specific ethnic group becomes proof that cultural contact or transfer occurred, no matter how unrepresentative such an object form might have actually been.[2]

Contrasting with the large number of regional monographs are studies that claim to cover all of Canada. However, the material being analysed is mainly from central Canada (Pocius 1982b:29; Symons 1975:106)—ironically affirming regionality.

ACADEMICS AND MATERIAL CULTURE SCHOLARSHIP

Besides the scholar-connoisseurs, there are the academics who conduct research within particular scholarly disciplines.[3] If the regionalist sees little connection with the objects of other areas, the disciplinarian is often reluctant to see links with the methods or theories of others. Indeed, in Canada certain disciplines compete to be *the* one in which objects are properly understood. Hence, there is even competition about what to call this pursuit: material history or material culture, although some have argued that one common methodology be adopted to cover all types of artifact research (Finley 1984:75; 1985:34–35). This concern with disciplinary boundaries is, not surprisingly, related to institutional power.

Canadian material culture scholars often lament the lack of research going on in this country: "Canada is far behind other societies in its artifact-based research" (Condon 1984:145). Ironically—considering the constant complaints about the Americanization of the Canadian academic community—Canadian scholars often turn to Americans to point the way. Three recent surveys of Canadian material culture research have specifically used Thomas Schlereth's book, *Material Culture Studies in America* (Schlereth 1982), as the model statement of what should be happening here (Condon 1984:138–41; Rider 1984:93; Rider 1986:254–56). However, it must be realized that this "textbook" is itself a cultural document that gives the outside observer the impression that there is a unified intellectual pursuit in the United States called material culture research. The fact that this anthology exists—and that there is nothing like it in Canada—is an indication to some scholars that a major unifying, intellectual movement is occurring in the United States which Canadians need to learn about and even follow.

Indeed, Schlereth's *Material Culture: A Research Guide* contains essays by a historian now in an American Studies program, a cultural geographer, an art historian, an architectural historian, and a folklorist (Schlereth 1985b). Certainly interdisciplinary rhetoric has led to action; researchers do roam freely over all of these disciplines, and borrow methods and theories. In the United States, leading material culture monographs indicate that scholars are conversant not just in their own discipline but in key works in art history, folklore, history, anthropology, and geography (see, for instance, the range of sources in: Upton 1986; Glassie 1975b; Ames 1977; Deetz 1977a; Prown 1982). Articles in leading journals such as *Winterthur Portfolio* or *Material Culture* reflect the diverse theoretical range of much contemporary interpretive research (e.g., Carson *et al.* 1981; Herman 1984; Carter 1987). Although there may be some doubts as to the possibility for true interdisciplinary research, given the extreme difficulty of keeping up with research in a number of disciplines, American publications clearly indicate that this is the ideal. The important point here is that it is not so much that disciplines themselves may co-operate more in the United States than in Canada, but that American material culture researchers believe they should be more attentive to the broad theoretical underpinnings of their enterprise.

There may be differences, as well, in the academic institutions of the two countries—and the types of research and theories considered appropriate in either place. Material culture studies in the United States have by and large been advanced by relatively new disciplines in the university context: American studies and folklore have been as much in the forefront as history, art history, or anthropology. These newer disciplines rushed in to fill a void, in many instances, of what had been too long neglected: the culture of the poor, the working class, the rural peasant, women—and the everyday material world.

Leading universities began to introduce new departments: folklore at the University of Pennsylvania; American studies at Pennsylvania, Yale and Brown; Afro-American studies at Yale; and a long list of others. While there are obvious specific historical reasons why each of these programs developed, academic expansion in the 1960s often encouraged the type of interdisciplinary programs that would include research on material culture.[4]

In some cases (such as folklore), these were full-fledged departments that hired faculty not to teach an interdisciplinary subject, but rather to address the parameters of new disciplines. The relatively recent academic basis for many such disciplines led, in turn, to a stress on interdisciplinary contact. As part of demonstrating their respectability within the university, these scholars in newer departments had to prove they were conversant with the ideas of the establishment disciplines, indeed could use them in their research. As Henry Glassie commented: "The most venturesome [folklorists] stole quietly away and spied on the anthropologists, who were spying on the linguists, who were spying on the physicists, who were reading Blake" (Glassie 1977:25). In one way, the scholars of these new disciplines sought legitimation by using a language understandable by more conventional colleagues. In other cases, however, scholars who had been trained in traditional disciplines found their disciplinary paradigms inadequate for an understanding of the artifact, and looked to others for answers.

Canada developed in different ways, operating under different academic traditions. In spite of the recent concern over the Americanization of Canadian universities, Canadian academic institutions owe their development as much to the British university system and its disciplinary arrangements. Canada's institutional culture was taken from British models in most areas, including education (Breton 1984:127–28). Indeed, Canada's social élite was often sent to England to be educated, and advanced degrees from Oxford or Cambridge were more reputable than those from Canadian institutions. If a person remained in Canada to be educated, the University of Toronto clearly was the most prestigious institution (Porter 1965:497–99). When expansion came to Canadian universities in the 1960s — as it had in the United States — new faculty were hired for existing programs rather than for new departments. Indeed, some may have felt that newer fields that did not exist in the revered British universities — such as folklore or the Canadian version of American studies — might simply be representative of American academic imperialism if they gained wide acceptance in Canada (Rush, Christensen and Malcolmson 1981:520–21). Canadian universities did not experience such extreme competition for students as did their American counterparts and thus few universities introduced these newer pursuits.

Since the beginning of this century, there have been Canadian scholars who have researched material culture, primarily of native groups, and, to a lesser extent, of Québec (Dickson 1986:53; McFeat 1976; McFeat 1980). These ethnographers were initially based in museums, but as the institutional basis for such scholars gradually shifted to the university during the post-war period, a parallel decline in an academic interest in the artifact among anthropologists occurred, with the adoption of new psychological and social anthropological approaches. Indeed, few university-based anthropologists today in either Canada or the United States have any familiarity with museums or the study of artifacts (Fenton 1974; Lurie 1981; Sturtevant 1973). Many historians are equally unsure of the relevance of objects to their research. At best, the historian might produce studies of the documents connected with objects, rather than histories of objects (Muise 1986:244).

Unlike American Studies or American Civilization Departments in the United States, Canadian Studies programs are, for the most part, taught by scholars in other departments (Kroker 1980:6). While there are exceptions (such as the program at Trent), Canadian Studies curricula generally are made up of courses from older disciplines that have paid little recent attention to the object. American Studies programs in the United States, on the other hand, have always considered the artifact a major topic of concern.

Some disciplines like folklore have still not made major inroads into Canadian academic institutions, in part because of their lack of acceptance within the British academic context. Folklore studies in Britain had been linked with disreputable theories or methods; one Canadian academic, echoing the current British attitude, has characterized folklore as "too often a silly little discipline, absorbed in a kind of mindless butterfly collecting, and lacking any explanatory power at all" (Leyton 1984:220). While folklorists have played a major role in artifact analysis in the United States, Canadian academics often still associate the study of folklore with the colourful performance traditions of fringe ethnic groups (Carpenter 1979; Symons 1975). Scholars from such older established disciplines as history and anthropology are still suspicious of the folklorist's ability to analyse cultural issues.

What this all means for the Canadian context is that material culture research as an all-embracing concept has been slow to develop largely because of the nature of the institutional framework. Artifact researchers are trained in a particular discipline, and few exercise the effort to learn the theories used outside their own intellectual camp. Historians read Braudel; anthropologists read Trigger; folklorists read Glassie; geographers read Kniffen; art historians read Gowans; yet, what must still become the norm is that all artifact researchers become familiar with all such theorists.[5] In many respects, then, material culture studies in Canadian universities remains multidisciplinary, rather than having become interdisciplinary (Jackel 1980:34; Mannion 1979).[6]

Account here must be taken of actual differences in the nature of the artifact data base used in research. For instance, art history, archaeology, and museum studies by and large use the object as their primary data source; therefore folklore, anthropology, and oral history that use fieldwork would seem to object-centred researchers to have little to offer beyond what can already be derived from the artifact *per se*. Why bother to interview object makers or users, if all one has or needs is the artifact? Another example: The disciplines that stress ethnography are accused of neglecting chronology and diachronic content, especially with their infrequent use of standard historiographic sources such as documents. A consequence is that anthropologists or folklorists will sometimes try to find out information from fieldwork that is better obtained from documents. Yet those disciplines that depend on documents are themselves sometimes considered ignorant of the actual material objects; the artifact is seen simply as an accessory to a history shaped by written sources, and a lack of ethnographic training makes fieldwork bewildering and finally unnecessary (Ennals 1986:238).

Ultimately, it may be that the intellectual climate of the Canadian university will restrict those who wish to move outside the normal bounds of research; such broadening is initially tolerated, but one's colleagues are often unable to judge it adequately, and therefore such work is quietly discouraged. Tenure and promotion are often based on external assessments by one's peers in a particular discipline. Will administrators (and colleagues) value comments by artifact researchers in other traditionally non-related disciplines who can often more appropriately evaluate the work of the material culture scholar?

THE MUSEUM AND THE ACADEMY

If the institutional framework of the Canadian university has limited and will continue to limit an awareness of the growing interest in artifact research across the country, then perhaps the museum context will answer the demand for new theories and approaches. In spite of reservations among some museum researchers regarding the need for new theories and methods, this museum world has certainly generated calls for new ideas in Canadian material culture research. At recent meetings of the Canadian Museums Association, the professional community has raised issues of fundamental concern regarding responsibility for artifact collection and analysis. A multidisciplinary plenary session on new theoretical approaches to the study of the artifact was a focus of the 1983 CMA meeting, followed two years later by the conference theme investigating "the nature of the object" and the interrelationship of museums, objects, and society.

However, in spite of this growing awareness of theoretical needs among certain segments of the Canadian museum community, there unfortunately remain lingering doubts as to how much public institutions will finally be able to do. For example, many members of the Canadian museums community did not find it necessary to attend the 1986 Winterthur/Memorial University material culture conference to hear prominent artifact researchers discuss new theories and methods. This is puzzling because, despite financial restrictions, most museum budgets do include provisions for professional development opportunities. Perhaps energies of major Canadian museums are moving more and more away from research toward the administrative realm of collections management, caught up in a curatorial schizophrenia that tears museum personnel between research and conservation (Ames 1986:18; Halpin 1983: 263). It may well be that artifact research will increasingly become an activity pursued only in spare time by those museum professionals who remain intellectually alive, often in spite of their institution. There seems to be a danger that museums are becoming more interested in directing their resources toward public entertainment, and less in providing equal support for ensuring the scholarship on which this entertainment should be based (Ames 1986:18). Research funds are often the first to be slashed in a museum (Rider 1986:253), and the remaining funding sometimes pushes the museum to safer, duller performances in their exhibits (Pryce-Jones 1977:39).

Nonetheless, the development of material culture studies in Canada may well proceed from the institutional basis of the museum, in part because museums in Canada are generally funded by governments rather than by private individuals. Public instit-utions will by their nature be oriented towards certain polemic topics: working class culture, folk objects, and local themes that are at times critical of élitist culture. The museum worker in Canada may not feel compelled to advance any particular version of culture. Like the Canadian political system, work can range ideologically from conservative glorifications of royalty to socialist condemnations of the corporate bosses of the industrial worker.[7]

This institutional context may be contrasted with the situation of a number of leading museums in the United States. Museums in Canada are usually provincial or national institutions that promote some vision of the region or nation; American museums are as often private organizations (Lurie 1981:181) based on the collection of wealthy individuals (Key 1973:74), thus sometimes becoming mon-uments to private taste and wealth (Fry 1972:107). One may well imagine that in this world, museum researchers might be hesitant to criticize a culture that permits such accumulation, a culture that often neglects the objects of ethnic or racial minorities unless, of course, they are extinct. Museums in the United States were often established to teach what were distinctively "American values"— values often at odds with new political systems and foreign immigrants (Kaplan 1982:48–53; Harris 1978:141). Boards of trus-tees at these museums exert an inordinate amount of ideological control, ensuring an avoidance of any politically unsettling research or even critical thinking (Glueck 1972). Thus, the museum in the United States often encourages the scholars of region and genre, for these researchers produce cautious as well as appropriate theories within such an institutional framework. American museums will often disconnect the past from the present and separate culture from politics within the museum; "history was to be confined to providing entertainment, nostalgia, or interesting insights into vanished ways of life" (Wallace 1986:155, 157; also see: Ettema 1982:135–44). With the movement in the 1960s and 1970s for alternative histories, such presentations have slowly changed in many instances, but the financial power of private individuals still often translates into apparently safe versions of culture.

The museum researcher in the United States may thus be more akin to the Canadian academic; each content to stay within the confines of the dominant intellectual conventions when it comes to looking at objects. Cultural criticism using the object can more likely occur within the American university or the Canadian museum. Although a *Material Culture Studies in Canada* has yet to be written, it can be imagined. A substantial amount of research is going on; if academics move beyond the confines of disciplinary audiences, and collectors and describers acknowledge the important questions that transcend the boundaries of their region or artifact type, Canadian material culture studies could become a disciplinary community of communities. Then, the common theoretical issues that link Canadian research will finally make clear a common thread that does, indeed, distinguish Canadian from American research on the artifact.

Notes

* This paper developed from a number of conversations with Ken Ames and Gene Metcalf while I was a NEH Fellow at Winterthur Museum in 1985. Bernie Herman and Mary Tivy offered criticisms on an earlier draft of this essay. Shane O'Dea read several versions, and provided a number of suggestions that improved the final form.

1. One historian reviewing a material culture conference several years ago had not heard of semiotics, and complained of the "jargonistic flimflammery" when this unknown term was used in a paper title; the author of the paper assumed that the meaning and methods of such an approach were common knowledge, and thus spent no time dwelling on the theory for theory's sake (Rider 1983:55).

2. For example, while Irish house types can certainly be found in Newfoundland (e.g., Mannion 1974:143–55), they seem to be statistically very small in numbers in certain areas of Irish settlement (Pocius 1982a).

3. My comments on the academic study of the artifact refer primarily to the situation in anglophone Canada. From the early twentieth century, the situation in Québec has often been much different, for disciplinary boundaries have frequently been secondary to the delineation and documentation of that which is considered distinctively Québecois (Handler 1985). Descriptive monographs on a wide range of material culture have been produced for a number of years (Espessat, Hardy & Ruddel 1972:508–12), and today scholars with diverse backgrounds in history, anthropology, archaeology and folklore work together at centres such as CELAT at the Université Laval on common Québecois

topics. To some critics, the Québec academic situation often borders on the extremes of the regionalist bias I have discussed, with little desire to relate the thorough and lengthy Québecois ethnographies to broader more fundamental issues.

4. The increased interest in artifact analysis in the United States came, as well, at a time (the 1960s) when academic institutions were expanding with an influx of baby boom students, and new departments—as well as all forms of interdisciplinary programs—were born (Schlereth 1982:27–28; Drury 1984). Universities began to compete openly for students, so programs were introduced in new topics to increase enrolment. Where undergraduate schools number in the thousands, and students many more times that, some institutions in the United States felt survival was possible only through new subject areas. Some may argue that they were victims of academic consumerism.

5. Examples abound of this insularity; a recent essay dealing with cognitive approaches to material culture shows no awareness of recent work by folklorists or art historians (Young 1985). Even more revealing, one leading historian working in a large Canadian museum who had been publicly critical at several national conferences of Henry Glassie's discussions of folk housing confided to me in private that he actually never read any of these studies.

6. This lack of interdisciplinary borrowing within the Canadian academic scene is not exaggerated. A clear mark of how little is read across disciplinary boundaries can be gauged from searching the footnotes of numerous recent material culture publications. Again, although there are exceptions, a glance through recent issues of journals such as the *Journal of Canadian Art History, Culture, Canadian Geographer*, the *Society for the Study of Architecture in Canada Bulletin* and even the *Material History Bulletin* indicates that scholars often depend on work in their own discipline rather than a broad synthesis from diverse approaches.

7. Two examples. The Miners' Museum in Glace Bay, Nova Scotia, had a very strong anti-capitalist pro-labour slant in many of its interpretations. In 1988, the Newfoundland Museum organized an exhibit around a specific working-class family who lived in St. John's in the 1880s, historical figures neither completely known nor exceptional (Pocius 1988).

Studying Material Culture Today   **15**

Henry Glassie

Material culture is the word for our study, the name for our movement, because the better term has been appropriated and narrowed.
Art, wrote Ralph Waldo Emerson in his early essay *Nature*, is a
blending of nature and will. In his sense, it is precisely art we study:
those objects that combine natural substances with human will.

The simple merger of human presence with nature is not
enough. A footprint in the mud or a gnawed bone tells us of bodies
moving. Art tells us of minds in motion as well as of bodies behaving.
It records will, intention. Intentions need not so register in awareness that they can be brought forth in commentary. People with
literal minds and limited imagination cannot hear the voices in
things, the screams of the stone gods prisoned behind glass in the
museum; they trust only the meanings that lie in stripes of prose
across pages. They live in the little world of words. In the past I
argued redundantly that those of literal minds could know only the
history of a prosperous literate minority, that the history of most
people, preserved in artifacts that are not documents, escaped their
histories. I was not wrong, nor have I abandoned that position, but
now, reflecting more, I worry that studies focused upon words,
whether written or spoken, leave out of account vast realms of
experience that do not fit into words at all, that can only be shaped
into artifacts. It is not alone the lower orders of society in recent
times and all people in the most ancient days who elude research

into documents. We miss the profound wordless experiences of all people when we concentrate exclusively on texts made out of language.

There are people, I know them, who think human beings think in words. Some may, sometimes I do, but usually I do not. Instead I think in images, quicker and more enormous than words, which I must struggle to reduce and transform into the conventions of speech and writing. Only some of the thinking of some kinds of people (the kinds who become linguists and historians and who write convincingly about all of us out of their variety of experience) finds itself expressed naturally in language.

Blessed with a feeling that needs to be communicated, the mind sends directions and the body moves using materials beyond the body to signal feelings to others. Using light, the shoulders shrug a gesture. Using air, the mouth moves to make meaningful sounds. Using wood or clay, the hand moves to make things. From this simple fact flows the artifact's special virtue. Since the artifact blends mind with permanent materials, with stone, not light or air, only artifacts last beyond the event and only artifacts—books, crockery, knapped flint—provide the basic resource for history.

I do not mean, as people seem sometimes to think I mean, that I am opposed to the use of documents or that I am in favour of purely artifactual, nondocumentary history. After all, documents are artifacts, and any serious historian will use all sources—oral testimony as well as artifacts with and without words—to get the tale told. The ideal for history is a disciplined synthesis of all resources, and my own best book integrated oral and material evidence and embraced such tiny facts as I could ferret out of writing to tell the history of a little Irish community. What I do oppose are the assumptions that there can be no real historical study when there are no documents, and that the history in documents is somehow more reliable than that in wordless artifacts, which leads, of course, to the assumption that the only real history is that of the literate. If the history of the literate is the real history, then history remains largely the story of prosperous males in the late West. Similarly, if the only real thought is one framed in words, then major varieties of cognition remain invisible to our philosophies. It is historical folly, when documents accompany artifacts, to ignore them and it is worse folly to believe they say the same thing and assume the document is the more accurate or articulate. Documents and wordless artifacts deserve separate analysis, followed by comparison to determine their patterns of complement and conflict. That comparison, I believe, generally shows them to provide different information with the artifactual information being greater, richer, deeper. An artist's letters are fascinating, but they are small things by comparison to the artist's paintings. A building contract is a petty thing by comparison to a building, a prescriptive essay on domestic decor is as nothing next to the actual interior of a home.

Those who favour wordy as opposed to wordless artifacts (most usually those raised in Jewish and Protestant traditions founded theologically upon the Word) may feel language to be truer, closer to the soul, than gestures or artifacts, but the process of expression seems the same. Language is not closer or farther than the artifact from the human essence yearning for expression and reception. There is no privilege in language beyond that we grant it by virtue of our intellectual tradition. Having made much myself of linguistic analogy in material culture study, I know that to be the result of the excellence of theoretical linguistics and not the result of any special quality in language. The artifact is as direct an expression, as true to the mind, as dear to the soul, as language, and, what is more, it bodies forth feelings, thoughts, and experiences elusive to language. Artifacts should not be reduced to sentences of prose, clear in their meanings. Poetry, explosive with vague profundity, is closer in its mode of significance to art, and music, moving more than allusive, would make as good a metaphoric source for material culture as language. It is a sadness of the Memorial University conference that Robert Plant Armstrong is dead, for better than anyone in our days he taught that art, that material culture incarnates essences of cultural rightness uncontained by even complex verbal formulations.

From Saint Thomas, for whom art was the skill that bound beauty to utility, to Emerson and William Morris and Bob Armstrong, there runs a Western tradition of thinking about artifacts to which we are the humble and excited heirs. We study the intentions in things, all of that in things which is will and not nature. Our job is separating out of objects that which is owed to willful intervention in the world. Then we accept the strange responsibility of putting into words that which is not verbal, that which resisted and escaped language.

There is nothing easy in our work, but its basic strategy is not hard to state. We hunt for pattern. Often those of literal minds will ask for the meaning of a single object. What, say, does a lone motif on an oriental rug mean? The answer is, Nothing. Nor does a single word mean anything. It means only within the structures of contrast and association of a linguistic system. Reduced to its essence, that is the great message of structuralism. Words and things mean nothing in isolation. They are arbitrary. Arbitrariness leaves them when they become parts of interconnected sets. That is why our work requires complexity and quantity. All objects are simultaneously sets of parts and parts of sets.

As a set of parts, every object can be broken down into elements, read as a composition, a structure. For that simple reason, the more complex a thing, the more decisions its composition required, the more it fights us and rises before us into an object created by another, a presence on its own right.

As parts of sets, all objects exist in context. There is no such thing as an object out of context. There are objects in the right context, in which they beam meanings from others, or in the wrong context, in which their power to instruct is diminished through weak or improper association, normally the associations we build for them casually out of our experience or learning which may or may not be germane to the thing under question. Seeing a composition of wood and steel and naming it an axe, we draw it into our concept of axeness; we make it imaginatively into a thing for the hewing of wood and cease pondering it. A tool, we say. But for the man who forged and helved it, the axe was something different, the realization of his tradition and skill, and for the man who used it, the axe may have been a token of status, not to be lowered into wood and mere usefulness.

This idea of context, dominant in the discipline of folklore from which much of the thinking in the material culture movement flows, is not simple. To do our work we need to distinguish carefully among varieties of context. In context, as parts of systems, things, like words, assemble significance. They become evidence of will, expressions of people and experiences perhaps to be found in no document.

One variety of context is personal. It is the context we shape for things, usually inappropriately, out of our own culture. As we shift a statue from its context in a temple, where its associations were sacred, and place it in a museum, where its associations become art historical, and then imaginatively pluck the statue out of the museum and relocate it in a progressive sequence leading ineluctably to ourselves, so we lift an axe out of a village ceremony, where it served as a mace of honour, and place it into the category we have built in our minds for axes and dismiss it as a tool. Old meanings are replaced by new ones, convincing because they are derived from the culture we share with our readers, but false nonetheless.

A second kind of context is conceptual. In it the object exists within the set of associations that constitute the mind of its creator. This context could be called cultural, for we normally conceive of the creator's mind in terms of culture. It has also been called abstract because this context is invisible, a structuring of ideas and principles, not of palpable things. The conceptual context does not lie out in the world as an arrangement of objects and bodies that can be photographed; it lies hidden thoroughly deep in the mind created by creators as they pass through the whole of their lives. Having watched his elders at work, having seen axes lying about, having seen them used in sundry projects, the creator abstracts from all that experience an idea of axe—a basic pattern attended by a range of variations—that is enacted in the creative moment of which the axe is the phenomenal residue.

A third kind of context is physical. It has been called behavioural, for it contains the body moving, and it has been called particularistic because each one is different, specific (while the abstract, conceptual context is general and redundantly applicable). The physical context is the accumulation of associations present to the senses. The axe lies on a table in the context of oily rags and wood chips. It is lifted by a hand with knuckles and veins and allowed to fall into a short section of tree. All this is external, and it is the obvious focus of the ethnographer, but it is perplexing to the historian.

As a thing of parts, the object always tells of its composer, the man who pounded steel and shaved wood. As a part of things, as an element in a larger composition, it may or may not provide further information about its maker. Found at a flea market, an old axe continues to babble of the maker it contains, but from its setting in the market we are drawn not closer to him but farther away, distracted into interesting thoughts about the merchants and consumers of antiques.

Out of its conceptual context, as it always is, out of relevant physical context, as it often is, the artifact is poised for misreading, vulnerable. It becomes easy to absorb into the observer's personal context, where scholars who should restrain themselves, limiting their consideration of a thing to its existence as a composition, a set of parts, struggle to imagine it in a lost physical context which is always no more than a fiction of their own wit. The alternative is easy to sketch. The artifact, having lost physical association is granted conceptual association by being made into a member of a set, a group of things among which it will be understood as an element in a system, the system being the recapitulation of a mind at work. As the word is comprehended as part of a language, so the artifact is comprehended as part of a material culture set that is recomposed into a system of creation and expression, a principled system in which some parts are variable and some are not. The ratio of the variable to the invariant, analogous to the ratio of personality to culture, designates the limits and functions of the set, which might then be called a style.

Academic proclivities and matters of taste cause differences in the evaluation of a set's aspects. Atemporally, the invariant is the typological, the variable is the expressive range, and customarily folklorists emphasize the typological while art historians emphasize the expressive. Temporally, the stable is the traditional, the shifting is the historical, and the folklorist will emphasize the one, the historian the other. But the set, as the materialization of culture, will display both stability and variability—matching the folklorist's old definition of folklore as that which, nearly paradoxically, held steady over time while varying fluidly with personalities and occasions. Following elder folkloristic wisdom, or simply looking plain upon artificial reality, we will know our task to be the assembly of sets containing artifacts that belong together because they express the same mind, because they rise out of the same culture, then recasting the sets as systems of stability and variability that allow us to account for the objects in the sets as the creations of real people. Simply, the patterns of redundancy and variation contained by objects are the will we separate from nature in our study of art.

I am leading us toward an understanding of what I take to be the main problem raised by the Memorial University conference. Productive understanding depends on our knowing that all artifacts are things of parts. Removed from nature, they require a technology of destruction and creation. Separated, they take on form. Left in nature's tones or smoothed or painted or embellished, they are decorated. Every object will, then, contain evidence of technological manipulation. It will have a form. It will have ornamental properties. As these aspects of all things are elaborated, the object increases in complexity, in conspicuous artfulness, and it becomes easier to read as a composition and, therefore, as the product of another person. We need to know, too, that the composition is made meaningful through association with other compositions, in comparison with which it becomes the containment of patterns of stability and variability. In practice, the associations are our own creations. We determine what things in a physical scene bear meaningfully upon other things. We construct sets of artifacts and recompose them into principled systems that recapitulate cultural dynamics.

Our challenge is to describe things so well that their complexity will prevent us from associating them glibly or falsely with things they do not belong with, as, say, folk art ineptly described can be associated with Sunday painting. Our second challenge is to connect things correctly. If we are lucky enough to meet things bound as their maker intended them to be bound with other phenomena, we will have much to learn from puzzling the physical context together, but even when they have sprung free of their original setting (which, being material, lasting, and often transportable it is characteristic for artifacts to do), they can still be located in conceptual sets within which, owing to their embodiment of will, they can bring us toward other cultures we need to know to keep our own decent and honest.

I hope it is out of affection for materials, and not merely because they seem easier to study, that we are drawn toward physical contexts more often than conceptual contexts and even use the word "context" synonymously with setting or scene. (Context, I repeat, is all of that, visible or not, which goes with the text—the one woven together by the other—to make it meaningful.) The ethnographer is naturally thrilled by rich physical contexts and is obliged to describe them completely. But even for the ethnographer, the conceptual context, the resource for creation and comprehension, is the richer goal. For historians, labour though they might to reconstruct physical contexts, the evidence borne by artifacts about physical context is slight and trivial by comparison with the evidence artifacts contain of conceptual context.

Envisioned as a composition, a set of parts, and as a thing in context, a part of sets, the artifact has been prepared for study. The next step is to loop composition and context into a single reciprocal system. Usually this looping is imagined as a sequential process. The object is made. Then it is placed in the world to accrue context. The scholar may gain a sense of completeness by shifting from the level of composition to the level of context, but the resultant satisfaction is an illusion. The theory of performance formulated by Dell Hymes will guide us into a correct procedure for looping. Context does not merely follow upon creation. In fact, an idea of context, an idea of a thing's fit among things, precedes the enactment of compositional competence. A builder does not employ the grammar-like "rules" for architectural design to make a house that just happens to shelter its inhabitants. Instead, a wish for a shelter, among other desires, prompts the architectural capacity. Function, as it were, both precedes and follows structure. The structured object may be followed by unanticipated functions (the tree toppled to make a basket for carrying corn may contribute to the denuding of a hillside that leads to a mudslide that destroys the cornfield and the need for baskets at harvest time), but other functions are built into the object. A thing may be used in all manner of ways, but some of those ways were designed into its creation. Creation entails use. Ideas of composition and context interpenetrate in the creative act, so the object is not only in context: context is in the object. Art is not mind purely; it is a record of the mind in the world, a blending of will and nature.

After we have seen things for themselves, then seen them in association, then unified their aloneness with their connectivity, we arrive at artifactual systems. Comparing them geographically, we have ethnology. Comparing them temporally, we have history. Put ethnology and history together and you defeat the fragmented, fractious academy and restore the study of humankind to the level of its noble beginnings in old Herodotus.

So far I have said nothing new. All I have done is to rehearse some of our dogma in order to set the Memorial University conference into its context.

Like the maker of a house or axe, the maker of a paper on material culture works at the end of a tradition, historically, and in a social moment, culturally. I take our tradition to be that which has carried from the Middle Ages to the present a broad idea of art, refusing to allow art to become the rarefied expression of a mystically talented few or the possession of a few wealthy white men. For William Morris who transformed the medieval idea into a modern one, art was the joy found in work. Late in the stream of thought that bore him too, we study axes as well as paintings, teapots as well as statues, as blendings of nature and will, as significant, and we are led to recognizing our own writings as art, so that contemplating our work we gain insight into the work of others, wishing for painters the seriousness of the scholar, wishing for industrial labourers the joy of the peasant girl at the loom.

The material culture movement of which we are all part belongs to a tradition of science, contemplation, and action dedicated to broadening the idea of art. As that tradition rises in this moment, refracted and distracted by the culture of our own times, it tells both of our heritage and ourselves; it urges us forward on our task.

Look into the papers of the Memorial University conference and you will find in them abundant signs of the vitality of our old tradition and you will find signs too of our own culture. Some of the manifestations of our culture I find dreary. There are false claims of originality, expressive of our insecure individualism. There are pugnacious, combative tropes, the corpses of flayed strawmen, and there are facile economic explanations—all expressive of the competitive, capitalistic dimensions of our culture. Rising out of our culture and filtering through several of the papers there is also an interesting, currently fashionable concept: consumption.

The material culture movement of today, though anticipated by progressive thinkers like Ruth Bunzel, Fred Kniffen, E. Estyn Evans, James Marston Fitch, Charles Montgomery, and Alan Gowans, is largely a product of the 1960s. Then, you will remember, the ideology focused people compassionately beyond themselves. It follows that studies, like my own, would be of people unlike us, elderly basket-makers, dead housewrights. Anxious about community and creativity, we were led back to a rediscovery of the great romantic thinkers who were similarly preoccupied, and outward into encounters with people, as Mike Jones was with chairmakers in Kentucky, who still made artifacts with their minds and hands.

Any magazine will inform you that we have drifted since then toward conservatism. That is more true for bourgeois intellectuals like ourselves and the journalists we allow to tell us about ourselves than it is true for the majority of Americans, still it is true enough to suggest an explanation for why now, late in the 1980s and early 1990s, we are focusing more upon users of things than makers of things. The mode of conservatism is the argument out of the self. Government policy is but the private opinion of politicians writ large. Satisfactory worldviews and moral codes are derived from limited individual experience. Thinking begins and often ends in the personal context. My life is like this, therefore human life is like this. It is enough to know ourselves. Such thinking created the need for anthropology, sociology, folklore, and a host of compensatory histories: black history, women's history, African history, Asian history, oral history, artifactual history. When the life of the English gentleman was life itself, when his society was society, his taste was culture, then the history leading to his creation was history. But when his society became only one of hundreds of societies, we came to need new ways to study other people, people who had little political power perhaps, whose appearance in the documentary record was fleeting, slight, and marginal. Now if we allow ourselves to define modern life by our own lives, we will tumble into the old trap, losing all we have gained. Nobody, we say, makes things by hand anymore; now it is all industrial production and consumption. It may feel like that to us because we are consumers more than we are creators, but we must not forget what a small portion of the world's population we represent. My research takes me now to Turkey where handmade excellence is neither a memory nor a marginal pleasure; it is central to modern life. I have been to Bangladesh. There, even more completely, the world for most people is handmade, homemade, and beautiful. Before you say such places are small and peripheral and do not matter, consider that the population of Turkey is twice that of Canada, and the population of Bangladesh is twice that of Turkey. No, the modern world remains a place of handskills, and we will be glad that it does should any of the catastrophes currently being concocted by the superpowers come to pass. The reason to come to grips with industrial production and consumerism is not because they define the modern world (even if they seem to define our tiny corner of it), but because a complete idea of material culture must entail industrial production as well as hand production, consumption as well as creation.

Out of our conservative self-fascination, then, rises a good new focus for material culture study. Many of the papers in the Memorial University conference evince a shift from making to use, from people unlike ourselves who create things (though, remember, we are creators of material culture papers) to people like ourselves who consume them. Upon reflection, I discover the same change in my own work, from my book on Virginia houses, written in 1972, to my book on Ballymenone, published in 1982, where I announced a shift in vernacular architecture study from male house builders to female homemakers.

Our problem is use. It is a profound reality of material culture study that all things are multifunctional and that one set of functions is always utilitarian. All things are made to use. The axe is made to rive wood or to be carried in ceremonial procession. The painting is made to sell, to reinforce the status of painter and patron, to pass the terrible time.

Use divides. Some of use (the analog is manifest function) is part of creation. It is predicted and built into the object which then coerces response. If used in the way its creator anticipated, the object unifies the maker and user in a communicative bond, but, even if the patron provides detailed direction, it is the creator who realizes the work, which, then, expresses, not the user, but the creator who contains the user as an inward concept. Use is submerged in the process of the creation of artifacts much as the reaction of the audience is incorporated into the telling of a story that exists at last with only the storyteller to blame.

Try as we might to construct users out of artifacts, artifacts are about their creators. A new Ford automobile tells of its designer and manufacturer, just as an antique chair does. The makers may have tried to anticipate use, but the car and chair will be consumed for a thousand reasons, and before they are used they provide no information about their consumers. We may make the Ford into an emblem of American culture, but it is an expression of its creators and the peculiar incorporation of their ideas about consumption into the process of design and manufacture.

Now put a thing into use. The car is purchased; it is polished, bumped, wrecked. From rubbing or rust or wear patterns, we might recover hints about use and users, but not much and not much of importance. Most of the car remains the product of the Ford Motor Company; the consumer exists only as stains and dents and ashes in the ashtrays. When we begin to learn about consumers is when they abandon the role of consumer and become creators. Then we watch drivers and from their habits of automotive operation gain notions about their personalities, and if we spend enough time with enough drivers, we will derive patterns of stability and variability which, correctly, we take to be expressive of the culture of drivers of cars. In such a study the car would be a tool in a creative act. It is to driving as a fiddle is to a tune. From the fiddle alone, from scars on the neck, we might learn a little about habits of playing, but the yield is slight. The fiddle tells us mostly about fiddle makers. Fiddling tells us about fiddlers. The car tells us about the manufacturer. Driving tells us about the driver who is not a consumer of cars but a creator of driving behaviours. Industrial products express designers and makers. When we watch consumers behave, we are watching the use of industrial objects, but "use" is a creative act that employs the creative act of another, as driving uses the car, as the basketmaker uses an axe, as the shopper uses money. Little about shopping behaviour or the culture of shoppers is to be learned from the shapes of bills, their colours, or the pictures they carry.

It turns out that our old focus upon creativity, learned from observing and interviewing men who made baskets and chairs out of wood, remains apt. As the old man uses an axe to split ash for a basket he hangs outside his shop as a sign of his capacity, so does the consumer of a Ford use it to drive to market or park at the curb as a symbol of his working self.

Take the person out of the picture, leaving only the basket, only the car, and the only person we can learn much about is the one who made it. The consumer is reduced either to an idea in the creator's mind or to a few smudgy fingerprints. But suppose the consumer in using the object in a creative act recreates it. In my day, the kid who bought a Ford bought an old one and with help from Manny, Moe, and Jack recreated it, removing chrome ornaments, filling holes with lead, painting it in splotches of barn-red primer, then, rarely, giving it the lacquered finish of his dreams. Thus recreated, the Ford became expressive of a second culture. The culture of the manufacturer and that of the teenager came to exist simultaneously in automotive fabric.

The customized car—that is what we called them—like the old house altered or the wide landscape, embodies creative layering, the wills of many makers. One way to approach the material culture of the industrial age is through study of remaking. Consequently, fresh studies in vernacular architecture take into account urban row-houses and suburban ranchers, but their authors concentrate on the way the rowhouse has been modified to express ethnic culture or the way suburban ranchers are made livable by their occupants. The user's will endures in the creative act of alteration. The purchase of a house is conditioned by too many considerations. Only patient interviewing can lead us into an understanding of the reasons governing consumption. But a home, somewhat changed, somewhat not, decorated, filled with things, becomes, as a unit, a composition, a bearer of information about its user who is not its user but one of its creators.

Use becomes creation as objects are altered radically. And use becomes creation when objects become parts of objects, when the context becomes a composition. The commodity alone, unchanged, expresses its maker. You buy a Ford. In the Ford abides information, not about you (you might have wanted a BMW), but about the Ford Motor Company. But if you buy a Ford and then make it one element in a set, gathering objects into a household unit, you have created a new entity, which as a whole is your creation.

The old man went into the woods, selected a tree he did not make, felled it, split it, made it into a basket. The consumer goes to the market, selects a car she did not make, drives it home and there incorporates it into a unit, a collection that is her creation. Emotionally, the process differs, tactically it is the same. Even if we do not make cars or recreate them through customization, we locate cars in sets of possessions, and, while the particular elements tell little about us, just as the tree itself told us little about the basketmaker, the final composition is, as a single object, a creation of our own. It is not the shirt bought off the rack that is you, but the shirt as a component in a composition of attire that informs on you. Sets of clothing, the environments that go near us, and sets of commodities built into domestic environments—these are the created objects, the material folk culture of industrial civilization. They are our mirrors; we see ourselves in them. They are our lenses; others read us through them.

The collection is our key expressive mode. Others make the parts, but we make the wholes. The painting expresses the painter;

the collection of paintings expresses the collector. The television alone expresses its Japanese manufacturer; the television as part of a collection that is the household expresses its creator, the house-holder.

Using the word "goods" to summarize paintings and televisions rather than the word "artifacts" we manifest the emphases in our culture. The artifact is what the artisan makes with art. Goods are artifacts used as commodities. The person who consistently uses "artifact" implicitly stresses one aspect of all things: they are made. The person who uses "goods" stresses another: they are owned and traded. All things are both artifacts and goods, and all theories of material culture need to account for both. The student of artifacts studies them as creations, as blendings of nature and will, and slights their use and the economic systems of which they are part. The student of goods studies them as aspects of commerce, slighting their creators and avoiding the dreadful moral issues raised in the contemplation of systems of production. The current emphasis on goods provides a valuable corrective to material culture studies. But an exclusive concentration on goods would be a vicious betrayal of our intellectual tradition.

Studying creative acts, with the old basketmaker as our guide, we need to add to the basketmaker's act, two other varieties of creativity. His is the creation out of nature, the prime artifactual act, but it is paralleled in acts of recreation, when the car is customized, the house remodelled, and in the construction of collections, when things are not made out of bits of nature but out of artifacts.

It is wrong, I believe, to call one of these acts "creativity" and the others "use." Rather, each is a variety of creativity that yields an object—a basket, a chopped car, the decor of an office in a university building—that expresses a mind at playful work.

The pattern I find in the Memorial University conference is this. We are continuing to develop along traditional lines, working to keep the idea of art broad, open, democratic. In its current phase this tradition, as a result of influence from its moment, has come to concern itself with industrial objects and consumers as much as with handmade objects and creators. The new focus is apt and productive, but it should not mislead us into thinking we must reject our scholarly past, for it has prepared us perfectly to deal with new phenomena, the most important among which I believe to be the collection—the domestic environment in contradistinction to the house—and it should not trick us into the belief that the little world we inhabit is the world. While we create collections of things made by other people in order to express ourselves, all across the globe people no less real than ourselves are going up into the woods and down to the river to chop out lumps of nature to fashion into artifacts that express their wills at wonderful war with nature.

Our goal is to keep the idea of art wide and useful, so that the old man's basket, the teenager's modified coupe, the old lady's beautiful kitchen made of junk, and our own earnest writings will all be taken seriously. On the way to that end the Memorial University conference, organized by Jerry Pocius and gathering scholars from Canada and the United States into useful colloquy, will be seen one day as a major landmark.

References

Adams, George 1800 *Astronomical and Geographical Essays.* 4th ed., Philadelphia: Young.

Alpers, Svetlana 1983 *The Art of Describing: Dutch Art in the Seventeenth Century.* Chicago: University of Chicago Press.

Ames, Kenneth L. 1977 *Beyond Necessity: Art in the Folk Tradition.* New York: Norton.

_____ 1978 "Meaning in Artifacts: Hall Furnishings in Victorian America." *Journal of Interdisciplinary History*, 9(1):19–46.

_____ 1980 "Material Culture as Non-Verbal Communication: A Historical Case Study." *Journal of American Culture*, 3:619-41.

Ames, Michael M. 1986 *Museums, the Public and Anthropology: A Study in the Anthropology of Anthropology.* Ranchi Anthropology Series 9. Vancouver: University of British Columbia Press.

Anderson, Joan J. 1961 "A Collection of the Poems of Jonathan Odell with a Biographical and Critical Introduction." Master's thesis, University of British Columbia.

Architectural History, First Presbyterian Church of Elizabeth, New Jersey. 1947 Prepared by the office of Gugler, Kimball, and Husted.

Arendt, Hannah 1958 *The Human Condition.* Chicago: University of Chicago Press.

Armstrong, Robert Plant 1971 *The Affecting Presence: An Essay in Humanistic Anthropology.* Urbana: University of Illinois Press.

_____ 1975 *Wellspring: On the Myth and Source of Culture.* Berkeley: University of California Press.

_____ 1981 *The Powers of Presence: Consciousness, Myth and Affecting Presence.* Philadelphia: University of Pennsylvania Press.

Audet, Bernard 1981 "La maison de l'Ile d'Orléans: Aspects et équipement intérieur, 1647–1715." Master's thesis, Université Laval.

Auerbach, Erich 1953 *Mimesis*. Princeton: Princeton University Press.

Bailey, Alfred Goldsworthy 1983 "Jonathan Odell." *Dictionary of Canadian Biography*, V:628–31.

Baker, Ray Palmer 1920 *A History of English Canadian Literature to Confederation*. Cambridge: Harvard University Press.

Baxandall, Michael 1985 *Patterns of Intention: On the Historical Explanation of Pictures*. New Haven: Yale University Press.

Becker, Howard 1982 *Art Worlds*. Berkeley: University of California Press.

Bellah, Robert N. 1967 "Civil Religion in America." *Daedalus*, 96(1):1-21.

Bériau, Oscar A. 1943 "Home Weaving in Canada." *Canadian Geographical Journal*, 27(1):19–29.

Bishop, Robert C. 1977 *Folk Painters of America*. New York: Greenwich House.

Blackbeard, Bill and Martin Williams 1977 *The Smithsonian Collection of Newspaper Comics*. Washington: Smithsonian Press; New York: Harry N. Abrams.

Bolton, Theodore and Irwin F. Cortelyou 1955 *Ezra Ames of Albany: Portrait Painter, Craftsman, Royal Arch Mason, Banker, 1768-1836*. New York: New York Historical Society.

Bourdieu, Pierre 1984 *Distinction: A Social Critique of the Judgment of Taste*. Trans. Richard Nice. Cambridge: Harvard University Press.

Bowden, P.J. 1956–7 "Wool Supply and the Woollen Industry." *Economic History Review*, 2(29):44–58.

Branch, Edgar M. (ed.) 1969 *Clemens of the "Call": Mark Twain in San Francisco*. Berkeley: University of California Press.

Braudel, Fernand 1973 *Capitalism and Material Life, 1400–1800*. Trans. Miriam Kochan. New York: Harper and Row.

_____ 1977 *Afterthoughts on Material Civilization and Capitalism*. Trans. Patricia M. Ranum. Baltimore: Johns Hopkins University Press.

_____ 1981 *Civilization and Capitalism, 15th-18th Centuries* vol 1 *The Structures of Everyday Life*. Rev. Siân Reynolds. New York: Harper and Row.

Brawne, Michael 1965 *The New Museum: Architecture and Design*. New York: Praeger.

Breton, Raymond 1984 "The Production and Allocation of Symbolic Resources: An Analysis of the Linguistic and Ethnocultural Fields in Canada." *Canadian Review of Sociology and Anthropology*, 21(2):123–44.

Bridenbaugh, Carl 1962 *Mitre and Sceptre: Transatlantic Faiths, Ideals, Personalities and Politics, 1689-1774*. New York: Oxford University Press.

Bromberger, Christian 1979 "Technologie et analyse sémantique des objets pour une sémio-technologie." *L'Homme*, 19(1):105–240.

Bronner, Simon J. (ed.) 1985 *American Material Culture and Folklife: A Prologue and Dialogue*. American Material Culture and Folklife Series. Ann Arbor: UMI Press.

Bunzel, Ruth 1929 Rpt. *The Pueblo Potter: A Study of Creative Imagination in Primitive Art*. New York: Dover, 1972.

Burnham, Dorothy K. 1980 *Warp and Weft*. Toronto: Royal Ontario Museum.

Burnham, Harold B. 1971 "Bolton 'Quilts' or 'Caddows': A Nineteenth Century Cottage Industry." *C.I.E.T.A. Bulletin*, 34:22–29.

_____ and Dorothy K. Burnham 1972 *"Keep Me Warm One Night": Early Handweaving in Eastern Canada*. Toronto: University of Toronto Press.

Burr, Nelson 1954 *The Anglican Church in New Jersey: The Decorative Feature*. Philadelphia: Church Historical Society.

Bushman, Richard L. 1984 "American High-style and Vernacular Cultures." In Jack P. Greene and J.R. Pole (eds.), *Colonial British America: Essays in the New History of the Early Modern Era*. Baltimore: Johns Hopkins University Press.

Cafferty, Pastoria S. 1971 "Loyalist Rhapsodies: The Poetry of Stansbury and Odell." Ph.D. thesis, George Washington University.

Calhoun, Daniel 1973 *The Intelligence of a People*. Princeton: Princeton University Press.

Canada 1876 *Censuses of Canada, 1665–1871*, 5 vols. Ottawa: I.B. Taylor.

_____ 1914 *Documents Relating to the Constitutional History of Canada, 1765–1791* 1914 Ottawa: Parmlee.

Cannizzo, Jeanne 1987 *Living in the Past*. (printed transcript) Toronto: Canadian Broadcasting Corporation.

Carpenter, Carole Henderson 1979 *Many Voices: A Study of Folklore Activities in Canada and Their Role in Canadian Culture*. Canadian Centre for Folk Culture Studies Paper 26. Ottawa: National Museums of Canada.

Carson, Cary *et al.* 1981 "Impermanent Architecture in the Southern American Colonies." *Winterthur Portfolio*, 16(2&3):135–96.

Carson, Cary 1984 "Chesapeake Themes in the History of Early American Material Life." Paper presented at "Maryland, A Product of Two Worlds" Conference, St. Mary's City, Maryland, 19 May.

Carter, Thomas 1987 "'It Was in the Way, So We Took It Out': Remodeling as Social Commentary." *Material Culture*, 19(2&3):113–25.

Chaldecott, J.A. 1951 *Handbook of George III Collection of Scientific Instruments*. London: H.M.S.O.

Clifford, James 1988 *The Predicament of Culture*. Cambridge: Harvard University Press.

Cogswell, Fred 1976 "The Maritime Provinces." In Carl F. Klinck (ed.) *Literary History of Canada: Canadian Literature in English*, vol. 1. Toronto: University of Toronto Press.

Cohen, Sheldon S. and Larry Gerlach 1974 "Princeton and the Coming of the American Revolution." *New Jersey History*, 92:69–92.

Coleman, D.C. 1969 "An Innovation and its Diffusion: The 'New Draperies.'" *Economic History Review*, 2(22):417–29.

Condon, Ann Gorman 1983 *The Envy of the American States: The Loyalist Dream for New Brunswick*. Fredericton: New Ireland Press.

_____ 1984 "What the Object Knew: Material History Studies in Canada." *Acadiensis*, 13(2):136–46.

_____ (ed.) 1986 "'The Young Robin Hood Society': A Political Satire by Edward Winslow." *Acadiensis*, 15(2):120–43.

Coomaraswamy, Ananda K. 1935 *The Transformation of Nature in Art*. Cambridge: Harvard University Press.

Copleston, Frederick 1964 *A History of Philosophy, vol. 5, Modern Philosophy: The British Philosophers, II, Berkeley to Hume*. Garden City, New York: Image Books.

Cott, Nancy F. 1977 *The Bonds of Womanhood: "Woman's Sphere" in New England, 1780-1835*. New Haven: Yale University Press.

Cotter, John 1972 "Above-Ground Archaeology." *American Quarterly*, 26(3):266–80.

Cyr, Lise and Yvan Chouinard 1976 *Le forgeron Emile Asselin*. Québec: Ministère des Affaires culturelles.

Daniels, Les 1971 *Comix: A History of Comic Books in America*. New York: Bonanza.

Davies, Gwendolyn 1987 "'Consolation to Distress': Loyalist Literary Activity in the Maritimes." *Acadiensis*, 16(2):51–69.

Dechêne, Louise 1974 *Habitants et marchands de Montréal au XVIIe siècle*. Montréal: Plon.

Deetz, James 1967 *Invitation to Archaeology*. Garden City, New York: Natural History Press.

_____ 1977a *In Small Things Forgotten: The Archaeology of Early American Life*. Garden City, New York: Anchor Press/Doubleday.

_____ 1977b "Material Culture and Archaeology—What's the Difference?" In Leland Ferguson (ed.), *Historical Archaeology and the Importance of Material Things*. Society for Historical Archaeology Special Publications 2. N.p.: Society for Historical Archaeology.

Dickson, Lovat 1986 *The Museum Makers: The Story of the Royal Ontario Museum*. Toronto: Royal Ontario Museum.

Diploma in Material History: A Programme Proposal 1983 Saint John: Department of History, University of New Brunswick

Doherty, Robert 1977 *Society and Power: Five New England Towns, 1800-1860.* Amherst: University of Massachusetts Press.

Dolgin, Janet L., David S. Kemnitzer, and David M. Schneider (eds.) 1977 *Symbolic Anthropology: A Reader in the Study of Symbols and Meanings.* New York: Columbia University Press.

Dorson, Richard (ed.) 1972 *Folklore and Folklife: An Introduction.* Chicago: University of Chicago Press.

_____ 1976 "Is Folklore a Discipline?" *Folklore and Fakelore: Essays Toward A Discipline of Folk Studies.* Cambridge: Harvard University Press.

Douglas, Mary and Baron Isherwood 1979 *The World of Goods: Toward An Anthropology of Consumption.* New York: Norton.

Drury, George 1984 "No Answer." In Sohnya Sayres *et al.* (eds.), *The 60s Without Apology.* Minneapolis: University of Minnesota Press.

Duncan, Carol and Alan Wallach 1978 "The Museum of Modern Art as Late Capitalist Ritual." *Marxist Perspectives,* 1(4):28–51.

Dunnell, Robert C. 1978 "Style and Function: A Fundamental Dichotomy." *American Antiquity,* 43(2):192–202.

Dupont, Jean-Claude 1974 *Le pain d'habitant.* Montréal: Leméac.

_____ 1975 *Le sucre du pays.* Montréal: Leméac.

_____ 1977 *Héritage d'Acadie.* Montréal: Leméac.

_____ 1979 *L'artisan forgeron.* Québec: Les Presses de l'université Laval.

_____ and Jacques Mathieu 1986 *Héritage de la francophonie: Les traditions orales.* Québec: Les Presses de l'université Laval.

Dupree, A. Hunter 1981 Review of *A History of Technology,* vols. VI and VII. *Journal of Interdisciplinary History,* 11(4):685–94.

Dwyer, Jane Powell (ed.) 1975 *The Cashinahua of Eastern Peru.* Studies in Anthropology and Material Culture, vol. 1. Providence: Haffenreffer Museum of Anthropology, Brown University.

Eames, Penelope 1977 *Furniture in England, France and the Netherlands from the Twelfth to the Fifteenth Century.* London: Furniture History Society.

Edelberg, Cynthia Dubin 1983 "The Shaping of a Political Poet: Five New Found Verses by Jonathan Odell." *Early American Literature,* 18:45–70.

_____ 1987 *Jonathan Odell: Loyalist Poet of the Revolution.* Durham: Duke University Press.

Eliade, Mircea 1977 *Forgerons et alchimistes.* Paris: Flamarion.

Elliot, Robert S. 1985 "Towards a Material History Methodology." *Material History Bulletin*, 22:31–40.

Ellis, Joseph S. 1979 *After the Revolution: Profiles in Early American Culture.* New York: Norton.

Emerson, Ralph Waldo 1836 Rpt. *Nature.* East Aurora: Roycrofters, 1905.

Ennals, Peter 1986 "Inside the Front Door: Recent Approaches and Themes for Interpreting Past Housing." In Philip Buckner (ed.), *Teaching Maritime Studies.* Fredericton: Acadiensis Press.

Espessat, Helene, Jean-Pierre Hardy and David-Thiery Ruddel 1972 "Le monde du travail au Québec au XVIIIe et au XIXe siècles: historiographie et état de le question." *Revue d'histoire de l'Amérique française,* 25(4):499–539.

Ettema, Michael J. 1982 "History, Nostalgia, and American Furniture." *Winterthur Portfolio,* 17(2–3):135–44.

Evans, E. Estyn 1951 Rpt. *Mourne Country: Landscape and Life in South Down.* Dundalk: Dundalgan Press, 1967.

Fenton, William N. 1974 "The Advancement of Material Culture Studies in Modern Anthropological Research." In Miles Richardson (ed.), *The Human Mirror: Material and Spatial Images of Man.* Baton Rouge: Louisiana State University Press.

Fernandez, James 1971 "The Mission of Metaphor in Expressive Culture." *Current Anthropology,* 15(2):119–45.

Finley, A. Gregg 1984 "Material History and Museums: A Curatorial Perspective in Doctoral Research." *Material History Bulletin,* 20:75–79.

_____ 1985 "Material History and Curatorship: Problems and Prospects." *Muse,* 3(3):34–39.

Fisher, Philip 1975 "The Future's Past." *New Literary History,* 6:587–606.

Fitch, James Marston 1982 *Historic Preservation: Curatorial Management of the Built World.* New York: McGraw-Hill.

Fleming, E. McClung 1969 "History 803: The Artifact in American History," Unpublished Course Outline, Winterthur Program in Early American Culture.

_____ 1974 "Artifact Study: A Proposed Model." *Winterthur Portfolio,* 9:153–173.

Flexner, James Thomas 1954 Rpt. *History of American Painting, Vol. 2, The Light of Distant Skies.* New York: Dover, 1969.

Ford, Georgeann Bishop 1935 "In the Days of Our Ancestors." Unpublished typescript, Mudd Archives, Princeton University.

Francina, Francis (ed.) 1983 *Pollock and After.* New York: Harper and Row.

Fréchette, Louis 1909 "La maison hantée." *L'Almanach du Peuple.* Montreal: Beauchemin.

Fry, Edward F. 1972 "The Dilemmas of the Curator." In Brian O'Doherty (ed.), *Museums in Crisis*. New York: Braziller.

Garrett, Wendell D. 1960 *Apthorp House, 1760–1960*. Cambridge: Adams House, Harvard University.

_____ 1964 "John Adams and the Limited Role of Art." *Winterthur Portfolio*, 1:242–55.

_____ 1970 "The Matter of Consumers' Taste." In John D. Morse (ed.), *Country Cabinetwork and Simple City Furniture*. Winterthur Conference Report 1969. Charlottesville: University Press of Virginia, for Winterthur Museum.

Geertz, Clifford 1973a "Ideology as a Cultural System." *The Interpretation of Cultures*. New York: Basic Books.

_____ 1973b "Religion as a Cultural System." *The Interpretation of Cultures*. New York: Basic Books.

_____ 1983 "Art as a Cultural System." *Local Knowledge*. New York: Basic Books.

Gerardi, Donald F.M. 1977–78 "The King's College Controversy, 1753–1756, and the Ideological Roots of Toryism in New York." *Perspectives in American History*, 7:149–96.

Gibbs, Robert, (ed.) 1982 *The New Brunswick Poems of Jonathan Odell*. Kingston, Ontario.

Glassie, Henry 1967 "William Houck, Maker of Pounded Ash Adirondack Pack-Baskets." *Keystone Folklore Quarterly*, 12(1):23–54.

_____ 1969 *Pattern in the Material Folk Culture of the Eastern United States*. University of Pennsylvania Publications in Folklore and Folklife. Philadelphia: University of Pennsylvania Press.

_____ 1973 "Structure and Function, Folklore and the Artifact." *Semiotica*, 7(4):313–51.

_____ 1974 "The Variation of Concepts within Tradition: Barn Building in Otsego County, New York." In H.J.Walker and W. G. Haag (eds.), *Geoscience and Man, Volume V: Man and Cultural Heritage*. Baton Rouge: Louisiana State University, School of Geoscience.

_____ 1975a "Barns Across Southern England: A Note on Trans-Atlantic Comparison and Architectural Meanings." *Pioneer America*, 7(1):9–19.

_____ 1975b *Folk Housing in Middle Virginia: A Structural Analysis of Historic Artifacts*. Knoxville: University of Tennessee Press.

_____ 1977 "Archaeology and Folklore: Common Anxieties, Common Hopes." In Leland Ferguson (ed.), *Historical Archaeology and the Importance of Material Things*. Society for Historical Archaeology Special Publications 2. N.p.: Society for Historical Archaeology.

_____ 1982a "Folk Art." In Thomas J. Schlereth (ed.), *Material Culture*

Studies in America. Nashville: American Association for State and Local History.

_____ 1982b *Passing the Time in Ballymenone: Culture and History of an Ulster Community.* Publications of the American Folklore Society, n.s. 4. Philadelphia: University of Pennsylvania Press.

_____ 1986 "The Idea of Folk Art." In John Vlach and Simon Bronner (eds.), *Folk Art and Art Worlds.* Ann Arbor: UMI Research Press.

_____ 1989 *The Spirit of Folk Art.* New York: Harry N. Abrams.

Glenie, James 1800 "A Creed for ST. JOHN N.B.." Mudd Archives, Princeton University.

Glueck, Grace 1972 "Power and Esthetics: The Trustee." In Brian O'Doherty (ed.), *Museums in Crisis.* New York: Braziller.

Gowans, Alan 1966 *The Restless Art.* Philadelphia: Lippincott.

_____ 1971 *Unchanging Arts: New Forms of the Traditional Functions of Art in Society.* Philadelphia: Lippincott.

_____ 1979 "Popeye and the American Dream." *Prospects,* 4:549–57.

_____ 1983 *Learning to See: Historical Perspectives on Modern Popular/Commercial Arts.* Bowling Green, Ohio: Popular Press.

_____ 1983 *Prophetic Allegory: Popeye and the American Dream.* Watkins Glen, New York: American Life Foundation.

Gramsci, Antonio 1971 *Selections from the Prison Notebooks of Antonio Gramsci.* Eds. Quintin Hoare and Geoffrey Nowell Smith. New York: International Publishers.

Guild, James 1937 "From Tunbridge, Vermont to London, England—The Journal of James Guild, Peddler, Tinker, School Master, Portrait Painter, from 1818 to 1824." *Proceedings of the Vermont Historical Society,* 5:249-313.

Habermas, J. 1984 *The Theory of Communicative Action.* Trans. Thomas McCarthy. Boston: Beacon Press.

Hachey, Paul A. 1980 *The New Brunswick Landscape Print, 1760–1800.* Fredericton: Beaverbrook.

Hadjinicolaou, N. 1978 *Art History and Class Struggle.* London: Pluto Press.

Halpin, Marjorie M. 1983 "Anthropology as Artifact." In Frank Manning (ed.), *Consciousness and Inquiry: Ethnology and Canadian Realities.* Canadian Ethnology Service Paper 89E. Ottawa: National Museums of Canada.

Handler, Richard 1985 "On Having a Culture: Nationalism and the Preservation of Québec's Patrimoine." In George W. Stocking, Jr. (ed.), *Objects and Others: Essays on Museums and Material Culture.* History of Anthropology 2. Madison: University of Wisconsin Press.

Handsman, Russell G. 1983 "Historical Archaeology and Capitalism, Subscriptions and Separations: The Production of Individualism." *North American Archaeologist*, 4(1):63–79.

Harding, Chester 1866 *My Egotistigraphy*. Cambridge, Mass.: John Wilson.

Hardy, Jean-Pierre and David-Thiery Ruddel 1977 *Les Apprentis artisans à Québec, 1660–1815*. Montréal: Les Presses de l'Université du Québec.

Harris, Neil 1978 "Museums, Merchandising, and Popular Taste: The Struggle for Influence." In Ian M.G. Quimby (ed.), *Material Culture and the Study of American Life*. New York: Norton, for Winterthur Museum.

Haskell, Francis 1976 *Rediscoveries in Art: Some Aspects of Taste, Fashion and Collecting in England and France*. Ithaca: Cornell University Press.

Hebdige, Dick 1979 *Subculture: The Meaning of Style*. London: Methuen.

Hélias, Pierre-Jakez 1978 *The Horse of Pride: Life in a Breton Village*. Trans. June Guicharnaud. New Haven: Yale University Press.

Herman, Bernard L. 1984 "Multiple Materials, Multiple Meanings: The Fortunes of Thomas Mendenhall." *Winterthur Portfolio*, 19(1):67–86.

_____ 1987 *Architecture and Rural Life in Central Delaware, 1700–1900*. Knoxville: University of Tennessee Press.

Hersey, George L. 1972 *High Victorian Gothic: A Study in Associationalism*. Baltimore: Johns Hopkins University Press.

Hills, George Morgan 1876 *History of the Church in Burlington, New Jersey*. Trenton: Sharp.

Hindle, Brooke 1956 *The Pursuit of Science in Revolutionary America, 1735–1789*. Chapel Hill: University of North Carolina Press.

_____ 1978 "How Much Is a Piece of The True Cross Worth?" In Ian M. G. Quimby (ed.), *Material Culture and the Study of American Life*. New York: Norton, for Winterthur Museum.

_____ 1981 *Emulation and Invention*. New York: New York University Press.

Hogarth, William 1753 *The Analysis of Beauty: Written with a View of Fixing the Fluctuating Ideas of Taste*. London: Reeves.

Holmes, Oliver Wendell 1861 "Sun-painting and Sun-sculpture." *Atlantic Monthly*, 8:13-29.

Hood, Adrienne Dora 1988 "Organization and Extent of Textile Manufacture in Eighteenth-Century, Rural Pennsylvania: A Case Study of Chester County." Ph.D. dissertation, University of California, San Diego.

Horn, Maurice (ed.) 1976 *The World Encyclopedia of Comics*. New York: Avon.

Horne, Donald 1984 *The Great Museum*. London: Pluto Press.

Hoskins, W.G. 1955 *The Making of the English Landscape*. London: Hodder and Stoughton.

_____ 1965 *Provincial England: Essays in Social and Economic History*. London: Macmillan.

Hume, David 1779 *Dialogues Concerning Natural Religion*. Library of Classics No. 5. New York: Hafner.

Hymes, Dell 1974 *Foundations in Sociolinguistics: An Ethnographic Approach*. Philadelphia: University of Pennsylvania Press.

Inge, M. Thomas 1975 "American Comic Art: A Bibliography." *Choice*, 11(11):1581–93.

Jackel, Susan 1980 "Making Connections." *Journal of Canadian Studies*, 15(3):34–38.

James, John 1982 *Chartres: The Masons Who Built a Legend*. London: Routledge and Kegan Paul.

Jervis, Simon 1976 "The Americanization of American Art?" *Apollo*, 104(175):182–89.

Jicha, Hubert F., III, and Valerie Cesna 1986 *Agricultural Buildings and Complexes in Mill Creek Hundred [New Castle County, Delaware], 1800-1840*. National Register of Historic Places Nomination prepared for the Delaware Division of Historical and Cultural Affairs.

Jones, Michael Owen 1989 *Craftsman of the Cumberlands: Tradition and Creativity*. Lexington: University Press of Kentucky.

Jones. W.T. 1961 *The Romantic Syndrome: Toward a New Method in Cultural Anthropology and History*. The Hague: Humanities Press.

Kaplan, Wendy 1982 "R.T.H. Halsey: An Ideology of Collecting American Decorative Arts." *Winterthur Portfolio*, 17(1):43–53.

Key, Archie F. 1973 *Beyond Four Walls: The Origins and Development of Canadian Museums*. Toronto: McClelland and Stewart.

Kniffen, Fred B. 1965 "Folk Housing: Key to Diffusion." In Dell Upton and John Michael Vlach (eds.), *Common Places: Readings in American Vernacular Architecture*. Athens: University of Georgia Press, 1986.

_____ 1990 *Cultural Diffusion and Landscapes: Selections by Fred B. Kniffen*. Eds. H. Jesse Walker and Randall A. Detro. Baton Rouge: LSU Geoscience and Man Press.

Kroker, Arthur 1980 "Migration from the Disciplines." *Journal of Canadian Studies*, 15(3):3–10.

Kubler, George 1969 "Time's Perfection and Colonial Art," *1968 Winterthur Conference Report: Spanish, French, and English Traditions in The Colonial Silver of North America*. Winterthur: Winterthur Museum.

Labaree, Leonard, et al. 1959 *The Papers of Benjamin Franklin, vol. 16*. New Haven: Yale University Press.

La Fabrication artisanale des tissus: Appareils et techniques 1974 Québec: Musée du Québec.

Lambert, Sheila (ed.) *House of Commons Sessional Papers*, LXXXIII.

Lankton, Larry 1981 "Reading History From the Hardware," *The Edison Institute Herald*, 10(3):23–29.

Larson, Neil G. 1980 "The Politics of Style: Rural Portraiture in the Hudson Valley, 1825–1850." Master's thesis, University of Delaware.

Lavoie, Thomas, Gaston Bergeron and Michelle Côté 1985 *Les parlers français de Charlevoix, du Saguenay, du Lac-Saint-Jean et de la Côte Nord*. Québec: Ministère des Communications.

Leone, Mark 1983 "Method as Message." *Museum News*, 62(1):35–41.

Leroi-Gourhan, André 1971 *L'homme et la matière*. Paris: Albin Michel.

Lewis, Peirce F. 1975 "Common Houses, Cultural Spoor." *Landscape*, 19(2):1–22.

Lewis, R.W.B. 1955 *The American Adam*. Chicago: University of Chicago Press.

Leyton, Elliott H. 1984 Review of *Irish Folk History* and *Passing the Time in Ballymenone*. *Ethnohistory*, 31(3):220–21.

Lipman, Jean 1980 "Foreword." In Jean Lipman and Tom Armstrong (eds). *American Folk Painters of Three Centuries*. New York: Hudson Hills.

Longstreth, Richard 1984 "The Problem with 'Style.'" *The Forum: Bulletin of the Committee on Preservation*, 61–2.

Lurie, Nancy Oestreich 1981 "Museumland Revisited." *Human Organization*, 40(2):180–87.

Mackiewicz, Susan 1985 "Property Is the Great Idol of Mankind, However They May Profess Their Regard For Liberty and Religion: The Material Lives of Philadelphia Elites, 1700–1775." Presented at the Delaware Seminar, Department of American Civilization, University of Delaware, Newark, Delaware, Spring.

MacLachlan, James L., et al. 1976 *Princetonians: A Biographical Dictionary*, vol. 1. Princeton: Princeton University Press.

Mannion, John J. 1974 *Irish Settlements in Eastern Canada: A Study of Cultural Transfer and Adaptation*. University of Toronto Department of Geography Research Publications 12. Toronto: University of Toronto Press.

_____ 1979 "Multidisciplinary Dimensions in Material History." *Material History Bulletin*, 8:21–25.

Maquet, Jacques 1979 "Art by Metamorphosis." *African Arts*, 12(4):32–36, 90–91.

_____ 1986 *The Aesthetic Experience*. New Haven: Yale University Press.

Marcus, George and Michael Fischer 1986 *Anthropology as Cultural Critique*. Chicago: University of Chicago Press.

Mathieu, Jocelyne 1983 "Les ustensiles domestiques comparés, Perche-Québec, XVIIe, XVIIIe siècles." Ph.D. dissertation, Ecole des Hautes Etudes en sciences sociales.

McAlester, Virginia and Lee McAlester 1984 *A Field Guide to American Houses*. New York: Knopf.

McCallum, John 1980 *Unequal Beginnings: Agriculture and Economic Development in Quebec and Ontario until 1870*. Toronto: University of Toronto Press.

McCoubrey, John W. (ed.) 1965 *American Art, 1700-1960: Sources and Documents*. Englewood Cliffs, N.J.: Prentice-Hall.

McFeat, Tom 1976 "The National Museum and Canadian Anthropology." In J. Freedman (ed.), *The History of Canadian Anthropology*. Proceedings 3. N.p.: Canadian Ethnology Society.

_____ 1980 *Three Hundred Years of Anthropology in Canada*. Occasional Papers in Anthropology 7. Halifax: Dept. of Anthropology, Saint Mary's University.

McKendrick, Neil, John Brewer, and J. H. Plumb 1982 *The Birth of a Consumer Society: The Commercialization of Eighteenth-century England*. London: Europa.

Meltzer, David J. 1981 "A Study of Style and Function in a Class of Tools." *Journal of Field Archaeology*, 8(3):313–26.

Michel, Jack 1981 "'In a Manner and Fashion Suitable to their Degree': A Preliminary Investigation of the Material Culture of Early Rural Pennsylvania." *Working Papers from the Regional Economic History Research Center*, 5:1–83.

_____ 1985 *The Regional Organization of Delaware Agriculture, 1849*. Philadelphia: author.

Mills, George 1957 "Art: An Introduction to Qualitative Anthropology." In Charlotte M. Otten (ed.), *Anthropology and Art: Readings in Cross-cultural Aesthetics*. American Museum Sourcebooks in Anthropology. Garden City, New York: Natural History Press, 1971.

Morris, James 1979 *Pax Britannica*. New York: Penguin.

Morris, William 1882 *Hopes and Fear for Art*. London: Ellis and White.

_____ 1888 *Signs of Change*. London: Reeves and Turner.

Moussette, Marcel 1983 *Le chauffage domestique au Canada, des origines à l'industrialisation*. Québec: Les Presses de l'Université Laval.

Muise, D.A. 1986 "Material Culture and the Teaching of Maritime Studies." In Philip Buckner (ed.), *Teaching Maritime Studies*. Fredericton: Acadiensis Press.

Mukarovsky, Jan 1966 "The Essence of the Visual Arts." In Ladislav Matejka and Irwin R. Titunik (eds.), *Semiotics of Art: Prague School Contributions*. Cambridge: MIT Press, 1976.

Naipaul, V.S. 1980 *A Bend in the River*. New York: Penguin.

Nelson, Dean *et al.* 1983 *Orphans Court Valuations, 1760–1850, Kent County, Delaware*. Dover: Delaware Bureau of Museums.

Noble, David W. 1968 *The Eternal Adam and the New World Garden*. New York: George Braziller.

Odell, Jonathan n.d. "My Pedigree." New Brunswick Museum Archives.

_____ 1805 *An Essay on the Elements, Accents & Prosody, of the English Language: intended to have been printed as an Introduction to Mr. Boucher's Supplement to Dr. Johnson's Dictionary*. London: Privately published.

"Old First" Church of Newark, New Jersey n.d. Mudd Archives, Princeton University.

O'Neil, William B. 1960 *Primitive into Painter: Life and Letters of John Toole*. Charlottesville: University Press of Virginia.

Panoff, Michel and Michel Perrin 1973 *Dictionnaire de l'ethnologie*. Paris: Michel Payot.

Peat, Wilbur D. 1954 *Pioneer Painters of Indiana*. Indianapolis: Art Association.

Perry, George and Alan Aldridge 1967 *The Penguin Book of Comics: A Slight History*. Harmondsworth: Penguin Books, 1971.

Pessen, Edward 1969 *Jacksonian America: Society, Personality, and Politics*. Homewood, Ill.: Dorsey Press.

_____ 1973 *Riches, Class, and Power before the Civil War*. Lexington, Mass.: Heath.

Pitt-Rivers, A. Lane-Fox 1906 "On the Evolution of Culture." In J. L. Meyers (ed.), *The Evolution of Culture and Other Essays*. Oxford: Clarendon Press.

Pocius, Gerald L. 1982a "Architecture on Newfoundland's Southern Shore: Diversity and the Emergence of New World Forms." In Camille Wells (ed.), *Perspectives in Vernacular Architecture*. Annapolis: Vernacular Architecture Forum.

_____ 1982b "Material Folk Culture Research in English Canada: Antiques, Aficionados, and Beyond." *Canadian Folklore canadien*, 4(1&2):27–41.

_____ 1988 *The Working World of Egbert Warren: St. John's Life at the Turn of the Century*. St. John's: Newfoundland Museum.

Podro, Michael 1982 *The Critical Historians of Art*. New Haven: Yale University Press.

Porter, John 1965 *The Vertical Mosaic: An Analysis of Social Class and Power in Canada*. Toronto: University of Toronto Press.

Price, Sally 1989 *Primitive Art in Civilized Places*. Chicago: University of Chicago Press.

Prown, Jules D. 1980 "Style as Evidence." *Winterthur Portfolio,* 15(3):197-210.

_____ 1982 "Mind in Matter: An Introduction to Material Culture Theory and Method." *Winterthur Portfolio,* 17(1):1-19.

_____ 1985 "Material Culture Studies: A Symposium." *Material Culture,* 17(2/3):79.

Pryce-Jones, Hugh 1977 "New Public Demands." In Ted Poulos (ed.), *Conference Proceedings for 2001: The Museum and the Canadian Public.* Ottawa: Canadian Museums Association.

Quimby, Ian M.G. (ed.) 1978 *Material Culture and the Study of American Life.* New York: Norton, for Winterthur Museum.

Randall, Willard Sterne 1984 *A Little Revenge: Benjamin Franklin and his Son.* Boston: Little, Brown.

Rathje, William L. 1981 "A Manifesto for Modern Material Culture Studies." In Richard A. Gould and Michael B. Schiffer (eds.), *Modern Material Culture: The Archaeology of Us.* New York: Academic Press.

Raymond, William Obder (ed.) 1901 *The Winslow Papers.* Saint John, N.B.: Sun, for New Brunswick Historical Society.

Reitberger, Reinhold C. and Wolfgang J. Fuchs 1971 *Anatomie eines Massenmediums.* Munich: Heinz Moos.

_____ 1974 *Tegneserier: En eksspansions historie.* Aarhus, Denmark.

Renaud, P.E. 1928 *Les Origins économiques du Canada.* Namère: Erault.

Richardson, Douglas Scott 1966 "Christ Church Cathedral, Fredericton, New Brunswick." Master's thesis, Yale University.

Ricoeur, Paul 1970 *Freud and Philosophy: An Essay on Interpretation.* Trans. Denis Savage. New Haven: Yale University Press.

_____ 1974 *The Conflict of Interpretations: Essays in Hermeneutics,* Ed. Don Ihde. Evanston: Northwestern University Press.

_____ 1981 *Hermeneutics and the Human Sciences: Essays on Language, Action, and Interpretation.* Ed. and trans. John B. Thompson. New York: Cambridge University Press.

Rider, Peter E. 1983 "1983 Atlantic Workshop." *Material History Bulletin,* 18:54-57.

_____ 1984 "The Concrete Clio: Definition of a Field of History." *Material History Bulletin,* 20:92-96.

_____ 1986 "Maritime Material Culture Studies in Heritage Resource Institutions." In Philip Buckner (ed.), *Teaching Maritime Studies.* Fredericton: Acadiensis Press.

Robbins, Daniel 1976 "Folk Sculpture Without Folk." In H. Hemphill (ed.), *Folk Sculpture U.S.A.* Brooklyn: Brooklyn Museum.

Roberts, Warren 1985 "Material Culture Studies: A Symposium." *Material Culture*, 17(2/3):89–93.

Robinson, Dwight E. 1960 "The Styling and Transmission of Fashions Historically Considered: Winckelmann, Hamilton and Wedgwood in the 'Greek Revival.'" *Journal of Economic History*, 20(4):576-87.

Rossiter, W. S. 1967 *A Century of Population Growth*. Baltimore: Genealogical Publishing.

Rubin, Barbara 1979 *Los Angeles in Installments: Forest Lawn*. Santa Monica, Ca.: West Side Publications.

Ruddel, David-Thiery 1983 "The Domestic Textile Industry in the Region and City of Québec, 1792–1835." *Material History Bulletin*, 17:95–125.

_____ 1987 *Québec City, 1765–1832: The Evolution of a Colonial Town*. Ottawa: Canadian Museum of Civilization.

_____ 1990a "Domestic Textile Production in Colonial Québec, 1608–1840." *Material History Bulletin*, 31:39–49.

_____ 1990b "Consumer Trends, Clothing, Textiles, and Equipment in the Montreal Area, 1792–1835." *Material History Bulletin*, 32:45–65.

Rush, G.B., E. Christensen and J. Malcolmson 1981 "Lament for a Notion: The Development of Social Science in Canada." *Canadian Review of Sociology and Anthropology*, 18(4):519–44.

Sackett, James R. 1977 "The Meaning of Style in Archaeology: A General Model." *American Antiquity*, 42(3):369-80.

Saint, Andrew 1983 *The Image of the Architect*. New Haven: Yale University Press.

St. George, Robert Blair (ed.) 1988 *Material Life in America, 1600–1860*. Boston: Northeastern University Press.

Sargent, Winthrop (ed.) 1860 *The Loyalist Verses of Joseph Stansbury and Doctor Jonathan Odell, Relating to the American Revolution*. Albany: Munsell.

Savage, Henry Littleton (ed.) 1956 *Nassau Hall, 1756-1956*. Princeton: Princeton University Press.

Scarry, Elaine 1985 *The Body in Pain: The Making and Unmaking of the World*. New York: Oxford University Press.

Schapiro, Meyer 1953 "Style." In A.L. Kroeber (ed.), *Anthropology Today: An Encyclopedic Inventory*. Chicago: University of Chicago Press.

Schlereth, Thomas J. 1982 "Material Culture Studies in America, 1876–1976." In Thomas J. Schlereth (ed.), *Material Culture Studies in America*. Nashville: American Association for State and Local History.

_____ 1985a "Material Culture Research and Historical Explanation." *Public Historian*, 7(4):21–30.

_____ (ed.) 1985b *Material Culture: A Research Guide*. Lawrence: University Press of Kansas.

Schwartz, Paula S., H. John Michel, Jr., and Bernard L. Herman 1986 *A Place in Time: Continuity and Change in Mid-Nineteenth Century Delaware*. Dover, DE.: Delaware Agricultural Museum.

Séguin, Robert-Lionel 1972 *Les ustensiles en Nouvelle-France*. Montreal: Leméac.

Siders, Rebecca and Bernard L. Herman (eds. and comps.) 1985 *Orphans Court Valuations, 1760–1830, New Castle County, Delaware*. Newark: Center for Historic Architecture and Engineering, University of Delaware.

_____ 1986 *Orphans Court Valuations, 1760–1830, Sussex County, Delaware*. Newark: Center for Historic Architecture and Engineering, University of Delaware.

Smith, Cyril S. 1980 *From Art to Science: Seventy-Two Objects Illustration the Nature of Discovery*. Cambridge: Harvard University Press.

Smith, E. Baldwin 1950 Rpt. *The Dome: A Study in the History of Ideas*. Princeton: Princeton University Press, 1971.

_____ 1956 *Architectural Symbolism of Imperial Rome and the Middle Ages*. Princeton: Princeton University Press.

Smith, Merritt Roe 1977 *The Harper's Ferry Armory and the New Technology: The Challenge of Change*. Ithaca: Cornell University Press.

Smith, Stuart Allen 1981 "Loyalist Architecture of British North America." *Canada's Visual History Series*, Vol. 43, Ottawa: National Film Board of Canada, and National Museum of Man.

Soltow, Lee 1975 *Men and Wealth in the United States*. New Haven: Yale University Press.

Sperber, Dan 1977 *Rethinking Symbolism*, trans. Alice L. Morton. Cambridge: Cambridge University Press.

SPG 1787–1791 Letters to the Society, Records of the Society for the Propagation of the Gospel, vols. 22–24, Provincial Archives of New Brunswick, Microfilm 10007.

Strong, Roy 1969 *The English Icon: Elizabethan and Jacobean Portraiture*. New York: Pantheon.

Sturtevant, William C. 1973 "Museums as Anthropological Data Banks." In Alden Redfield (ed.), *Anthropology Beyond the University*. Southern Anthropological Society Proceedings 7. Athens: University of Georgia Press, for Southern Anthropological Society.

Susman, Warren 1984 *Culture as History: The Transformation of American Society in the Twentieth Century*. New York: Pantheon.

Symons, T.H.B. 1975 *To Know Ourselves: The Report of the Commission on Canadian Studies*. Ottawa: Association of Universities and Colleges of Canada.

Tilton, James 1789 "Answers to Queries on the Present State of Husbandry and Agriculture in the Delaware State." *The Columbian Magazine*, (3):156–60, 217–20.

Tivy, Mary 1988 "The Quality of Research is Definitely Strained: Collections Research in Ontario Community Museums." *Material History Bulletin*, 27:61–68.

Tondriau, Julien 1964 *L'occultisme*. Verviers, Belgium: Gerard & Cie.

Tryon, R.M. 1917 *Household Manufactures in the United States, 1640–1860*. Chicago: University of Chicago Press.

Tuckerman, Henry T. 1867 *American Artist-life*. New York: Putnam.

Turner, Frederick 1984 "Escape from Modernism." *Harper's Magazine*, 269(1614):47–55.

Turner, Robert D. 1984 "The Limitations of Material History: A Museological Perspective." *Material History Bulletin*, 20:87–92.

Twain, Mark 1883 Rpt. *Life on the Mississippi*. New York: Penguin, 1984.

Tyler, Moses Coit 1897 Rpt. *The Literary History of the American Revolution, 1763–1783*. New York: Burt Franklin, 1988.

Updike, John 1972 *Museums and Women*. New York: Knopf.

Upton, Dell 1979 "Towards a Performance Theory of Vernacular Architecture in Early Tidewater Virginia." *Folklore Forum*, 12(2–3):173-96.

_____ 1984 "Pattern Books and Professionalism: Aspects of the Transformation of American Domestic Architecture, 1800-1860." *Winterthur Portfolio*, 19(2–3):107-50.

_____ 1985a "Material Culture Studies: A Symposium." *Material Culture*, 17(2/3):85–87.

_____ 1985b "The Power of Things: Recent Studies in American Vernacular Architecture." In Thomas J. Schlereth (ed.), *Material Culture: A Research Guide*. Lawrence: University Press of Kansas.

_____ 1986 *Holy Things and Profane: Anglican Parish Churches in Colonial Virginia*. New York: Architectural History Foundation; Cambridge: MIT Press.

_____ and John Michael Vlach (eds.) 1986 *Common Places: Readings in American Vernacular Architecture*. Athens: University of Georgia Press.

Varenne, J. M. 1980 *La magie des objets*. Paris: Hachette.

Velder, A. and M. José Lamothe 1976 *Le livre de l'outil*. Paris: Denoël/Gauthier.

Verville, M. de 1977 *Système descriptif des objets domestiques français*. Paris, Editions des Musées nationaux.

Vincent, Thomas B. (ed.) 1978 *Narrative Verse Satire in Maritime Canada, 1779–1814*. Ottawa: Tecumseh Press.

_____ 1980 *Jonathan Odell: An Annotated Chronology of the Poems, 1759–1814*. Kingston: Loyal Colonies Press.

Vlach, John Michael 1988 *Plain Painters: Making Sense of American Folk Art*. Washington: Smithsonian Institution Press.

Wagner, Roy 1981 *The Invention of Culture*. Chicago: University of Chicago Press.

Wallace, Mike 1985 "Mickey Mouse History: Portraying the Past at Disney World." *Radical History Review*, 32:33–57.

Wallace, Michael 1986 "History Museums in the United States." In Susan Porter Benson, Stephen Brier, and Roy Rosenzweig (eds.) *Presenting the Past: Essays on History and the Public*. Philadelphia: Temple University Press.

Walsh, Lorena S. 1981 "The Material Life of the Early American Housewife," Paper presented at the Conference on Women in Early America, Colonial Williamsburg Foundation and the Institute for Early American History and Culture, Williamsburg, Virginia, November.

Watson, Robert L. 1984 *Christ Church Cathedral, Fredericton: A History*. Fredericton: Christ Church Cathedral.

Wertenbaker, Thomas J. 1946 *Princeton, 1746–1896*. Princeton: Princeton University Press.

Wetherill, Lorna 1986 "A Possession of One's Own: Women and Consumer Behaviour in England, 1660–1740." *Journal of British Studies*, 25(2): 131–56.

Whiffen, Marcus 1969 *American Architecture Since 1780: A Guide to the Styles*. Cambridge: MIT Press.

White, David M. and Robert H. Abel 1963 *The Funnies: An American Idiom*. New York: Macmillan.

Williams, Raymond 1973 "Base and Superstructure." *New Left Review*, 82:3–16.

Williams, Rosalind H. 1982 *Dream Worlds: Mass Consumption in Late Nineteenth-century France*. Berkeley: University of California Press.

Wood, Elizabeth B. 1967 "Pots and Pans History: Relating Manuscripts and Printed Sources to the Study of Domestic Art Objects." *American Archivist*, 30(3):431–42.

Yarmolinsky, Avrahm 1930 *Picturesque United States, 1811, 1812, 1813: Being a Memoir of Paul Svinin*. New York: William Edwin Rudge.

Young, David E. 1985 "The need for a Cognitive Approach to the Study of Material Culture." *Culture*, 5(2):53-67.

Index

ISER BOOKS

Studies

Papers

Mailing Address:
ISER Books (Institute of Social and Economic Research)
Memorial University of Newfoundland
St. John's, Newfoundland, Canada, A1C 5S7